WHITEWASH

This book puts the language used in popular film, TV, press, radio, popular music and the Internet, as well as that spoken by key leaders, under the spotlight. It questions how these various mediums construct and normalise a language and order of white privilege which may appear universal but which is actually highly selective and exclusionary in its effects. Taking specific examples and presenting new factual evidence, it studies the racial politics that lie behind much of the communication in the public arena.

John Gabriel also describes and re-values the larger questions and debates surrounding the relationship between media communication and more general economic and political developments. Under chapter headings such as 'Genealogies of whiteness' and 'The fringe and the fabric: the politics of white pride' comparative case studies in both England and the US draw on contemporary political controversies and are used to explore the specific dynamics of the relationship between racialised forms of media discourse and political and economic change. He also explores the use made of the media by oppositional community and campaign organisations. What is ultimately revealed is the existence of a 'white' language, both coded and overt, which re-casts and re-invents dominant representations of whiteness.

Whitewash is a timely and controversial addition to a growing area of interest in sociological studies. It will therefore be essential reading to all media and racial politics students, as well as those wishing to know more about the hidden languages that seem to be increasingly invading the discourse of politics and the media.

John Gabriel is Head of the Department of Cultural Studies and Sociology at the University of Birmingham. He is the author of *Racism, Culture, Markets* and is highly regarded as an expert on racial politics and its place in society and the media.

WHITEWASH

Racialized politics and the media

John Gabriel

London and New York

First published 1998
by Routledge
11 New Fetter Lane, London EC4P 4EE

Simultaneously published in the USA and Canada
by Routledge
29 West 35th Street, New York, NY 10001

Typeset in Baskerville by Routledge
Printed and bound in Great Britain by TJ International,
Padstow, Cornwall

British Library Cataloguing in Publication Data
A catalogue record for this book is available from the British Library

Library of Congress Cataloguing in Publication Data
Gabriel, John, 1951–
Whitewash: racialized politics and the media/John Gabriel.
p.   cm.
Includes bibliographical references (p.   ) and index.
1. Mass media and race relations – United States. 2. Mass media – Political aspects –
United States. 3. United States – Politics and government – 1993–   4. Mass media
and race relations – Great Britain. 5. Mass media – Political aspects – Great Britain.
6. Great Britain – Politics and government – 1979–
I. Title.
P94.5.M552U634   1998
302.23'0973–dc21   97–42943
CIP

ISBN 0–415–14969–x (hbk)
ISBN 0–415–14970–3 (pbk)

CONTENTS

ACKNOWLEDGEMENTS

I would like to thank Mari Shullaw and Jo Mattingly at Routledge for their support and efficiency shown throughout the duration of this project. I would also like to thank the anonymous readers at Routledge for their very helpful comments on my proposal and manuscript and to Stephen Small, in particular, whose extremely detailed comments on the manuscript were invaluable.

I am very fortunate to have had the support of colleagues and friends in the Department of Cultural Studies and Sociology; Ann Gray, Michael Green, Stuart Hanson, Jo Van Every, Mark Erickson, Yvonne Jacobs, Jorge Larrain, Malika Mehdid, David Parker and Marie Walsh. Many of the ideas for this book came as a result of teaching courses with my close friend and colleague, Gargi Bhattacharyya and I would like to give her special thanks. I would also like to thank other friends and colleagues who have inspired and encouraged me over the years: Floya Anthias, Gideon Ben-Tovim, Dave Mills, Janet Morgan, Hugh Wisdom and Thelma Flores.

I am very grateful indeed to those library staff and archivists at Columbia University and to Rebecca Hankins and Katherine G. Wilkins at the Amistad Center, Tulane, LA. Thanks also, to Teresa Garcia at the Audio Video Reporting Services, Los Angeles, for all her help. I am also indebted to those community activists who gave up their valuable time to be interviewed. Thanks to all those at: WBAI community radio; Pacifica Radio; Fairness and Accuracy In Reporting; the Race Relations Unit, Birmingham City Council; Newham Monitoring Project; the Campaign agaisnt the Asylum Bill; the Louisiana Coalition against Racism and Nazism; the local California Campaigns against Propositions 209 and 187; and the Southern Poverty Law Center.

I would like to thank Jim and Joan Linkogle for their warm hospitality during my countless trips to the US and to Jim, in particular, for helping me to gain access to material on the Oregon Citizen's Association. I would like to pay special thanks to my mother, Pauline, and to my sister, Sally Townsley, for their love, support and encouragement throughout my life. And finally, a very big thank you to Stephanie Linkogle for her support, innumerable insights, friendly criticisms and help in the preparation of the manuscript.

INTRODUCTION

Over the past thirty years, both academic and common-sense definitions of 'race' and ethnicity have suffered from a certain myopia. In the 1960s, for example, the term 'race music' meant 'black music'. In the 1980s in Birmingham, England, an ex-university student wrote a guide to the City's 'ethnic' restaurants which assiduously avoided any food which might conceivably be described as English and/or American – hence no reference to fish and chips and certainly no McDonald's! In the 1990s the terms 'race' and 'ethnic' and even 'multiculturalism' continue to be used as if they only apply to anyone but 'whites' and anything other than 'white' culture. However, it is not just that some groups or cultures or identities have been ethnically or racially marked whilst others have not. Terms like 'racism' and processes of 'racialisation' have so monopolised debate that black identities are seen in unitary terms and equated with or restricted to the negative impact of racism. This reductionism has had two important consequences, one of which has been to compartmentalise being racialised from becoming other things, including being gendered and/or sexed. The other consequence of defining terms such as 'race', 'ethnic', etc., so narrowly has been to hide the ethnic characteristics of 'whiteness' and (to think about) *its* racial formation.

A number of research strategies have addressed this myopia. One has been to acknowledge the variety of racisms beyond those most widely discussed. For example, whilst a brief glance through Lewis Curtis's *Apes and Angels* (1971) quickly confirms the historical significance of anti-Irish racism, more contemporary forms have been largely hidden from the academic and public sphere. Mary Hickman's research project for the Commission for Racial Equality has been a welcome, if overdue, acknowledgement of the need to conduct research and develop policy agendas with respect to diasporic Irish communities in England in the late twentieth century. However, to extend the definition of racism to include some white ethnicities might only compound the view that racial groups, for all their diversity, are no more than the sum of the effects of racism.

Another approach, therefore, working with a revived concept of ethnicity, has been to look at the more dynamic, proactive, forms of cultural expression and diversity. Cross-cultural fertilisation provides an important source of ethnic identity rather than simply hanging on to and reproducing old ethnic divisions. The analysis of 'routes' rather than roots becomes a more effective way of understanding new ethnic configurations. Such work, invoking concepts of diaspora and hybridity, has begun to dislodge hermetically sealed versions of ethnic origin and difference, and to recognise the reciprocal and symbiotic relationships between cultures (Hall 1991; Gilroy 1993a, 1993b; Brah 1996). The idea of 'hybridity' has acquired particular resonance for those of mixed ethnic background illustrated by the golfer Tiger Woods, who, rather than be thought of as the first black to win the US Masters golf tournament, preferred to describe himself as a 'Cablinaisian'. This was a term of his own invention to describe his Caucasian, Black, Indian and Asian background (*Guardian* 24 April 1997). This idea of hybridity, however, simply acknowledges the complexity of background rather than thinking about the formation of identity through ongoing inter- and trans-cultural influences and the significance of symbolic and fluid, rather than fixed, boundaries. Avtar Brah's use of the idea of 'diasporic space' is an attempt to capture the contingency and complexity of such identities which also have a gender and class dimension to them (Brah 1996: 208ff.).

In 1988 Richard Dyer wrote an article about whiteness in popular culture. Whiteness? The very idea of talking about whiteness as an ethnicity in its own right initially caused eyebrows to furrow, followed by long, sometimes stupefied, sometimes uncomfortable, silences. Such an occasion springs to mind when, in 1994, a colleague and I showed a video of the 'Britpop' band, Blur, and asked students to comment on who or what was 'racially marked', how and why. According to Dyer, the power of whiteness lies precisely in its ability to render itself invisible, or normal. Whilst Dyer's analysis focused on popular media representations and film in particular, Ruth Frankenberg has explored whiteness in terms of other locations; the material, cultural and subjective (1993). The overall aim of her study was to 'make visible processes by which the stability of whiteness is secured and reproduced' (1993: 242). This was explored through in-depth interviews in which her white subjects revealed the ways in which their lives and the meanings attached to them had been shaped by race, even though many employed discursive strategies for evading race. Dijk's work also includes examples of such denials as part of a wider discussion of semantic strategies and rhetorical devices operating within the press (Dijk 1991: 187ff.; see also Dijk 1993: 76ff).

It is probably no coincidence that this body of research reflects a focus on whiteness which is normally associated with the extremes of right-wing politics. Why? What has precipitated such changes in consciousness? Howard Winant has described the historical moment of the mid 1990s as 'the incipient crisis of whiteness' (1994: 283). There are a number of aspects to this. The fact that whites are numerically becoming a minority in the US provides an important material dimension to these anxieties. Moreover, white anxieties are fuelled by a growing and widely held view (amongst whites) that not being white is associated with privileges (affirmative action, multiculturalism), and summed up in the claim that 'being white means you are less likely to get financial aid' (cited in Winant 1994: 285). According to Winant, the idea that whiteness may be a handicap is 'quite unprecedented' but it also means that white racial identity will inevitably grow in salience.

Demographic changes, including migration, are but one important aspect of 'globalisation'. Diasporic communities have been increasingly defining and shaping mainstream culture. Struggles for colonial independence have brought in their wake new forms of interdependence as well as old forms of dependence. At the same time, discourses of 'post'-colonialism have served to undermine traditional narratives of nation, and of national and ethnic origin, and challenged the major tenets (universalism, rationality, essentialism) of modernity. The growth in significance of transnational corporations and power blocs and the ever-proliferating empires of media corporations and information technologies have shown little respect for national borders. Old and new media technologies have transformed the relationship between time and space, the local and the global. A new politics of representation has emerged in which cultural producers (film-makers, artists, journalists, etc.), entrepreneurs and community organisations of hitherto marginal or excluded ethnicities have begun to promote complex and diverse (diasporic) forms of cultural expression whilst simultaneously challenging dominant, monocultural world views. Together such trends have undermined the view that national identities are culturally homogeneous and hence have challenged many of the privileges inscribed in eurocentric thought.

In this book I will explore the hidden and, in some cases, not so hidden expressions and assertions of whiteness. I will refer to whiteness both as knowledge and as state of being, despite the ambiguity of the latter and its reliance on self-perception and definition by others. (In other words whiteness as a state of being is also dependent on knowledge claims.) What both epistemologies and ontologies of whiteness share in common is their exclusionary characteristics. Some discourses set out with the intention of demarcating racial boundaries and of promoting whiteness. Such would be the case in white supremacist discourse which is discussed in Chapter 6. Others work more subtly, often not making explicit reference to being white or defending whiteness, but maintaining its dominance through denial and absence. As Jessie Daniels points out 'themes of race, class, gender, and sexuality that appear in extremist white supremacist discourse resonate effectively in mainstream politics, advertising, academia, and popular culture' (1997: 7). Discourses of the nation, whether these be expressed in the context of a debate on immigration, a national sporting event, or what passes for a national cultural form like 'Britpop' or 'British film', have proved important sites for the defence of white ethnicity.

The culture that provided privileges and order for a class of white men is being challenged, and that class is fighting back. The ontology of whiteness (whiteness as subject – with the proviso, I shall argue, that some of whiteness's best advocates are black) is coming to the defence of the epistemology (whiteness as knowledge). Unprecedently, white men are being told to get in line with groups over whom they have hitherto implicitly assumed some rightful advantage. Now the mechanisms of white privilege, e.g. alumni scholarships, Ivy league or Oxbridge networks, the 'old school chums' and next of kin networks that Patricia Williams referred to in her

Reith Lectures (1997), or the subtleties of dress and language codes, or what counts as useful knowledge, are all being seen for what they are – not part of the 'invisible' natural order of things but mechanisms (on a much larger and more pervasive scale than affirmative or positive action), which have historically secured the advantage of white men and, in different ways, white women.

The concept of racialisation has been defined by Robert Miles as a process:

> where a group has been signified as a distinct category or type of human being by reference to real or alleged biological characteristics, a significa- tion that has usually been accompanied by an explicit or implicit use of the discourse of 'race'.
>
> (1993: 135)

Stephen Small distinguishes this, the *process* of racialisation, that is the unfolding patterns of attributing racial differences to groups, from the *problematic* of racialisa- tion, which includes different theoretical perspectives for explaining racialised barriers, boundaries and identities (Small 1994: 33). *Whitewash* refers to both to the process and works within a loose problematic of racialisation. What distinguishes it in terms of process is its focus on the construction of *white* racialised identities – processes which are sometimes implicit and concealed behind the racialisation of 'others'. It develops within a problematic of racialisation which explores the role of cultural, including media processes in the context of rapid global economic and political change in the formation, re-assertion, and transformation of whiteness. 'Racial' is used as an adjective to describe the consequences of racialisation, e.g. 'racial' attacks. It is *not* a reference to biological or physical characteristics *per se*.

'Anglo' and 'Anglicisation' are more troublesome terms. I have used them to refer to a particular cultural strain of whiteness, which is distinguishable from other white European ethnicities. Historically, however, there are important differ- ences in terms of forms and patterns of racialisation amongst the latter, e.g. between northern and southern European, Irish and German ethnic or national identities. In what follows I have tried to acknowledge these specificities where appropriate and relevant whilst at the same time holding on to the idea of domi- nant versions of whiteness. In the US, the term 'black' Americans refers to people of African descent, whereas in Britain the term has been used more 'inclusively' (although some writers have denied this) to refer to those of African Caribbean, African and south Asian background. The category, Asian-Americans, on the other hand, refers to people of south-east Asian background in the US , whereas in Britain it refers to people from the Indian sub-continent (hence the qualification, 'south Asian'). I shall use these terms in accordance with these common under- standings.

The discourses of whiteness can be seen as both a backlash against such devel- opments and a re-assertion of older forms of supremacy, exclusion and denial. In saying this, I am not suggesting that whiteness works for all 'whites' in the same way. Not all white ethnicities are dominant and not all 'whites' are privileged. Just as blackness, Jewishness, Irishness, etc., defy definitions in terms of a stable and fixed set of ethnic attributes, so too whiteness must be thought of as heterogeneous, hybrid, fluid and contingent, however much its more conscious defenders might deny this. Moreover, whiteness has a different exchange value depending on other social locations, including class, gender, ethnicity and able-bodiedness. This poses a paradox for a book on whiteness such as this. I set out with the intention of examining processes of white racial formation whilst at the same time wanting to reject the idea of whiteness as a unitary or absolute category. The apparent contradiction can be resolved, I would argue, by thinking of whiteness *as an essentialising strategy* (by no means always pursued consciously) to defend and maintain white privilege. '*Whitewash*' refers to the process of cultural bleaching and hence the book's concern with *how* such dominant versions of nation and ethnicity are made.

By way of summarising the above I will distinguish five related, as I shall argue, uses of whiteness in what follows.

White pride politics   Which entails the conscious pursuit of and celebration of whiteness and which is explicitly racist.

Normative whiteness   The two discourses of interest in this book are *liberal universalism* and *national identity*. The latter includes both formal political discourses and popular cultural forms, e.g. sport, music and film. Such discourses may not be explicitly racist but nevertheless implicitly racialise values, aesthetics and forms of inclusion and exclusion. A particularly important shift in normative whiteness has been the extent to which it has become more visibly racialised through campaigns, such as those concerning the English language, immigration and multiculturalism.

Ontological whiteness   The state of 'being white' begs immediate qualification. Firstly, other social divisions, e.g. gender and class, are constituted simultaneously which makes it necessary to talk about whiteness only in relationship to other constructions. Furthermore, 'being white' is not a once-and-for-all categorisation for anyone, although it is contested in some cases more than others. Despite these problems, it remains the case that privileges are bestowed on those commonly assumed to be 'white'.

Progressive whiteness   There are risks in generalising here but I am referring to a politics (with a small and a large 'P') which condemns white pride and normative versions of whiteness yet in which 'whites' continue to dominate both ideologically and organisationally.

Subaltern whiteness   Much of my discussion of 'minority whiteness' will be around Irish and Jewish ethnicities. Even here it is important to bear in mind that such groups have been the object of racism (as both 'white' *and* 'black' ethnicities) as well as colluding in it.

Such a categorisation also has implications for understanding different forms of resistance and alternatives to whiteness which will be explored throughout this book. These include:

1   hybridising/disaggregating whiteness
2   the politics of representation
3   anti-racist politics

Hybridising/disaggregating whiteness and anti-racist politics are sometimes consciously pursued but often challenge or subvert dominant norms and values by default. In this book, I am particularly interested in more conventional forms of political mobilisations against both white pride politics and normative whiteness, particularly, in the case of the latter, as it becomes more visible.

What, it might be asked at the outset, are the advantages of using the concept of whiteness in preference to that of racism? Is whiteness not just another euphemism for racism? There is certainly overlap between the two terms, particularly given my interest in the exclusionary effects of unitary versions of whiteness. However, there are more compelling reasons for foregrounding whiteness as an object of analysis and debate. The first, already mentioned, is that racism has come to define those groups on its receiving end, to the exclusion of other sources of identity and processes of cultural change. The discourse of 'race relations' has invariably turned complex, dynamic, heterogeneous communities into homogeneous, passive recipients of racism. This point applies to whiteness too, for whilst white ethnicity has its racist elements, racism cannot be said to exhaust its social identities or complex (in reality, hybrid) cultural practices. Moreover, the experiences and practices of subaltern white ethnicities only serve to compound the problem of conceiving whiteness and racism as synonymous. Thirdly, the fact that antiracism is but one of three ways of challenging whiteness suggests that the phenomenon of whiteness is not just about racism *per se* but about forms of representation and versions of ethnicity which are capable of being re-worked, subverted and undermined through cultural and institutional practices that fall outside the confines of anti-racist politics.

The decision to explore these issues on both sides of the Atlantic arose, in part, out of an interest in global forms of interdependence and dependence and the role of the US, in particular, in shaping these developments. The rapidity and intensity of global communications has made it increasingly difficult to talk about societies as entities, let alone discrete entities which can form the basis of a comparative study. My interest is more in the relationship between the two countries than a comparison. Much has been written about the cultural influences of the US on the rest of the world including England, and this has been seen as increasingly one way and hegemonic as the twentieth century has progressed. Some would see such influences for the better, others for the worse. My aim is to explore this relationship, setting it against a longer-term perspective which invokes the idea of *intertwined* histories, and of processes of Anglicisation as much as Americanisation. But those global changes referred to above invite us to think about other kinds of relationships, not just between societies, which are increasingly fraught and arguably contrived entities but also between the 'local' and the 'global'. Both these terms are relative, in that the 'local' for example can refer to a particular city or district or it may refer to a domestic space, or to a city or region ('The South', 'Europe'), or to the US and England, depending on the relationship under consideration. By exploring processes of white cultural formation within and across both countries, it becomes possible to identify those factors which are specific to the locality and which might be the result of wider trans- or supra-national processes.

The first aspect to the US–British cultural axis worth noting relates to 'Americanisation', a process widely regarded as a form of imperialism. Conservative critics like the Leavises bemoaned the impact of US culture as did Edward Thompson, the Marxist historian, who criticised both 'Star Wars' and the use of British air bases to launch an attack on Libya as examples of the negative influences of US global domination, and the subordination of British to US interests. Amongst the intellectual avant-garde of post-modernism, too, there is a strong anti-American current, most powerfully expressed in Jean Baudrillard's essay on America, in which he describes the US as a giant hologram (Baudrillard 1988).

Against these critics has emerged a tradition within cultural studies, more willing to recognise the subversive potential of the US on British culture. Duncan Webster (1988), following Dick Hebdidge, has explored different ways in which US culture has served to radicalise British culture. Hebdidge, for instance, has examined how representations of teenagers in the cinema and television of the 1950s, evoked lastingly in the screen characters played by James Dean, the novels of Jack Kerouac and the beat poetry of Allan Ginsberg, provided all kinds of subversive forms for Britain's emerging post-war youth sub-cultures (cited in Webster 1988: 182ff.). Webster develops this idea with reference to the crime genre in TV, films and novels. What US popular culture did, he argues, was to take murder out of the parlour, the library or the living room and on to the street, thus bringing it within reach of working-class readers and audiences. US culture, in this sense, was a threat in class terms. The crime fiction of British writers like Dorothy Sayers and Agatha Christie reflected their familiarity with middle-class lifestyles. Although class was not the overt issue on which British taste was being judged by its custodians like the BBC, it was not far beneath the surface (Webster 1988: 190).

A second feature of the relationship between the US and Britain, has been their intertwined racialised histories. In the post-1945 period in particular, the 'US experience' has been an important reference point for British political debate. When British commentators look into their crystal ball for tomorrow's 'racial' problems (and their solutions), they invariably cast an eye across the Atlantic to the situation in the US. For example, supporters of race relations (anti-discrimination) legislation in British parliamentary debates in the 1960s and 1970s, cited street uprisings in the inner cities of Los Angeles and Chicago as evidence of the need for social reform at home. As events transpired, these race relations laws did not prevent the uprisings of the 1980s, which became a feature of the social landscape in Britain.

A recurrent theme of British press reporting after the Los Angeles uprising in May 1992 was its implications for Britain. John Taylor, defeated Conservative candidate for Cheltenham in the general election, wrote a piece in the *Sunday*

Express entitled COULD IT HAPPEN HERE? (3 May 1992), in which he talked about the breakdown of family life as a contributory factor. Many of the callers to BBC Radio 4's programme *Call Nick Ross* (5 May 1992) attributed the 'riots' to 'too many immigrants'. In this instance, the discourse about numbers, problems and threats on this side of the Atlantic was used to make sense of what was happening in Los Angeles. The prospect of a repeat of Los Angeles on mainland Britain was worked around other linked themes, notably white fear (WHITES RUN TO BUY GUNS, *Sunday Express*, 3 May 1992) and through powerful visual representations of white victims of black violence. The deluge of coverage in these terms quickly superseded the original catalyst for the uprising: the acquittal of four white policemen charged with offences relating to the beating of a black motorist, Rodney King, despite a video recording of the incident which had been regarded by most as incontrovertible proof of their guilt.

The US thus adds an important global dimension to our understanding of English racial cultures. The relationship described so far is a complex one. The globalisation of media networks means that it is increasingly harder to talk about the influence of one culture over another. Rather it makes more sense to speak of the incorporation of the one culture into the other. The US has become an integral part of British culture, not only through the export of its cultural products (television, film and music) but also through the investment of its multinational corporations in the UK. In countless ways, from fast food to computer games, the US shapes ways of life and British cultural identity. But the process cuts both ways. Anglocentrism has inspired white formations in the US just as British punk music became significant for chicano gangs in Los Angeles in the 1980s. The Internet too offers opportunities for cultural exchanges and the emergence of transnational white identities.

It should be clear now that although *Whitewash* is not about the media *per se*, its focus on the cultural *formation* of imagined white communities means that much of what follows will inevitably draw on media examples. Discourses of whiteness comprise a repertoire of assumptions and beliefs, recurring images and interpellations which 'hail' some and not others, all deployed through an array of distinct forms and genres. Following Wetherell and Potter's study (1992), discourses might be understood in terms of: their capacity to identify, regulate and construct (not just represent) social groups; their ability to provide resources for making evaluations and constructing factual versions; their success in creating the impetus and motivation to act; their capacity to constitute 'truth' and to maintain social relations and disadvantage (Wetherell and Potter 1992: 90ff.).

However, as Frankenberg points out, racialised discourses of whiteness not only vary over time and space, they are also relational. In other words they are constructed in terms of other discourses. Frankenberg is particularly concerned with how whiteness is constructed in relation to gender and sexuality. A further aspect to the contingent nature of discourse is its capacity to be understood differently across diverse social groups. As Wetherell and Potter stress, it is the situated use rather than the once and for all abstract reading of discourse that counts.

These comments on discourse help to locate the media within a more developed and complex cultural circuit which forms the framework for organising the book's chapters. Media representations are part and parcel of everyday culture including the material fabric of institutional culture. Media do not merely 'report' economic restructuring, political upheavals, environmental crises, migration and displacement and the expansion of media technologies linked to the transformation of cultural landmarks (customs, institutions, values). They have done so in ways which have enhanced the experience of dilution, loss, purposelessness and imminent catastrophe. The media has thus played a key role in buttressing whiteness with selective versions of national culture: by mobilising deep-seated anxieties and insecurities whilst simultaneously seeking to counter such anxieties with discourses which serve to purge culture of its syncretic forms. *Whitewash* is intended to capture such processes as they feed off as well as nourish anxieties and uncertainties associated with modern and post-modern change. Whiteness has been formed, re-formed and contested under such conditions and the aim of this book is to illustrate such processes with reference to those issues of particular significance in the constitution of the white imaginary in the last decade of the twentieth century. What *Whitewash* does not attempt is to theorise the relationship between the realm of representations and some discrete material sphere in general terms, but rather aims to explore interfusing patterns in particular historical circumstances.

Chapter 1 takes up some of these more general debates and ideas with particular reference to their recurring themes: ideas of whiteness; the relationship between the local and the global; and the role assigned to the media in theories of culture. Chapter 2 takes a step back to look at historical constructions of whiteness. This serves not only to underpin what follows but to illustrate the importance of thinking about white identities as contingent and constantly adaptable to different sets of historical circumstances.

Chapter 3 takes a defining, constitutive moment in the history of whiteness as its focus – the backlash culture of the 1980s and 1990s characterised by debates around political correctness and antiracism. However, more overt political discourses are not the only ways in which such interests come to be understood and addressed and I look at one national sporting event, the European Football Championships held in England in 1996 to illustrate the significance of popular cultural sites in discourses of whiteness. Chapter 4 looks at how white interests have been mobilised around the issue of immigration, not just as an issue *per se* but through recurrent imagery and metaphor which fuels anxieties around the policing of bodies as well as national borders.

Although the book as a whole is concerned with 'policing' in a general, non-institutional sense of the term, policing itself is taken up explicitly in Chapter 5. Institutional histories in both the US and England provide a useful example of those intertwining histories referred to above. They also illustrate the ways in which sections of the media have orchestrated, in unison with police and successive governments, to racialise crime and how this in turn has materialised in the 'canteen' (i.e. on the job) police culture. Much of the discourse around whiteness has hitherto been coded; the language of whiteness is hidden beneath a discourse which is seemingly more neutral, e.g. welfare, crime, etc. In Chapter 6 I look at those attempts to make explicit a defence of whiteness and to mobilise white interests around the political organisations of the far right.

Throughout the book my aim is to integrate the analysis of the dominant version of whiteness with community strategies of resistance, the overall aim of which has been to dismantle dominant versions of whiteness. The organisations and groups looked at here include a community radio station, two media pressure groups, grass roots anti-fascist and anti-racist groups and alliances, national campaign organisations and a local authority race relations unit. I am particularly interested in the ways in which these organisations, etc., have consciously and explicitly used the media to deconstruct and mobilise against white 'interests'. Their priorities vary but include: the displacement of white norms; the creation of space for cultural expression; redressing resource inequalities; and anti-racism. It might be argued that their overriding concern with the pursuit of equality and inclusiveness (i.e. universal values) would undermine attempts to pursue and express difference. Such a tension only exists if the concepts (of equality and difference) remain abstract and unhinged to particular political circumstances. I hope to show that the organisations discussed throughout this book, whilst differing in their priorities, nevertheless remain committed to establishing conditions that make it easier to pursue difference in some instances and sameness in others.

1

GLOBALISATION, ETHNIC IDENTITIES AND THE MEDIA

June Jordan has described how her understanding of whiteness changed from associating it with extremist groups like The Aryan Nation or the British National Party to something much more mundane and everyday (1995). She wrote, 'I came to recognise media constructions such as "The Heartland" or "Politically Correct" or "The Welfare Queen" or " Illegal Alien" or "Terrorist" or "The Bell Curve" for what they were: multiplying scattershots intended to defend one unifying desire – to establish and preserve white supremacy as our bottom line' (1995: 21). The difference here is that the 'whiteness' found in mundane, everyday culture is less obvious and visible. In fact, as Dyer argues, its power lies in its unspokenness and/or its deployment through code. This interest in whiteness from a left or an academic perspective is part of wider acknowledgement that white English are, indeed, just another ethnic group (Hall 1991: 21).

Taking the categorisation of *white pride* and *normative, ontological, progressive* and *subaltern* whiteness as its starting point, this section will explore some of the ways in which whiteness has been theorised. This will begin to provide what Stephen Small refers to as a paradigm of (white) racialisation that is explored in subsequent chapters. The second section will begin to develop an account of the shift in consciousness, referred to above, and, in particular, of those global conditions which have brought whiteness into sharper relief. The media's integral role in the formation of new ethnic identities and, relatedly, political alignments, has fractured old identities built around the nation and the locality. Not surprisingly, therefore, nationalism, nation states and national identities have proved important ideological and political sites for the formation and re-affirmation of whiteness. I will explore this with reference to both economic and political theories of nationalism and with reference to everyday mobilisations of national sentiment witnessed in the European Football Championships 1996, in section three. Theories which emphasise *dominant* culture, including media culture, often pay undue regard to complex, contradictory and dynamic forces at work and hence overlook, sometimes preclude, the analysis of contestation and counter-mobilisation. With this in mind, section four explores different forms of resistance, with particular reference to the campaign against the use of sweatshop labour in New York's designer fashion industry.

11

The invisible whiteness of being

As I suggested above, the general focus on whiteness re-directs our gaze away from those groups invariably problematised in race relations discourses. The concepts of race relations, racism, discrimination, prejudice etc., although not inevitably, have invariably encouraged the production of a sociological knowledge of the 'victim'. Whiteness, on the contrary, problematises the perpetrators and related processes. Toni Morrison makes this point when she says rather than look at the impact of racism on blacks it is important to examine the impact of racism on those who perpetuate it (1992: 11). However, according to Jordan, white supremacy goes beyond racism: 'it means that God put you on the planet to rule, to dominate, and occupy the center of the national and international universe – because you're white' (1995: 21).[1] But if, as is widely acknowledged, black identity cannot be reduced to the impact of racism, then neither can whiteness be reduced to perpetuating it. So what *is* whiteness? To address this, I will review some of the recent and not so recent attempts to theorise whiteness. I have organised this section around ten key themes in the discourse of whiteness, loosely based on John Fiske's helpful discussion (1994). The aim is both to raise questions as well as to set the parameters for the analysis which follows.

Theme 1 Whiteness does not refer to a fixed set of ethnic characteristics, but to strategic deployment of power or the space from which a variety of positions can be taken (Fiske 1994: 42). Such 'positions' are inevitably relational, so that in Ruth Frankenberg's terms, whiteness is constructed precisely by the way in which it positions others at its borders. In this sense, it is 'fundamentally a relational category' (1993: 231). Moreover, positionality is constructed through discourse which shapes personal identity. The power to both define and regulate subjectivity and how this is accomplished through institutions lies at the heart of Michel Foucault's work on prisons and asylums for the mentally ill (1971; 1979). Surveillance, therefore, that is the ability to turn individuals into objects of information and thus amenable to constant scrutiny, is an integral aspect of whiteness. The latter cannot be understood outside of the discursive, regulatory and technological means at its disposal to position itself through others.

New media technologies and the proliferation of ever-sophisticated interrelated systems of communication thus provide potential mechanisms for the regulation, dissemination and contestation for whiteness. We might ask as a preliminary question, do such technologies enhance democratic processes, including greater accountability and scope for resistance or do they merely provide the means for greater surveillance, this time on a global scale? A sceptical or at least cautious response is not unreasonable at this point, particularly given the military's role in the development of many of these new technologies and their subsequent use as interconnected databases for both surveillance and the storing of information on personal finance or debt, criminal records, etc. (Thompson 1995: 134).

The use of such technology is implied in legislation on immigration and asylum both in the US and the UK. How else will employers and public sector workers be able to track the citizenship status of their employees or clients other than with a click of the mouse and by accessing growing data banks of personal records? And who will arouse the suspicions of this growing army of information gatherers, if not those already under suspicion thanks to processes of racialisation? Such legislative trends provide an example of new, racialised forms of surveillance, to which information technologies are currently harnessed. Anthony Giddens introduces the idea of *moral totalism* to describe attempts to associate authoritarian values with the essential characteristics of a culture. Information flows (or rather restricted and selective information flows including, notably, hostility to out-groups) are a prerequisite for the formation of such values. The success of the media in forging continuities between marginal (e.g. white pride) and mainstream (e.g. neo-conservative or liberal) values is an important theme running through subsequent chapters.

But, we might ask, how do white, other than dominant white, ethnicities fit into this problematic of whiteness? In his study, *Ethnic Identity: the transformation of white America*, Richard Alba argues that attachment to ethnic origins has become increasingly symbolic for all European ethnic groups, partly as a result of education and intermarriage (1990: 291), so that now just the symbols of ethnicity (e.g. religious festivals, customs and discourses of family origins) remain. Allegiances have correspondingly shifted from the community to ethnic identity which was more privatised, individualistic and subject to personal choice. (Although Alba did recognise that there were important differences in ethnic salience between groups, so that northern Europeans (e.g. English, French, Germans) showed less 'ethnicity' than those from southern and eastern Europe (e.g. Italians, Jews and Poles).) In the place of old ethnic ties, what Alba refers to as 'European ethnicity' emerged. This occurred during the period of the Civil Rights movement, i.e. precisely at a time when hitherto allegedly universal notions of fairness were being called into question (1990: 317). By way of re-enforcing this point Alba argued that Asian, Latin American and Caribbean immigration also encouraged whites to define themselves in ethnic terms (ibid.: 318). Alba's conclusions thus coincide with one of this book's key arguments regarding the growing salience of ethnicity to whiteness.

Theme 2   The power of whiteness lies in a set of discursive techniques, including: *exnomination*, that is the power not to be named; *naturalization*, through which whiteness establishes itself as the norm by defining 'others' and not itself; and *universalization*, where whiteness alone can make sense of a problem and its understanding becomes *the* understanding (Fiske 1994: 43). It is possible to think of numerous instances of events, customs, traditions, which somehow do not count as expressions of national and/or ethnic culture, whilst others invariably do. For example, one of Ruth Frankenberg's interviewees revealingly described St Patrick's day as a national celebration but not Thanksgiving (1993: 191). In her examination of whiteness in 'American' literature, Toni Morrison observes that in South Africa to call someone a South African means little without white, black or

13

coloured to prefix it. In the US (and in England for that matter) quite the reverse holds. She goes on, 'American means white and Africanist people struggle to make the term applicable to themselves with ethnicity and hyphen after hyphen' (1992: 47). W.E.B. Dubois, writing some sixty years prior to this develops a similar critique of the notion of Americanisation when he writes,

> What the powerful and privileged mean by Americanization is the deter-
> mination to make the English New England stock dominant in the
> United States . . . it is but a renewal of the Anglo-Saxon cult; the worship
> of the Nordic totem, the disfranchisement of Negro, Jew, Irishman,
> Italian, Hungarian, Asiatic and South Sea islander – the world rule of the
> Nordic white through brute force.
>
> (in Sundquist 1996: 384)

Richard Dyer was amongst the first British writers to make explicit reference to 'white' in an article about film (1988). His main argument is that to ignore white ethnicity is to redouble its hegemony by denying it. This *invisibility*, which closely relates to techniques of exnomination and naturalisation, is a key discursive mech-anism in the construction of whiteness. In Dyer's words, 'whiteness is often revealed as emptiness, absence, denial or even a kind of death' (ibid.: 44). In the first of her Reith lectures, Patricia Williams put it another way when she said that one of the privileges of whiteness was to appear 'unraced' (1997).

Theme 3   One of the reasons why whiteness keeps itself so well hidden is because it works through other discourses. Fiske makes particular reference to sexuality (1994: 45). One of the analytical advantages of whiteness is the scope it provides to explore how subjects are simultaneously gendered and racialised. Heterosexuality, too, is constituted through discourses of whiteness, as I shall argue with reference to anti-Semitism and to the homophobic politics of Oregon's Christian Alliance. At a more subliminal level, however, it has been argued that sexuality is integrally bound up with the discourse of whiteness both in terms of language and practice. David Sibley (1995), for instance, has made some persuasive connections between the 'body sexual' and the 'body politic' in which terms of images of defilement, degeneration and contamination dominate the discourses of both. Likewise, Barnor Hesse analyses the 'white' underpinnings of racial harassment with refer-ence to the significance of body imagery in racialised constructions of city spaces. He writes, 'in the context of racial harassment the body of the other is viewed as a surface of inscription for the shrunken visibility of a white appropriation of the city' (1997: 98). Threats of city spaces being overrun, that is (of being) 'violated' and 'penetrated', make racial harassment the 'inevitable paranoiac anticipation of those events' (ibid.: 99). Psychoanalytic discourse (with its focus on the conscious/unconscious and the mechanisms of projection, displacement and denial) has thus become an important site for analysing and exploring the origins and forms of whiteness.

14

Theme 4 Taking this last point further, the psychological basis of whiteness has been attributed to deep-seated insecurities, anxieties and fears. These are then expressed in numerous, neurosis-driven expressions of whiteness, of which one example, taken from above, would be surveillance. The aim of racialised forms of surveillance would be to allay white fears through the ability to know without being known (Hesse 1997). But whiteness is not just based on fear but elicits it too. This is powerfully evoked in the writings of Frantz Fanon and W.E.B. Dubois who both have much to say about whiteness through their own consciousness of blackness.[2] In *Black Skin White Masks*, Frantz Fanon describes his reaction to being shouted at by a young white boy with the words, 'Look at the nigger . . . Mama a Negro' and how such comments 'imprisoned him' and 'sealed him into that crushing objecthood' (1986: 113ff.). As a result, he argued, 'the white world, the only honourable one, barred me from all participation' (ibid.). For Fanon whiteness meant subjectivities defined both through and by others as well as the internalisation of guilt.[3] However, whiteness is more than induced guilt, according to Fanon. It is also corrupt and de-humanising, as he implies when he writes, 'when whites feel they have become too mechanised they turn to men of colour for human sustenance' (ibid.: 129). Writing earlier in the century, Dubois also noted that whiteness not only positioned blacks but positioned whites in constraining ways. The latter were thus forced to live out their racist subjectivities and in so doing they were imprisoned in their own whiteness.

Theme 5 There is a complex relationship between being 'white' and acting 'white'. Whilst whiteness is defined more by what it does than what it is, Fiske also recognises that white skin has brought 'disproportionate access to that power base' (Fiske 1994: 49). However, the problem of defining whiteness both in physical terms, i.e. skin colour, and as a socially constructed identity, has encouraged Marylin Frye (1995) to coin the term 'whiteliness' to distinguish the constructed from the physical aspect of whiteness. In doing so she draws the analogy between maleness and masculinity, the former referring to physical differences, the latter to a social (or gendered) construct. Whiteness thus refers to some physical state, whiteliness to the ideology of white domination. The advantage of Frye's distinction is that it makes it easier to talk about racialised whiteness in non-essential terms, whilst at the same time acknowledging the existence of pigment differences.[4] However, whilst few would deny the physical category of maleness,[5] white skin pigment is a more elusive property not only because allegedly white ethnic groups, notably the Irish and the Jews have, in some historical circumstances, been defined as black, but also because many who might pass for 'white' see themselves as physically black. Moreover, 'racialised' marks have not just used skin, but other alleged physical and cultural differences. Both anti-Irish racism and anti-Semitism again testify to these complexities. Victoria Davion's reservations about the use of the term whiteliness are relevant here. As a Jewish woman, she has written about how she associated whiteliness not with herself but with the other. Anti-Semitism encouraged her to succumb to whiteliness but not to benefit from its mechanisms of oppression which, on the contrary, worked to deny or fracture her sense of Jewishness (Davion 1995: 137).

Theme 6   Following this last point, whiteness is not a monolith, as work around gender and politics has demonstrated. For example, Mary Hickman and Bronwen Walter have persuasively shown how social scientists have eschewed anti-Irish racism whilst simultaneously developing their analysis of gendered forms of such racism (1995). Vron Ware (1992) too, has explored the ways in which ideas and meanings became historically associated with white womanhood and its related sense of superiority. Contemporary examples include media representations of women in Muslim countries which implicitly contrast the backwardness of Islamic countries with western freedom. Such ideas which also circulate in popular films like Michael Radford's *White Mischief* (1987) can be traced back to the colonial era. During this period white women were seen as conduits of the race (Ware 1992: 37), an idea which complemented those of pure stock and racial contamination espoused by eugenicists. White women were thus seen as particularly vulnerable and hence in need of protection (ibid.: 8–9). This reached fever pitch, according to Ware, in the aftermath of the so-called 'Indian Mutiny' of 1857 with the fear of sexual assault becoming a powerful indicator of wider control of the colonies (ibid.: 38). Nevertheless, alongside these dominant versions of white femininity, there exist accounts of white women who defied this role, lived independent lives (hence often attracting scandal) and who supported and committed their energies to black women and to liberation struggles (ibid.: 42).

Whiteness is not a monolith (although it might function on occasions as such) but a disaggregated set of world views or ideologies. Ruth Frankenberg found evidence of this in her study of white women. In it she distinguished two 'white' perspectives; colour evasion and colour cognisance (each with its own internal differences) both of which were a reaction to a third perspective, essentialised racism (1993: ch. 6). Frankenberg and others have not only recognised the diversity of whiteness, they have argued that whiteness cannot be defined in terms of a set of fixed ethnic characteristics but something which can only be defined relationally and historically. Hence, an important idea in both Ware and Frankenberg's work is the idea that *whiteness is a social construct*. Like blackness it is not about biological differences *per se* but on the cultural meanings often, but not always, associated with skin differences. Blackness and whiteness in this sense are political concepts and just as Stuart Hall said he did not think of himself as black until the 1970s so others might only now be seeing themselves as white. Frankenberg captures the changing and diverse attachments to different ethnicity depending on time and place, by her use of the terms 'social and political salience' (1993: 214–15). According to David Roediger (1991) it is ironic that at the present time appeals to whiteness are at their height at the very time when white cultures are so vacuous and have so little to shout about. It may not have much to shout about but an important argument in what follows is that we should not mistake what is hidden or implicit for what is absent or vacuous.

Where does this leave relationships between white perspectives across the mainstream political spectrum? Jordan argues that seemingly respectable politicians like Pete Wilson in California and Newt Gingrich have more in common with the convicted Oklahoma bomber Timothy McVeigh than we might first assume. In addition, there may be surprising continuities with liberal perspectives, illustrated in defences of white liberalism against the excesses of black nationalism and anti-racism in the respective writings of Robert Hughes (1993) in the US and Melanie Phillips (1994) in England. Donald Warren writes about the emergence of what he calls 'Middle American Radicals' characterised by a 'loose web of anger' as 'private fears (begin) to translate into public protest' (1995: 127–8). The campaign to assert and defend the primacy of English language use in the US is one such protest. In subsequent chapters, I will explore both distinctions and convergences between the more visible, extreme versions of whiteness and the latter's more coded, conservative and even liberal manifestations.

Theme 7 Fiske emphasises the point that media events, as he refers to his examples, all have a material dimension. Whiteness thus works in both representational and material domains (1994: 50). The intention in *Whitewash* is to illustrate the ways in which whiteness expresses itself through representation but that these cannot be understood without reference to wider political and economic conditions. I will begin to explore these later in this chapter but the book is organised around the analysis of events, campaigns and practices, which treats both symbolic and material realms as interdependent and inseparable. Whiteness means the power to position, through representation and practice as Walter Rodney's Guyana testifies. There, whiteness spelt privilege and jobs be it working for transnational companies or universities (1988).

Theme 8 Whiteness has been undermined by what has been referred to as a *politics of representation*. Stuart Hall distinguishes this from *the relations of representation* which is more concerned with issues of bias, positive and negative images and access to media institutions. The 'politics of representation' has been more concerned with the production of diverse forms of representation which in effect challenge stereotypical, essentialised notions of black identity or monolithic versions of black culture, and even the notion of black itself (1992: 253). Such politics are to be found in all spheres of representation, including film (see e.g. Shohat and Stam 1994; Diawara 1993; Bhattacharyya and Gabriel 1994), photography (see e.g. Gilroy 1993b), television, press, radio (see e.g. Riggins 1992), art (see e.g. Gilroy 1993a; Jordan and Weedon 1995), music (e.g. Dines and Humez 1995; Gilroy 1993b; Dent 1992; Wallace 1990), and literature (e.g. Birch 1994; Cobham and Collins 1990). Apart from constituting forms of cultural expression in their own right, this new 'phase' as Hall describes the politics of representation, whatever its aim, has become an all-important corrective to the attempts within whiteness to define, subsume and appropriate other ethnicities in its own terms.

Theme 9   Other strategies contest whiteness more directly. For example, the idea of (white) racial purity has been subverted by the notion of whiteness as a hybrid category, both biologically and culturally. Patricia Williams recalled an incident when a Haitian statesman was asked by an official from the US what percentage of Haiti was white to which he replied 'ninety five per cent'. When he was asked to explain his answer, the Haitian turned the question back on the official and asked how black was defined in the US. The official replied, 'anyone with a black ancestor' to which the statesman retorted 'Well, that's exactly how we measure whiteness' (Williams 1997b: 4–5). Dominant versions of English whiteness are also being contested by other white ethnicities. One example of this has been the Celtic revival in Scotland, Ireland and Wales. This has been expressed in an increase in the demand to learn Gaelic, television stations in Ireland such as 'Teilifis na Gaelige' and SC4 in Wales, as well as a growth in popularity in Celtic dance, literature, poetry and music (*Observer*, 17 November 1996).

Theme 10   Finally, we might think about the future prospects for whiteness? According to Fiske, whites are going to have to come out of their ethnic niche and do a bit of assimilating themselves. But should the aim be, as Roediger (1994) suggests, to abolish whiteness? Is it something we can simply remove like an unwanted blemish? And/or should we begin to disaggregate the monolith of whiteness as both Vron Ware and Ruth Frankenberg begin to do in terms of gender? I will be returning to these questions through an examination of the media strategies of organisations campaigns and pressure groups. My aim will be to look at the cultural making of whiteness and how its 'interest' groups are formed and transformed through media and political activity.

It is clear form the writings of Fanon and Dubois that the terms 'white' and 'whiteness' have been around in black discourses of race and ethnicity for some time. George Fredrickson also used the term white supremacy in his historical study of the US and South Africa to refer, not just to white extremism but to the 'systematic and self-conscious efforts to make race or color a qualification for membership in the civil community' (1981: xi). What is more recent, perhaps, is the increasing acknowledgement of white and whiteness as distinctive and significant concepts for understanding contemporary social relations and cultural processes. They refer not just to self-conscious processes but also to invisible, often unconscious assumptions regarding ethnic and/or racial difference invariably couched in terms of superiority. They refer not only to the ideologies of the extreme right, but to what passes for the norm. White and whiteness acknowledge that such norms are in fact ethnically loaded and express a particular set of cultural assumptions and values. That they pass for the norm or the universal gives them greater legitimacy. It also hides deeply embedded assumptions of superiority. The question is what is it about the present conjuncture that makes whiteness an object of popular, political and academic interest?

Globalisation, the media and the crisis of whiteness

One possible explanation (for the interest in whiteness) is to be found in a set of new global conditions described by, amongst others, Stuart Hall (1991). These conditions include: the liberation and independence of former colonies and the resultant decentring of the west; the alienating effects of mass culture, both in terms of the growth of bureaucracies over which individuals have less and less control and the commodification and standardisation of consumer goods; a growing lack of security and powerlessness at work, typified in short-term contracts, fluctuating hours and redundancies; the commodification of culture resulting in the blurring of the distinction between 'high' and 'low', i.e. between elitist and popular, culture; global migrations or diasporas, brought about by political and economic pressures but with far-reaching cultural consequences, too; and spatial compression brought about by ever more efficient means of disseminating media and cultural products. The combined effects of these conditions have encouraged, if not forced, western culture to reflect on itself as just another culture, not the only culture, not even *the* culture, but just one amongst many. The rapidity and scale of these changes have inevitably played on deep-seated fears and anxieties, both ontological securities and material privileges, which in turn have been 'managed' through the strategies of denial, displacement, and projection referred to above. The fear of the 'disappearance of blondes' harks back to the early twentieth century when social Darwinists encouraged immigration of those of 'Nordic stock' to the US to off-set the impact of immigration of 'celts', 'slavs' and those from southern Europe (Bendersky 1995: 139).

What, specifically, can be said of the media's role in these global processes and the resultant 'crisis of whiteness'? We can begin to address this with reference to two debates surrounding the media which recur in the literature. The first is concerned with the relationship between the media and 'reality' and is thus of general significance in a book concerned with both representations and materialisations of whiteness. John Fiske (1994) refers to the O.J. Simpson case as a media *event* by which he means that part of the 'reality' of the case must be understood in terms of its mediation. For example, the freeway car chase involving the Los Angeles police in hot pursuit of O.J. Simpson, of course, happened, but it can only be understood with reference to its live television transmission across the world. The real and the mediated in this sense are inseparable. Moreover, the significance of particular media events is derived from their ability to resonate deep-seated fears and anxieties within the psyche of white America. The 'O.J. case' could thus be understood as an embodiment of the 'white fascination with and terror of the Black male and his embodiment of a racial-sexual threat to white law and order' (ibid.: xv). The representation of the black male as object of both terror and desire has been integral to the ideology of whiteness and re-told in many different narrative settings. Some of these narratives will be discussed at greater length in subsequent chapters.

According to Douglas Kellner media cultures have to be understood in terms of the relationship between text and context. His concern is 'not only reading media culture in a socio-political and economic context, but seeing how the internal constituents of its texts either encode relations of power and domination . . . or contain a contradictory mixture of forms that promote domination and resistance' (ibid.: 56). Jean Baudrillard takes the idea of 'mediated' as 'real' culture to its conclusion, when he argues that the pervasiveness of media in all its forms detaches us from 'reality', or rather takes on a hyperreality of its own, a condition expressed in his idea of a simulacrum (1983). Whilst many would not go this far, few would deny the all-important role played by the media, a view summed up by Zygmunt Bauman when he writes of it as 'the most powerful influence on the shape of contemporary culture' (1992: 31).

If we are looking for male embodiments of contemporary media culture, we might pause at the television characters Beavis and Butthead, members of a generation raised on media culture and whose textual references are yet more television programmes. 'Bereft of any cultivated taste, judgement, or rationality, and without ethical or political values, the characters react in literally mindless fashion and appear to lack almost all cognitive and communicative skills' (Kellner 1995: 143). In the words of *Newsweek*, a weekly magazine aimed more at the international professional and business classes than generation X, 'the downward spiral of the living white male surely ends here' (cited in ibid.). If we are looking for whiteness in the everyday and mundane, then at some point, space should be found to explore identities alleged to epitomise post-modern white masculinity.

A second approach to the study of the media has been to chart the remarkable growth of global communications empires and to debate their cultural impact. Despite well-publicised battles like Betamax versus VHS (video cassettes), Apple and IBM (personal computers), and Microsoft and its software competitors, there is an indisputable trend towards monopoly. According to Morley and Robins, 'we are seeing the emergence of truly global, decentred, corporations in which diverse media products (film and television, press and publishing, music and video) are being combined into overarching communications empires' (1995: 32). The interdependence of old and new media and the integration of new technologies within the media is worth emphasising. Ian Parker gives the example of the newspaper industry which 'simply could not function in its present form without reliance on a communications system involving interlinked computers, telesatellites, telephone, telefacsimile (FAX) and MODEM services, and printing systems' (Parker 1994: 49). The suppliers are part of an interrelated network (not always working in unison) which includes government agencies and industrial lobbying groups (Lull 1995: 116–17). The significance of these 'media systems' which are organisationally and ideologically linked and which can both support and contest dominant versions of whiteness, will be explored in subsequent chapters.

Arguments about media monopolisation have predictably fed into the heated controversies surrounding 'cultural imperialism', an idea which has come to be associated with the work, amongst others, of Herbert Schiller. In his early writing Schiller blamed the global dumping of consumerist values on the US military–industrial complex. In more recent work he has modified his argument to acknowledge the role of transnational corporations which may not be US-owned. For example, in 1996, Columbia, Tristar and CBS were owned by the Japanese company Sony. Likewise, MCA and Universal, until being taken over by Seagram, were owned by Matshushita. Moreover, international information flows are not just one way, from the US to the rest of the world, but multi-directional. For example, Brazilian, Mexican and Argentinean television are exported to Latin America and, via satellite, to Europe. Nevertheless, Schiller has stuck with the general thrust of the imperialist argument, that it is part of a process which through saturation of (white) western norms, and the increasing role of information technology in particular, leads to the destruction of local cultures (1986). A number of authors (Tomlinson 1991; Thompson 1995; Lull 1995) have criticised the cultural imperialist arguments on three grounds. Firstly, Schiller, etc., are said to mistakenly adhere to a romanticised view of the third world as 'authentic' and 'untainted' by outside influences (Thompson 1995: 169–70). Secondly, advocates of the imperialism thesis patronise Third World subjects by both speaking for them and by presuming to know what is in their interests (Tomlinson 1991: 113ff.). Instead Thompson calls for an analysis which explores the relationship between 'structured patterns of global communication, on the one hand, and the local conditions under which media products are appropriated, on the other' (1995: 174). Thirdly, advocates of the cultural imperialism thesis tend to reduce dominant 'imperial' values to consumerism, and hence to economics. In fact, as Thompson points out again, other values, including nationalism and anti-communism have proved equally significant in the post-World War II period (ibid.: 167).

Edward Herman and Noam Chomsky's 'propaganda model' is, in part, an attempt to offer a more sophisticated explanation of the processes and mechanisms which ensure the maintenance of dominant economic and political interests and hence the imperialistic tendencies of the west and the US in particular (1994: 1ff.). In elaborating their thesis, they identify five filters which serve to censor, if not to silence marginal ideologies and sectors. These include: *size* of media conglomerates (which prohibits most individuals from gaining access to electronic or digital technologies to disseminate their views); *advertising* which binds information providers to a hidden, and sometimes not so hidden, agenda which conforms both directly and indirectly to the values of the advertisers; the reliance on a pool of *experts* whose views have come to dominate the perspectives on offer; the prospects of '*flak*' which may result from publishing 'out of turn'; and, finally, *anti-communism*, which may seem less relevant in the 1990s after the collapse of the Berlin Wall but which, they argue, remains a significant fifth filter.

In what follows, I will make use of the ideas of both the imperialist thesis *and* its critics. Whilst 'cultural imperialism' has the merit of explaining the capacity of whiteness to 'exnominate', 'naturalise' and 'universalise', what it (and Herman and Chomsky) are less able to do is to accommodate and account for an oppositional, alternative politics. Later, in this and subsequent chapters, I will argue that both representational and materialised forms of whiteness result from the combined effects of both monopolising and imperialising tendencies including filtering processes, on the one hand, *and* the exploitation of the inevitable contradictions to which they give rise, on the other. In the meantime, I want to consider one further explanation for the visibility of whiteness at the present time; the rearguard action of nation states, including and notably the US and England, in their attempts to create monocultural and racial versions of the nation and national identity in the face of globalisation.

Nationalism, nation states and national identity

In a humorous, albeit salutary polemic on the state of the British Conservative Party, written just months before its defeat in the 1997 general election, Bill Schwarz argued that the Party's short-term success might well hinge on mad cows, a fact which he attributed to the significance of English nationalism:

> The roast-beef-eating Englishman – the no-nonsense carnivore – has a long history. The blood of the beef and the blood of the Englishman have intermingled in many symbolic repertoires of the nation. Beef. Blood. Semen . . . . To suggest that some unseen contamination has occurred, and that the nation has silently been poisoned from within, calls for a renewed authoritarianism. It calls for intransigence against the 'foreign' enemy as well as summoning up fantasies of quislings at home, who might dare to suggest that English stock has become contaminated.
>
> (1996: 15)

The language of contamination in relationship to the British/English nation/national stock is not new but the context is. It is one marked by a political crisis within the Conservative Party and reflected in the conflict over both Europe and national sovereignty. It is also tied up with divisions over economic policies related to: disinvestment in British manufacturing; the emergence of the OPEC oil producing countries and later the 'tiger economies' of south-east Asia; and pressure from international financial agencies. In 1996, the beef crisis, working with older narratives of nation and race, was just the latest manifestation of a longer-term crisis; that of globalisation and its impact on national identity and the nation state. Stuart Hall and others refer to a number of trends which are of particular relevance for the future of nation states. These include both the economic decline of countries like the UK and the internationalisation of economy. The latter, in turn, can be broken down into seven features. Firstly, there has been a growth in the significance of both transnational companies and global production processes. A second feature has been the emergence of a financial network, described by Richard Barnet and John Cavanagh as a 'constantly changing maze of currency transactions, global securities, master cards, euroyen, swaps, ruffs, and an ever more innovative array of speculative devices for repackaging and selling money' (1994: 17). Contracting out and franchising off sections or stages of business activity has been a third characteristic of these new conditions. Fourthly, there has been an expansion of global markets and fifthly bodies like the International Monetary Fund and World Bank have grown in significance. The migration of labour has been a sixth characteristic and finally, there has been an increased awareness of ecological interdependency, of the kind witnessed at Chernobyl (Hall 1991: 22–3).

Nationalist and religious revivals can thus be understood as a backlash against a world in which 'national leaders no longer have the ability to comprehend, much less control, these giants (global corporations)' (Barnet and Cavanagh 1994: 19). Hall describes Thatcherism as an example of such defensive exclusivism, which he argues was driven by racism (1991: 26). Barnet and Cavanagh add that such reactions are often expressed through religious as well as nationalistic discourse (1994: 20). The impression given in some of these arguments is that nationalism, in all its ethnic, including religious, forms, is but a blip in the inexorable shift towards a new global order. According to Etienne Balibar, such global conditions as those cited above have provoked a crisis of national identity and nationalist backlash throughout the west which has been witnessed in the emergence of the far right in Europe and in the election of right-wing governments (1991). Similarly in central and eastern Europe, the end of Soviet hegemony gave rise to nationalisms both within the former USSR and elsewhere in eastern Europe. In particular, problems arose when claims to nationhood and ethnic lines did not territorially coincide which created new and revived forms of discrimination, for example against the Russians in the Baltic states, the Poles in Lithuania, and, taken to its genocidal (euphemistically termed 'ethnic cleansing') extreme, against the Muslims in the former Yugoslavia. These global conditions have relatedly provided an important backdrop to the rise of religious fundamentalism, which in turn has prompted a re-assertion of western, liberal values.[6]

It is important to distinguish nation state from nationalism in this discussion, for whilst nationalism may be regarded as an anachronism, the idea that the nation state is in its death throes has been challenged by Paul Hirst and Graham Thompson who argue that the world economy, for all the transnational links, remains an inter(*national*) system (1995). The authors suggest a number of ways in which nation states perform what is regarded as a pivotal role in international relations. These are: by providing legitimacy for supra-national entities; by regulating populations; by speaking for peoples; and through the possession of territory. However, whilst nation states remain significant, nationalism, according to Hirst and Thompson, is the political ideology of losers. Rather than integral to the politics of the present, it promotes a politics of the past based on ideas of cultural control and homogeneity. It thus immediately puts itself at odds with the transnational, trans-cultural pressures of new communications technologies (ibid.: 419).

Besides the idea of homogeneity or unity, nationalism is also associated with the ideas of destiny, that of an original people and the right to organise within the territory of a nation state. However, beyond this broad consensus, more precise definitions of nationalism are tied to a range of differing explanatory perspectives.

Floya Anthias and Nira Yuval Davis (1992) refer to one such perspective as *primordialist* since it is based on the belief that there exists a biological/innate need in all of us to belong to something greater than ourselves. Roger Scruton, for example, argues that nationalism is part of our nature (1986). Anthony Smith goes one stage further. He says what is primordial or innate in us are our ethnicities (culture, language and tradition) and that this is what is behind the nationalistic impulse (1986).

Others associate nationalism with a particular historical period, namely that associated with the development of nation states. Anthias and Yuval Davis characterise this perspective as *modernist*, an apt description given the metaphor 'the engine of modernity' used by one author to describe nationalism (Nairn 1977). Nationalism, according to modernists, was a key feature of industrialisation and the creation of legal authority of nation states over territories once controlled by religious communities and guilds. Moreover, imperialism and the expansion of the empire in the nineteenth century derived their political legitimacy from nationalism which aimed to fuse political and cultural boundaries (Gellner 1983). Why, then, given the intense rivalry between nations and the fact that nationalism drew on traditions peculiar to each nation did nationalisms appear remarkably similar in form and development? Immanuel Wallerstein explains this apparent paradox with reference to the important principle of international co-operation which, despite all the rivalry, was a pre-condition for the development of nation states and nationalism (1991). Industrialism also brought with it the technological pre-conditions for nationalism, namely the means of dissemination. According to Benedict Anderson 'imagined communities' were constructed in the first instance thanks to the printing press, which helped to popularise culture and construct a sense of national identity between peoples who never met or knew each other from one end of their lives to the other (1983).

These perspectives have led writers to assess whether or not it is possible for any nationalist struggle to be described as just, a debate which has often turned on the possibility of extricating nationalism from its racist and patriarchal associations. According to Tom Nairn (1977), the interconnections of narratives of nation and race took root in the nineteenth century. Prior to then, he argues, ideas of race were just about lineage or descent. During this period race became inscribed with ideas of superiority which were then used to justify expanding empire and relations of subordination. Nineteenth-century nationalism thus became stamped by its collusion with imperialism. Likewise, Paul Gilroy (1987) argues that British nationalism was and is intrinsically racist because both are based on ideas of pure stock. Linked to this is the idea that both rely on drawing boundaries of insiders and outsiders and entail processes of inclusion and exclusion. In the case of post-war Britain, nationalism has helped to hide racism under a more acceptable discourse. The principle of citizenship, which underpins nationality laws, thus entails forms of exclusion which are both racialised and gendered. The *patriality* clause, not unlike the 'grandfather' voting clause in the US, restricted rights of immigration and citizenship to those with long-standing paternal ties to the UK, which invariably ruled out black commonwealth citizens and 'ruled in' white ex-patriots. The 'twelve month' immigration rule, which requires a couple to live together for a minimum of one year before the non-citizen has a right of settlement has left immigrant women in abusive relationships with the choice between domestic violence and deportation (Southall Black Sisters 1989).

Other writers, whilst acknowledging nationalism's downside, also recognise its potential as a part of a wider revolutionary and/or liberation discourse in colonial and post-colonial struggles. For example, Lynn Innes (1994) looks at how narratives of nation have been constructed in Irish and African literature and illustrates the ways in which nationalist, anti-colonial struggles were historically built on patriarchal assumptions in which women functioned as allegorical depositories of the nation alongside oedipal men claiming back their mothers/mistresses from the imperial aggressor. However, she argues, there is nothing intrinsically patriarchal in such cultural forms or in nationalism itself and goes on to examine contemporary playwrights in both Ireland and Africa who are engaged in a process of recuperating national literature, demystifying the national/feminine coupling and challenging both colonial patriarchs and anti-colonial warriors.

Before leaving this discussion of nationalism and national identity for the time being or rushing to dispatch these alleged, cultural dinosaurs to their graveyards, there is one further way of thinking about national identity. It is important to think about the ways ideas of nation and of national belonging are reinforced in everyday life. Barnor Hesse takes up this idea in his analysis of the racialisation of British/English national identity in the post-1945 period and its 'local' articulation. In particular such national or racial discourses 'harboured the underside of less well-scrutinised features of white appropriations of the city where configurations of cultural identity, locality and neighbourhood became icons of national contestation' (1997: 93). Hence the third way of approaching national identity is therefore through the narratives of nation. These are made up of stories, memories, images and symbols, i.e. through representation. Such stories try to convey what is distinctive about 'imagined communities'. They are part of a set of cultural processes of *construction* in which the media play a crucial institutional role. Such is the appeal of these narratives and their capacity to become embedded in people's consciousness, that national identity and nationalism can appear, as Smith and others suggest, something natural or innate. However, we must ask, which stories, memories, images and symbols attain national status, in what sense are they racially marked and how are they reinforced in everyday life?

'Euro '96'

I shall begin to address these questions with reference to media representations of a major European sporting event held in England in 1996, the European Football Championships ('Euro '96'), and its significant role in the confirmation and re-working of English national identities. Sixteen countries participated and approximately 250,000 supporters travelled to the championships from abroad.

25

Over one million people attended the games which were played at eight football grounds around England. Over six thousand media personnel attended including a BBC and ITV consortium, which beamed the matches to 6.68 billion viewers across 192 countries (UEFA 1996). National sentiments (pride, shame, loyalty, despair, ecstasy etc.) were mobilised and national allegiances strengthened through the deployment of a number of discursive mechanisms. Stories had to be told in ways which resonated with common-sense understandings of the wider political context and encapsulated perceived national values and characteristics. They were described in words, expressed visually and put to music. They drew boundaries, both implicitly and sometimes overtly, between insiders and outsiders, including a thin line between a parochial nationalism and a spirited internationalism.

Euro '96 was not the only battle waged by the English during the summer of 1996. Whilst English footballers were aiming to re-live victories against old European adversaries on the pitch, John Major and Douglas Hogg were doing battle with EU members over the ban on British beef. The latter was one in a succession of crises over Britain's relationship with the European Union, which divided the Conservative Government between pro- and anti-European factions and which ultimately contributed to its defeat in the 1997 general election. Margaret Thatcher had already proved that military and military-style 'achieve-ments' (the Falklands/Malvinas war, the miners' strike, and the tough stance in Northern Ireland) could reap rich domestic political rewards. Added to this, there was a popular belief that sporting success could bring election victory.[7] The scene was thus set for the media to frame both the football championships and the beef war as twin European battlefronts.[8] The fact that political destinies, however tenu-ously, were linked to sporting events, reflected both the fragility of the Conservative regime and the power of what was referred to as the 'feel good factor' (i.e. national sporting success) on political party fortunes. But what was it that 'felt good' exactly? Did it have something to do with a sense of being English and of being rooted in a national culture? Did the opportunity to display an array of national symbols, both past and present, serve to stir and promote a uniquely English sense of achievement, progress and purpose?

In Euro '96 English footballers were not so much embodiments of some English version of the American dream[9] as soldiers re-enacting a military conquest, be it the Crusades against Islam, the defeat of the Spanish Armada or the defeat of the Germans in World War II. Reports of English victories at Euro '96 and previews of their games were thus dominated by metaphoric language of war and the reincarnation of footballers as military heroes. The English press thus mobilised support for the English team through an appeal to a sense of national identity rooted in the British Empire. The following were amongst the many press headlines surrounding England's games with Spain and Germany, which set out to revive particular memories, and thereby to remind readers what it meant to be English:

SEAMAN SINKS ARMADA (*Observer*, 23 June 1996)

LET'S BLITZ FRITZ (*Sun*, 24 June 1996)
ACHTUNG SURRENDER (*Daily Mirror*, 24 June 1996)
MY ENGLAND LIONHEART (*Sun*, 25 June 1996)
BLOODIED BUT NOT BOWED (*Daily Mirror*, 27 June 1996)

The *Daily Mirror* went as far as to declare football war on Germany with an editorial written in the style of the pre-World War II declaration of war. Readers were informed that the German ambassador had been handed a note demanding the withdrawal of the German football team. The Editor, seeking to defuse accusations of xenophobia with light-hearted analogy, continued, 'I have to tell you that no such undertaking has been received and that consequently we are at soccer war with Germany. It is with heavy heart that we print this public declaration of hostilities . . . .' (24 June 1996).

In victory, English footballers were honoured as soldiers back from a campaign. The *Sun* had twenty two medals minted with the words 'Hero (Sun) 1996' around the edge. A spokesperson for the *Sun* was quoted as saying 'Every one of England's Euro '96 squad is a national hero . . . the team has raised national pride to new levels' (27 June 1996). England's defeat by Germany provoked street attacks on a Russian suspected of being German, German cars being overturned, and fighting with the police in Trafalgar Square leading to over 200 arrests (*Sky News*, 27 June 1996). Elsewhere, the media made much of the determination and passion of the English team's performance and its success in raising national pride.

Although the press (and one or two tabloids in particular) stood out in its xenophobic reaction to the tournament, television and radio's more aloof stance did not prevent these media from working on the same symbolic terrain. Hence, on the one hand, tabloid coverage was condemned and space given to Spanish supporters and German players to express their point of view. Reconciliation and integration were pointedly emphasised both at the grounds ('English and Spanish supporters here side by side and that's how it should be', BBC1, 23 June 1996) and in everyday life.[10] Nevertheless, whilst television by and large lacked tabloid xenophobia, its commentators also found it hard to resist the language of battle. In the build-up to the match against Spain, *Sky News* reported 'the men with three lions on their shirt are now roared on by supporters singing a new anthem, and expecting a Spanish conquest' (23 June 1996) whilst on the BBC, Barry Davies reported, 'while the opposition prepares for battle, one assumes that Terry Venables (the England coach) has found time to nip down to Plymouth Ho for a game of Bowls' (BBC1, 23 June 1996).[11] After England's victory, there was much talk of one of England's players, Stuart Pearce, whose character was summed up in the BBC after-match chat by Alan Hanson in these terms: 'if you were in the trenches, with Stuart alongside you, you'd want this guy over the top first. If you were fighting against him the white flag would go up right away' (BBC1, 23 June 1996).

What made Euro '96 distinct from other popular cultural, including many sporting events, was its *Englishness*. This was evident in very visible forms, for example in the unprecedented number of English (St George's) flags adorning pubs up and down the country and painted on faces, backs, chests and top hats. In contrast, there were relatively few Union Jacks around Wembley Stadium, a fact noted by one commentator (BBC1, 23 June 1996). This might be partly explained by Scotland's presence at the tournament, since the union flag is by definition Scotland's too, although this did not prevent the English team from appropriating the British national anthem for the pre-match pageants. There were other less overt expressions of Englishness, from footage of 1966 when England won the World Cup at Wembley and references to the re-capturing of an old community spirit to the Queen's presence at the final. The presence of national celebrities (from breakfast and children's show hosts to actors and pop idols) at the games or just being photographed wearing English scarves etc. broadened the mass appeal of the games and turned them into wider entertainment spectacles.[12] Music was very important in this respect. There were of course the anthems, both official and adopted: *Land of Hope and Glory, You'll Never Walk Alone, Always Look on the Bright Side of Life, We will Rock You* and *Football's Coming Home* whose appeal lay in part in its lyrical references back to 1966 and England's victory against Germany in the World Cup final. There were also the pop stars, such as Allison Moyet, Paul Young and Mick Hucknall who led the singing of the national anthem at the closing ceremony as well as the 'Britpop' musical backdrops to edited 'highlights' of the games.

There was something paradoxical in Euro '96. On the one hand, there was an undoubted snow-balling interest and enthusiasm in England's success, a trend which was reflected in some tabloid newspapers, half of whose pages were devoted to the tournament (e.g. *Daily Mirror*, 22 June 1996). Commentators reinforced this sense of universal interest with such comments as 'the hopes of the nation are there at Wembley', televised scenes and press photographs of euphoric fans watching from pubs on Spain's Costa Del Sol and country-wide reports of 'local' celebrations. The Englishness on display was a playful, carnivalesque, backs-against-the-wall Englishness, but it remained a monocultural, white Englishness. Significantly, this ethos, undoubtedly buttressed by England's success, had ensured that extreme forms of jingoism, notably the tabloid coverage prior to the semi-final against Germany and the violence which followed England's defeat, were widely condemned by media reporters and readers alike.

The marginalisation of the intoxicated, aggressive, white Englishman and his tabloid counterpart, probably helped by the alcohol ban in all stadiums, did broaden the base of interest and support as the tournament progressed. However, that base was never genuinely diversified. The occasional black face, the likes of Frank Bruno in the stand and Paul Ince on the pitch, could hardly detract from the dominant white masculinities on show at the tournament. Yet, as far as spectators were concerned, it was by no means the tough, physical, 'who's next?', kind of masculinity. Whatever their respective ethnic origins, David Baddiel and Frank Skinner, who recorded the tournament's adopted anthem, 'Football's Coming Home', came to emblematise an alternative version of masculinity; non-aggressive, somewhat awkward, comic (often self-deprecating) and, stylistically, 'ordinary'. For all its charms, it complemented the imperial, bellicose version associated with the players, and thus served to reinforce the overall dominance of white English masculinity which the tournament came to symbolise.[13]

Resistance and the relationship between the global and the local

Every Sunday afternoon in July and August, New Yorkers make for Central Park's Summer Stage which hosts an annual series of 'world music' concerts. In August 1996, two bhangra bands from Birmingham, England, DCS and Safri Boys, were playing. 'We had the Beatles in the '60s now we have bhangra in the '90s, the second British pop invasion' announced one of the organisers. 'World Music' from Birmingham! As a resident of Birmingham I felt implicated in the music, even though both bands appealed directly to their 'brothers' and, in the case of the Safri Boys, spoke mostly in Punjabi. Of course, the bands had no interest in hailing me. I was part of one of Summer Stage's diverse audiences: white western consumers of 'world music' who, in my case, happened to live in Birmingham, England. The bands, however, were much more concerned to make their global connections across the south Asian diaspora than foregrounding their Birmingham connection. And it worked. Hundreds of New York's Indian population (mostly from New York's Queens district), some in their seventies, danced and clapped their hands, evidently taking pride in this adaptation of their Punjabi dance and musical tradition. For many it was their first encounter with rock. Some described it as working class. Others found it more accessible than traditional bhangra. Whatever it was, the rock riffs and the infectiousness of the dhol beat brought their diverse audience to its feet and towards the stage. Some, for whom cut 'n' mix and scratching techniques had traditionally come in a different wrapping, looked entertained as well as bemused by these bhangra rappers from Brum.

Of course 'Britpop' invasions, like 'English' films (as the recent adaptations of the novels of Jane Austin, Charlotte Brontë and E.M. Forster testify) are not supposed to reflect too much diversity. That was what was so striking about the Central Park event. Could 'Britpop' really mean bhangra and not just Oasis, Blur and Pulp? For bhangra to gain access to the mainstream, those responsible for compiling popular music charts, which relate directly to radio play lists, will need to include those retail outlets in Britain which sell south Asian records in their millions. In the meantime, the success of such bands will be confined to their 'ethnic market' and the 'mainstream' will appear more inclusive than it is or could be. At least on this one occasion British bhangra was given the chance to express British cultural diversity to a predominantly US audience and in so doing was able to play mischievously with traditional understandings of 'Britpop', 'world music', 'cultural imperialism' and 'Americanisation'.

This New York story introduces the idea of resistance which has hitherto been missing from many of the above accounts of globalisation and media processes.

The question left over from a previous section remains: how can we acknowledge the dominance of particular paradigms, media conglomerates, corporate influence, etc., in the encoding of whiteness but still make sense of the uneven, exceptional, complex and varied impact of contradictory media forms? One way to understand the sources of such resistance is to study audiences and audience culture. Kellner addresses this point when he argues that the media cannot be understood without reference to a bigger cultural circuit which must include media audiences. 'Media cultural texts articulate social experiences, transcoding them into the medium of forms like television, film, or popular music. The texts are then appropriated by audiences which use certain resonant texts and images to articulate their own sense of style, look and identity' (1995: 150). A similar point is made by James Lull who argues that the media as 'ideology-dispensing institutions' are at the same time social institutions which do not speak with one voice nor are their social effects all predictable (1995: 114).

Moreover, the media is only one of a number of information sources. Daily life provides numerous sites, including the family, work, school as well as other, non-media-related, leisure activities. All sites offer ideas and ways of thinking that potentially infiltrate consciousness and affect action (Lull 1995: 18). Media ideologies thus form part of a broader repertoire of beliefs which are used in the construction of everyday life. What interested Lull was the way television watching removed its audience from the immediacy of its surroundings; what he calls the symbolic distancing from the spatial, temporal context of everyday life. The impact of this 'distancing', Lull argued, could be witnessed in events in China in the 1980s. The new-found ability of Chinese audiences to identify with lifestyles, ideas, characters on television, indirectly at least, contributed to the unrest which culminated in the uprising in Tiananmen Square in 1989 (Lull 1995: 123). Global media serve both to displace their audiences in terms of their relationship to their surroundings and to play a part in processes of reinsertion, thus re-embedding themselves into new forms of allegiance and identities (Giddens 1991: 141–2).

Ian Ang's analysis of audiences (1991) illustrates the difficulties entailed in defining an audience and attributing known characteristics to its television viewing. The 'dissolution of "television audience" as a solid entity became historically urgent when "anarchic" viewer practices such as zapping and zipping became visible . . . (i.e.) when it (the industry) had to come to terms with the irrevocably changeable and capricious nature of "watching television" as an activity' (1991: 154–5). Liebes and Katz' often-cited study of watching the US soap *Dallas* confirms the ways in which cultural values (associated with kinship and the family, perspectives on corporate wealth, interpersonal wellbeing) will influence viewers' reactions to the programme (1986).

Moreover, whilst Murdoch, Berlosconi and Bertelsmann sit on the thrones of vast media conglomerates there has also been a parallel decentralisation of key functions, notably production, which have been increasingly franchised out to local independent producers (Lull 1995: 33). The spaces opened up by this mixture of centripetal and centrifugal pressures have enabled the development of localised media production and, in some instances, the creation of radical production companies. But such optimism needs to be qualified. As Morley and Robins point out, externalisation and sub-contracting of production created, not independent and autonomous programme makers, but a casualised, segmented and precarious workforce. The conglomerates held on to distribution and sub-contracted the creativity and the risk which they have been able to purchase on their terms (1995: 33ff.).

It is possible, therefore, to approach the idea of resistance not just via the concept of the active audience but also through an analysis of the relationship between the global and the local. Unless we accept the most rigid version of the cultural imperialism argument, which talks exclusively in terms of unilateral takeover and/or cultural colonisation, there remains the need to find ways of imagining and conceptualising resistance. One place to start would be the generally held view that globalisation entails processes of both homogenisation and fragmentation and that 'neither is an impostor' (Axford 1995: 159). But how do both seemingly conflicting processes work simultaneously and with what consequences? These broad questions have been addressed in a number of interrelated ways, through an examination of: the nature of the locality; processes of indigenisation and reciprocity; new and old ethnicities; third cultures; the end of society; and media as defence mechanisms. In the chapters which follow I hope to show how the locality, which I will use to refer to different spatial and cultural locations, can resist encoded versions of whiteness. I will also illustrate how 'the locality' has been a very significant site in the formation of white pride identities in opposition to those associated with the alleged multicultural or liberal agendas of the nation state.

Instead of thinking about localities as 'places' which are internally homogeneous and where identities emerge out of material conditions including face to face interactions, a growing body of writers have encouraged us to think about the interrelationship between localities in web-like, net-like connections (Morley and Robins 1995: 129) where identities emerge out of both material and symbolic resources. This serves to break with the idea that place and culture inevitably go together. In so far as place has always been subject to external influence there has never been a perfect fit, but with the expansion of electronic communications, there is an evermore pressing case to understand the locality through the global.

The locality thus provides an important site for a negotiation or contestation both internally and with respect to external influences and it is this dynamic interplay which makes for unevenness and variation. The twin processes of 'indigenisation' and 'reciprocity' have provided the conceptual focus for an analysis of the local. In the first (cited in Axford 1995: 167), global corporations and products are adapted to local requirements. Axford takes the example of western banks seeking to adapt their business practices to the ethical norms of Islam (ibid.). Likewise, he cites the use of a Coca-Cola bottle to depict a pregnant woman used in religious ceremonies in Japan as another example of cultural reciprocity. Far from undermining local traditions western icons like Coca-Cola are used to maintain them (ibid.: 170). The locality does not have to be on the periphery or always thought of in terms of neighbourhood or 'face to face' ideas of community. As Featherstone argues, since communities differ by the style in which they are imagined (1995: 108), it is possible to think of national and even global spheres as 'local' in some instances. In other words, what defines the local is relational, an idea which serves to emphasise the symbolic rather than the fixed spatial, community boundaries (ibid.: 193).

Of course there are other responses to global pressures and processes, including ethnicism, nationalism and religious fundamentalism, all of which retreat back into a literal and dogmatic version of culture, history and morality (Featherstone 1995: 163). These responses add up to what Stuart Hall calls defensive exclusivism (1991: 25) and are by no means confined to the periphery. On the contrary subsequent chapters will reveal how such tactics are used in the mobilisation of white identities in the US and Britain. The role of institutions, notably the media, in shifting and contesting as well as anchoring white identities will also form an important part of what follows.

Designer fashion, media celebrities and sweatshop labour

By way of concluding this chapter, I will explore an event which caught the media's attention in the US in the summer of 1996. Briefly, the case involved the use of Honduran child labour to make clothes which subsequently bore the name of US television celebrity Kathie Lee Gifford. The case is relevant to this book for a number of reasons. Firstly it highlights the importance of understanding whiteness in terms of *privileged spaces*, in this case those occupied by domestic retailers, local manufacturers, celebrity sponsors and consumers. Such 'spaces' cut across traditional class and ethnic divisions and emphasise the need to see whiteness as contingent and fluid rather than fixed. Furthermore, the case illustrates the interpenetration of 'global' production and media products on the one hand and 'local' economies and cultures on the other. It also highlights the role of local pressure-group organisations in bringing the case to a much wider national and global audience and the strategic use of the media to promote their cause. The case proved newsworthy on a number of counts. It had *human interest*, through the attention paid to the exploitation of child labour. It also had *entertainment* value through the direct involvement of a national television celebrity and a strong *dramatic narrative* worked around the theme of the individual versus the system or, in this case, a four-person pressure group pitted against the multi-billion, multinational clothes manufacturers, retailers and sponsors.

For several years many, including government officials, had been trying unsuccessfully to highlight the conditions in the clothing manufacturing sweatshops. The children working in the Honduran sweatshops, for example, were paid thirty-one cents per hour (approximately twenty pence) working long shifts in unsafe environments with no rights and subject to daily verbal and physical harassment

(*Washington Post*, 30 May 1996; *New York Times*, 31 May 1996). According to US Department of Labor figures, US workers earning half the minimum wage were paid $2.13 for every shirt they produced whilst the shirts were sold for $27.50. In contrast, those working for the minimum wage earnt $4.25 for each shirt they manufactured, whilst the shirt was sold for $29.00 (*Newsday*, 16 June 1996). The comparison can be used either to illustrate the small difference in retail price it takes to pay the minimum wage or to illustrate the perversely low labour costs as a total of retail price. The situation worsens for some brand names produced outside the US. One of the best-known examples is Nike shoes which retail for up to $135 but which cost $5.60 to produce. Moreover, Nike's (predominantly young female) workforce make an average of eighty-two cents a day in its Indonesian factories (Barnet and Cavanagh 1994: 326).

The Kathie Lee case illustrates how a political issue often needs an injection of 'entertainment' value before it can capture the public's attention. This is noted in an article in New York's *Newsday*: ' "until Kathie Lee came along, it was a very hard story to sell" says Jeff Balinger, a worker-rights activist who has been documenting conditions in Nike's Indonesian plants since 1987'. Likewise, the US Labor Secretary, Robert Reich, had been campaigning against sweatshops for a year. The *Los Angeles Times* (16 June 1996) reported that despite using 'his office as a bully pulpit against sweatshops . . . his sermons were sparsely attended' and he was only able to mobilise popular support in the wake of the Gifford revelations. In fact, it had been a year since another notorious case of sweated labour was exposed when government officials raided the El Monte, California, compound (enclosed by barbed-wire housing) and took away seventy-two Thai 'indentured' female workers for imprisonment.[14] Despite its significance, this case had failed to generate the sustained media attention which accompanied the Kathie Lee revelations.

What gave the story its edge and made it so intriguing was not just that it involved a celebrity, Kathie Lee Gifford, but that the media, which had been instrumental in constructing the latter's squeaky-clean image, now cast her in the role of the accused. 'It took a celebrity like Kathie Lee to capture media and public attention' (Maria Echaveste in *Newsday*, 16 June 1996). Kathie Lee derived her status not just from the media but also from the fact that 'Kathie Lee' blouses, skirts and trousers were bought in the country's most successful retail outlet, Wallmart. According to the *Los Angeles Times* 'Gifford boasted that it was not unusual for the many stores to sell 100,000 of the same skirt in a week' (16 June 1996). This last comment reported in the *Los Angeles Times* may partly explain why the mainstream media offered little in the way of sympathy for Kathie Lee. The fact that she was not a journalist by profession may have given fellow hacks greater licence. It might have also had something to do with the fact that Kathie Lee was not just successful, or even a successful woman, but that she was also seemingly squeaky clean as well (the wording on her label stated that some of the proceeds of each sale would go to a children's charity), all of which added relish to the exposé.

On May 1, she tearfully raised the subject on *Live with Regis and Kathie Lee*[15] mixing her sobs with indignation. 'You can say that I'm ugly, you can say I'm not talented. But when you say I don't care about children, mister, you better answer your phone because my attorney is calling you today'. . . . Sweatshops where they exist are deplorable, she told her audience . . . . Anyway she preferred to spend her valuable time on her well-known work with children with AIDS . . . 'I cannot save the world Reege!'

(*Los Angeles Times*, 14 June 1996)

Lee's embarrassment was compounded when UNITE, the Union of Needle Trades, Industrial and Textile Employees revealed that employees at Seo Fashions in Manhattan, again manufacturing clothes bearing the Kathie Lee label, not only worked in similar sweatshop conditions but had not been paid for several weeks. Some were owed as much as $700. The workers, from Mexico and Ecuador, were undocumented and feared the personal ramifications of a public campaign (a dilemma which employers have exploited in order to keep profits up and costs down). The *Los Angeles Times* reported what happened when Lee Gifford got to hear of this:

this led to a mesmerising event. The next day Frank Gifford (ex-football star and Kathie's husband) waded through a hostile crowd in the filthy streets, raising his voice above chants of 'Kath-ee, where's our mon-ee!' and entered the decrepit Seo sweatshop with three $100 bills for each worker in a stack of white envelopes.

(*Los Angeles Times*, 14 June 1996)

The case was originally brought to the public attention thanks to the investigative campaigning role of the National Labor Committee, a foundation-funded organisation run by four staff from its Chelsea office in Manhattan and in particular the role of Charles Kernaghan, its Executive Director. Kernaghan based his campaign, both on Lee's celebrity status and on what he expected would be her 'decent American' response, that is to marshall her star status to do all she could to stop the abuses. Whilst the case put by Kernaghan was taken by the press both to name and explain the problem (with headlines like 28C AN HOUR and APPAREL FIRM'S DIRTY LAUNDRY (both from *Newsday*, 16 June 1996)), his own character was portrayed as less than honourable. 'Good guy crusader or devious fanatic?' asked *Women's Wear Daily*, whilst the *New York Times* noted that 'Kernaghan with a machine gun speaking style . . . often breaks into moralistic tirades – and has the air of a radical priest . . . (and) never finishing his (doctorate) dissertation' (18 June 1996). In this case the efforts of the mainstream media to caricature Kernaghan as a zealot and fanatic served to undermine his own credibility and that of his under-funded organisation (helping to ensure it stayed that way) whilst at the same time enhancing the media's critical, but conciliatory role.

The Donnahue Show (12 August 1996) which was devoted to the issue, epitomised this through its choice of invited guests (including representatives of women workers, workers themselves and the Secretary of Labor and a representative of the American Apparel Manufacturers Association), all of whom presented a unanimous indictment of sweatshop conditions, and its use of audience discussion to explore future strategies, including consumer boycotts.

The success of the Gifford campaign culminated in a law regulating the activities of manufacturers and opened the door to further campaigns. Meanwhile *The Gap* chain agreed to monitor its factories in El Salvador in which women were being paid eighteen cents an hour. In 1996 the National Labor Committee also launched a campaign against the use of Haitian labour at twenty-eight cents an hour. In an open letter to the CEO of Disney, Michael Eisner, Kernaghan described the plight of a woman who earnt $10.77 a week making Pocahontas shirts trying to feed, clothe, educate and provide medical care (the price of antibiotics is over $30) for her four young children. In addition to the letter, the NLC produced a video, *Micky Mouse Goes To Haiti*, which documented some of these experiences and working conditions at the NS Mart plant. Apart from the Disney campaign, pressure groups and trade unions hoped to capitalise on the increase in public awareness as a consequence of the Gifford affair and to name other celebrity sponsors, including African-American basketball star Michael Jordon, to use their media roles as a platform for a similar campaign against Reebok.

Any assessment of the campaign would need to address the fraught question of 'interests'. The apparent beneficiaries of the 'old sweatshop system' would appear to be local manufacturers, sponsors like Kathie Lee (whose income according to her own figures in 1995 from the sponsorship deal was $5 million) and consumers, although the latter as the Department of Labor statistics suggest would not have to pay that much more for workers to receive the minimum wage. It could also be argued that consumers, too, are exploited when it comes to price-inflated designer-label fashion wear, although there is an arguable element of choice in consumption, depending on income. Even the 'interests' of the workers themselves are complex. The decision for illegal immigrants to complain about conditions in Manhattan's garment quarter was not straightforward, nor is it for workers in central America and south-east Asia working for a few cents but mindful of the alternatives. The role of white progressives like Charles Kernaghan or liberals like Kathie Lee Gifford may have been oppositional to both dominant commercially motivated versions of whiteness but is also in conflict with some subaltern perspectives based on the legitimate fear of the consequences of a high-profile media-led strategy on their job security and immigration status.

In terms of the concerns of this book, the case illustrated an important (some would say regrettable) shift in political debate whereby the more an issue can entertain as well as educate the more likely it is to reach a wider audience and hence shape popular attitudes and behaviour. In this case politicians, trade unions and pressure groups had tried, without too much success, to raise the issue of sweatshops by relying on more orthodox political strategies. The success of the campaign lay in its ability to develop strategies which acknowledged the enormous potential media interest in a case involving Kathie Lee as well as the level of public interest and potential concern around issues of consumption and lifestyle. The entertainment value of this story resulted directly from the status of the accused: squeaky-clean media celebrity, Kathie Lee Gifford. For once the logic of newsworthiness encouraged the media to run with it even at the expense of one of its own 'personalities'. Secondly the case proved a good example of the global/local nexus. In this case and in others, clothes marketed globally are produced in global production sites, located according to economic perceptions of cheapness and efficiency. However, this does not mean capital always has to be exported. Cheap labour can be imported and a further twist to this story was the revelation that Kathie Lee Gifford's clothes were also being manufactured in Manhattan sweatshops. The case thus illustrates the critical relationship between media culture and politics and between material conditions and the world of designer labels, image, lifestyle, i.e. consumer culture.

There are other ways in which the Kathie Lee Gifford saga might serve to encapsulate a number of the ideas explored in this book. It illustrates how white spaces and positions of privilege (domestic retailers, local manufacturers, celebrity sponsors and consumers) can cut across ethnic and class divisions. In terms of consumption, in particular, new ethnicities, based less around skin and more around style, are made possible by designer clothes available to those with purchasing power in the global market place. In contrast, the role of Honduran and Thai workers, whether they work in sweatshops inside or outside the US, is critical to the maintenance of the above orders of privilege. The fact that, in the main, clothes production is carried out by women and in some cases by child labour illustrates the co-constitutive processes of gender and age as well as ethnicity at the level of production. Above all therefore, the case thus demonstrates the importance of seeing whiteness in contingent terms, i.e. it represents a strategic position which need not necessarily be skin-related and sometimes, although not always, is dependent on where you are located in the production/consumption process. It illustrates a variety of white perspectives which illustrate the heterogeneity of whiteness without denying the significance of its unifying tendencies. It alerts us to the dangers of emphasising consumer culture to the exclusion of questions of production. Finally it encourages us to see the ways in which, in this particular set of circumstances, white privilege is ensured not simply by the exploitation of 'Third World' but more specifically female and child labour.

Conclusions

Rather than try to provide a water-tight definition of whiteness, this chapter has aimed to present an overview of some recent uses of the concept in order to build a more exploratory framework for the remaining chapters. Whiteness has been understood:

- not as a set of ethnic characteristics but the deployment of power and/or space from which a variety of positions can be taken;
- as a set of discursive techniques understood both in the context of their cultural representation and institutional materialisation;
- as a current running across the political spectrum from white-pride politics, where whiteness is consciously celebrated, to more normative forms of white-ness;
- as underpinned by a set of anxieties and fears rooted in the unconscious and capable of mobilisation depending on circumstance;
- as both a constructed unity; and
- as a disaggregated, diverse and heterogeneous disunity which is nevertheless capable of mobilisation against its dominant counterpart. Cultural and polit-ical expressions and mobilisations by 'subaltern' white ethnicities is one example.

The argument emerging from this chapter is that, for reasons to do with global economic, political and cultural shifts, even normative forms of whiteness are becoming less hidden. 'Exnominated', 'universal' and 'naturalised' expressions of whiteness are slowly emerging from the closet. Furthermore, what appeared at one time to be distinct ideological positions around whiteness, now appear more on a continuum. 'White' politics which is fractured and mobilised along class and gendered lines is another. Finally, historicising white fictions (hybridising white-ness), linked to a politics of representation which challenges constructed unities are further sources of potential white disempowerment.

To explore why whiteness has become an object of increased attention in both academic and popular discourse, attention switched in section two to the concept of globalisation. The latter was used to refer to the interdependence witnessed in the growth of global institutions and trading blocs, migration on a scale never witnessed before, the rise of new satellite and digital media and information tech-nologies and the dominance of transnational corporations. Together, these new global conditions have served to mobilise white fears and anxieties which have expressed the re-assertion of old identities often based on racialised ideas of the nation. Identities are not just rooted in anxieties or in economic and political ruptures but are reinforced in the routines and symbolic events of everyday life. This idea of mobilisation and maintenance through symbolic events was illus-trated through the example of the 1996 European Football Championships.

Resistance to dominant forms of whiteness comes in many shapes and sizes and can be both theorised and illustrated empirically. New global conditions have, in themselves, thrown up the scope for new forms of contestation, for example, dias-poran music produced locally and disseminated globally challenges what passes for an allegedly ethnically homogeneous national musical tradition. Likewise theories which acknowledge the role of diverse readings of media products are based on the idea that ways of thinking, motivations and actions are complex distillations of background circumstances and predilection. Political realities are thus correspondingly uneven, even when Noam Chomsky's filters are working at maximum efficiency.

The Kathie Lee Gifford episode illustrated some of these global configurations, e.g. sweatshop labour in both Honduras *and* Manhattan, but it also illustrated the problems of trying to pin whiteness down without providing a sense of context to define it. In this case it, whiteness, though not named as such (one of its discursive tricks), was expressed as a set of positions which cut across class and ethnic divisions and from which whiteness embraced ownership, sponsorship and consumption, but not production. The case was more than about white in skin terms. For example, 'whites' were evidently not the only ones to wear Kathie Lee clothes. On the contrary, consumption patterns have been instrumental in re-aligning ethnic and class divisions. Whiteness in this case was expressed through its ability to control the distribution of privileges and measured in terms of access to a living wage and a healthy work environment. Its power also resided in its ability to hide behind the so-called neutrality of the market place. What the campaign against the use of sweatshop labour also illustrated is that such economic practices can be effectively challenged so long as those global shifts, notably the growth in significance of the media and relatedly entertainment politics, are built into strategies of resistance.

2

GENEALOGIES OF WHITENESS

The Museum of the Confederacy in Richmond, Virginia, was founded in 1896 as a 'shrine to the confederate cause and a memorial to the devotion of confederate women' (*Museum of the Confederacy Journal* 1996: 3). The dedication was thus worded because white women had been responsible for building and managing what was perceived by its founders to be a testimony to the (white) male confederates of the 1860s. The museum has unashamedly symbolised white supremacy, ever since, through its displays of confederate uniforms, weaponry and flags, as well as furnishings and ornaments which once decorated the finest of the South's plantation houses. Almost by way of countering this white supremacist historical narrative, which had evidently been embodied since its outset, the museum hosted an exhibition in 1991 under the title, 'Before Freedom Came: African American Life in the Ante-bellum South'. Photographs of slaves (names unknown) as well as the more repressive means of terror, e.g. slave harnesses and collars, were displayed.

Within the overall ethos of the museum, the exhibition appeared both anomalous and marginal, a point not lost on Jane Lazarre (1996), whose consciousness had already been shaped by her own Jewish background and personal ties. Whilst she had been profoundly moved by what she saw, Lazarre reflected on the significance of the museum once the exhibition was over. She wrote, 'now the Richmond Museum (once again) becomes a metaphor for American denial of the reality of slavery (and) of African American history as a central core of American history' (1996: 19). This anecdote serves to illustrate the ways in which histories are made through the selective construction and representation of 'tradition' in the public sphere, i.e. symptomatic of what Barnor Hesse refers to as 'white amnesia' (1997: 92). It also shows how cultural spaces like museums are racialised and gendered in terms of their production and forms of representation and that such institutions can promote ideas which are both supportive of and resistant to white solidarity, depending on what is exhibited and who decides to spend the $8 entrance fee.

The aim of this chapter is to shed light on the problematic of whiteness by exploring its genealogies. A number of ideas, already associated with whiteness, will be illustrated with reference to both key historical moments and analytical themes. The chapter will explore the ways in which whiteness has been hidden, i.e.

'exnominated', 'naturalised' and 'universalised' through its construction of otherness and its capacity to resonate across the whole political spectrum will be explored. In addition, the inseparability of whiteness from other social formations of class, gender and sexuality and the scope for some ethnicities to experience whiteness both as a subaltern and a dominant status will be highlighted. Whiteness is socially constructed and historically contingent, by this I mean its genealogies have been characterised by periods of discursive dormancy punctuated by periods of resuscitation and activity. To this end an analysis of politics as an important site for the mobilisation of racial fears and anxieties, invariably linked to economic discourses and played out through the media will be examined. Finally the chapter will explore how whiteness can be disaggregated through the notion of multiple readings and the politics of representation.

The chapter, as I have indicated, will be organised around both historical moments and analytical themes. After a brief overview of media histories, I will take 'slavery and empire' as key moments in the formation of whiteness in the US and England. This will be followed by a discussion of the contingency of whiteness ('disposable whiteness') and its articulation with other social categories ('sexing the race'). In conclusion, I will focus more on the contemporary period as a prelude to subsequent chapters, which will explore current developments in the formation of, and resistance to, whiteness ('post-liberation' whiteness). This will entail a discussion of different strategies for contesting and subverting the idea of whiteness as both unitary and dominant. The emphasis here will be on the possibility of both different subject positionings in relationship to discourses of whiteness and different strategies pursued, via cultural production, in the sphere of representation.

Media and the collective imagination of whiteness

In many respects both the US and England share a common history of racialisation which, as Stephen Small points out, comprises the entrenchment of racist images and a history of political and economic expansion via slavery (1994: 179). Racism, Ali Rattansi argues, was constitutive of the wider growth of modernity (1994: 19) and ideas of race were integral to ideas of progress, morality, reason and certainty on which the modernist project was built (see Goldberg 1993: 14ff.). Whiteness formed part and parcel of an invisible trade between the two countries from the sixteenth century onwards, a time when England first introduced the idea of 'race' to its American colonies. It became a significant thread in the histories of the two countries, reciprocal and intertwining processes of Anglicisation in the US and Americanisation in England within an overarching history of modernity, creating some remarkable parallels as well as differences.

In her detailed analysis of the structure of racist discourse in both the US and Holland, Philomena Essed (1991) focuses on the mechanisms which ensured the dominance of 'whitecentric' culture. Her comparative focus enabled her to assess the specific histories of both countries in terms of their impact on contemporary discourses of whiteness. The divergent histories were reflected in differences, both of understandings and perceptions of racism and structures of racist ideology. In particular, in the US, racism was admitted and resisted in more overt and explicit ways than in Holland. Essed attributes this, in part, to the legacy of both slavery and segregation which, in historical terms, were still relatively recent phenomenon. In Holland, where racism was constructed 'at a distance' until migration from the former Dutch colony of Surinam, there was a much greater tendency to deny racism and to bury it beneath a rhetoric of tolerance. In both cases, however, racisms were gendered and, as Essed maintains, 'it is likely that Dutch images of black women are also strongly influenced by US culture, in particular through literature, television series, and movies' (ibid.: 31). Images may not have had the same resonance dis-embedded from their context of origin but this does not prevent their being re-worked in spatially unfamiliar settings, thus supporting the idea of a trans-spatial culture.[1]

The maxim that all media is political and that all politics is mediated is revealing at a general level but less helpful in terms of particularities. Media and political institutions have their own histories which have thrown up some interesting anomalies and variations. For example, I will argue in subsequent chapters that talk radio in the US and the tabloid press in England have become distinct sites for the articulation of racialised themes and imagery which single them out from their media counterparts. To understand the peculiar histories of these institutions is beyond the scope of this book, although it must, in part, relate to their specific historical relationship to the state, their open, populist style of engagement with listeners and readers, and the attraction of demagogic, didactic, populist media personalities to berate, cajole, energise and mobilise their audiences. Rather, I will explore more broadly the distinctive role of different media *vis-à-vis* ideologies of whiteness and the wider context from which whiteness both draws inspiration and invites an identification.

The history of the mass media and its significance as a source of symbolic power is usually traced back to Gutenberg's press in Germany in the fifteenth century although printing actually dates back to earlier developments in south-east Asia in both China and Korea (Thompson 1995: 53). The rise of the nation state, not just as a political entity but as a source of collective identity, has been attributed to the capacity of the early printing presses to disseminate news to people who would otherwise have no knowledge or contact with each other. The press played a particularly important role in Britain, in challenging both the Catholic Church and the monarchy in the seventeenth century (ibid.: 65).

The growth of the mass media transformed ideas of space and time which had been rooted in physical spaces but were now disembedded, allowing distant events (both spatially and temporally) to become part of everyday life (Stevenson 1995: 130). The democratic and subversive potential of new media has long been a topic for debate. Pessimists have believed that even the allegedly more open 'bourgeois public sphere was effectively closed to all but the middle-class males who frequented the salons and coffee shops in the latter part of the 17th century' (Thompson 1995: 73). Jürgen Habermas has also argued that such potential was lost with the commercialisation of the media and the colonisation of the life world. The Frankfurt School, as a whole, argued that the media induced mass passivity and inhibited a radicalisation of consciousness, whilst reproducing dominant culture (Stevenson 1995: 52).

The mass media's history thus coincided with the history of the nation state. From the outset, the media relied on colonial narratives and the deployment of tropes, metaphors and allegories of empire and expansion. This 'Eurocentrism', as Shohat and Stam refer to it, provided a rationale for discourses of white supremacy and colonialism with popular cultural forms feeding off each other (1994: 3). For example, minstrel shows and vaudeville inspired many ideas taken up in silent films which both debased and ridiculed black life (Rhodes 1995: 37). Representations of otherness shifted in broad terms with wider historical events, whilst at the same time retaining residues or precipitates from the old colonial period (Shohat and Stam 1994: 15). For example, the shift from Sambo, a figure introduced into musical theatre in 1795, to rapist brute in nineteenth-century discourse coincided with the US Civil War, the struggle for abolition and corresponding images of the compliant, against that of the freed, slave (Rhodes 1995: 36).

In the US, penny newspapers which became popular in the early nineteenth century served the agenda of racial superiority (ibid.: 35) and, simultaneously, the formation of class interests and alliances. Alexander Saxton has argued that US mass-circulation dailies of the 1830s and 1840s promoted territorial expansion, northern working-men's interests and, although containing 'scatterings of anti-slavery material' (1990: 103) more typically peddled ideas of racial superiority. In doing so the press of the period, as well as the literature, represented the class alliance of southern planters and northern working men, i.e. the Jacksonian Democratic agenda (1990: 101ff.). Film had a distinctive role in processes of white identity formation in both the US and Britain in the nineteenth and early twentieth century. As Shohat and Stam argue, 'while the novel could play with words and narrative to engender an "aggrandized subject", the cinema entailed a new and powerful apparatus of gaze' (1994: 103). Not that imperialism was somehow inscribed in the projector or the celluloid but that,

> the context of imperial power shaped the uses to which both apparatus and celluloid were put. In an imperial context the apparatus tended to be deployed in ways flattering to the imperial subject as superior and invulnerable observer . . . transforming European spectators into armchair conquistadors, affirming their sense of power while turning the colonies into spectacle for the metropole's voyeuristic gaze.
>
> (Shohat and Stam 1994: 104)

Ideas of exclusion, hierarchy, and identity were thus valorised through visual imagery (Pieterse 1992: 226). The cinema assisted in the promotion of a national self-consciousness from the turn of the century, playing the role once taken by newspapers and novels. Film-viewing audiences, which Shohat and Stam describe as a 'gathering community' (1996: 155), thus provided the setting for group loyalties to form. The narratives were such that Euro-Americans could identify with the British Raj and English audiences with the exploits of the French foreign legion. In other words, western audiences could participate in the global imperial project (ibid.: 154). The result has been a history of cinema which has drawn heavily on themes of *infantilization* (Michael Curtiz's *Casablanca*, 1942), *rape and rescue* (D.W. Griffiths' *Birth of A Nation*, 1916),[2] *'penetration of virgin lands'* (King Vidor's *Bird of Paradise*, 1932) and *harem fantasies* (Gene Nelson's *Harum Scarum*, 1965) (Shohat and Stam 1996: 137ff.). Even on the basis of these fingernail sketches it is clear that plots were simultaneously racialised *and* gendered; the two were co-constituted in the discourses of imperial cinema. And even though the empires on which such films drew their inspiration have been lost in a formal political sense, the 'submerged imperial presence lives on in contemporary films' (ibid.: 121). In the Reagan/Bush and Thatcher eras, such themes re-surfaced in films like Steven Spielberg's *Indiana Jones* (1984) on the one side of the Atlantic and the Raj nostalgia genre on the other (ibid.: 123).

Empire and slavery

Although in general terms, whiteness was historically constituted through its relationship to 'otherness', England and the US differed in two important respects. In England whiteness was constructed, at least initially, through relationships with an overseas empire, i.e. relations forged at a distance but very much associated with an allegedly indigenous English identity.[3] In the US it was manufactured by a *settler* community, in part to distinguish itself from indigenous native and subsequently African-Americans, who, far from inhabiting some overseas colony, co-habited the same land mass. Hence, in England, an implicit consciousness of white identity was associated with the second-hand reports of voyagers who, from the sixteenth century onwards, provided descriptions themselves drawn on already existing associations of whiteness with purity, beauty and virtue and blackness with their opposites (Jordan 1974: 6). The pre-occupation with heathenism, promiscuity and cultural difference became the focus of intense curiosity and fantasy on the part of English traders, travellers and writers who simultaneously re-affirmed a white English ethnocentrism inscribed with its baggage of aesthetic and religious values. In his much quoted *History of Jamaica* of 1774, Edward Long projects sexual fears and fantasies into his 'Negroe' stereotype when he states:

> they are as libidinous and shameless as monkeys, or baboons . . . if lust
> can prompt such excesses (in England) . . . despite all the checks which
> national politeness and refined sentiment impose, how freely will it
> operate in the more genial soil of Africa . . . where the passions rage

without any control; and the retired wilderness presents opportunity to
gratify them without fear of detection.

(cited in Walvin 1971: 131)

But as Jordan points out, such ideas of sexuality were not new. As early as 1526,
Africans were described in the following terms: 'they have great swarmes of
harlots among them; whereupon a man may easily conjecture their manner of
living' (cited in Jordan 1974: 19). And, at the turn of the century, Othello's
embraces were described as the 'gross clasps of the lascivious moor' (ibid.). Art,
too, in the eighteenth century, conferred prominence and superiority on its white
subjects. In contrast, those of African descent were invariably used as foils to their
white counterparts, their blackness accentuating the 'white', both literally and alle-
gorically (Dabydeen 1987: 30).

Beyond the bounded space of the canvas or the controlling white gaze, the
more general prospect of a black presence in England met with a terror-driven
response which has been the hallmark of official responses to black immigration
ever since. In 1601, Elizabeth I issued a Royal Proclamation, stating that,

> the Queen's Majesty . . . in these hard time of dearth, is highly discon-
> tented to understand the great number of Negroes and blackamoors
> which are carried into this realm . . . and . . . that the same said kind of
> people shall be with all speed . . . discharged out of her Majesty's realms.

(cited in Walvin 1971: 64–5)

In the nineteenth century, forms of representation drew heavily on concurrent
developments in the self-defined science of racial classification and the scramble
for empire which, in the latter's case, both inspired and drew comfort from literary
representations of overseas adventurism. As Gaina Lewis argues, it is 'not so much
that "imperial culture" developed to promote imperialism, but that, as a pervasive
economic, social, political and cultural formation the imperial project could not
but influence how people thought, behaved and created' (1996: 13).

The novel played a particularly important role in the formation of both white
masculinity and femininity in nineteenth-century England. As Said asserts,

> by the 1840s the English novel had achieved eminence as the aesthetic
> form and as a major intellectual voice, so to speak, in English society . . .
> (novelists like Jane Austin, George Eliot and Mrs Gaskell) shaped the idea
> of England . . . and part of such an idea was the relationship between
> home and abroad.

(Said 1993: 85)

In novels of the imperial period, this relationship between home and abroad was
rooted in relations between 'whites' (whose whiteness remained assumed and
understood) and 'others'. For example, Jane Eyre's character was premised on a

44

knowledge of the slave-owning plantocracy and the racial theories which supported it. Her status was also significantly tied to the death of Bertha, Rochester's Jamaican wife, who set fire to herself (and the house) in order that 'Jane Eyre might become the feminist individualist heroine of British fiction' (cited in Young 1990: 165). Women like the Brontës were thus very much products of their imperial times. Whilst they transgressed their traditional feminine roles they did so, nevertheless, as *white* women. In *Mansfield Park*, the stability and prosperity associated with home is made possible because of what is happening abroad, namely on Thomas Bertram's slave plantation in Antigua. The latter is 'mysteriously necessary to the poise and beauty of Mansfield Park' (Said 1993: 69).

Elsewhere travellers' tales and the reports of traders, administrators and missionaries furnished novelists like Rider Haggard, J.M. Ballantyne, John Buchan and Arthur Conan Doyle with the means to constitute a version of white English masculinity compatible with the times. In stereotyping blackness, these authors collectively cultivated its opposite. White masculinity positions itself, if not explicitly, *by default* as superior, civilised, etc. So, we see *Prester John*, in Buchan's novel, describing Bushmen as 'one of the lowest of created types' (cited in Street 1986: 98). Elsewhere, we are told of the demonic and exotic qualities of the Africans in Conrad's *Heart of Darkness* (McClure 1986: 159), the indigenous peoples in both Ballantyne's *Coral Island* and Haggard's *King Solomon's Mines*,[4] and finally, the child-like characteristics of the Indians in Kipling's *Kim*. The fact that both Kipling and Conrad have also been read as anti-racist and anti-imperialist respectively underlines a previous point about whiteness. It is not just what is written *per se* but who writes, how it is read and by whom.

The development of print technology, publishing and newspaper industries and the increase in adult literacy made these stories of imperial adventure available to increasing numbers who read them in comics, magazines, newspapers as well as novels. Such was the popular success of some fictional characters that they were reproduced in numerous cultural forms. For example, the turn-of-the-century gollywog character, described in dictionaries as a grotesque, black figure, appeared in magazines, circus, theatre, in children's fiction and on marmalade jelly and jam jars from the turn of the century onwards (Pieterse 1992: 156–8).[5]

Advertising generally played an important complementary role in mediating these themes. For example, Victorian soap adverts provide allegorical settings in which the 'purification of the domestic body becomes a metaphor for the regeneration of the body politic' (McClintock 1995: 214). The black child was scrubbed white apart from his face, 'almost but not quite' in Homi Bhabha's terms, mimicking his white counterpart and thus ensuring the white child as heir to progress. What distinguished advertising, or commodity racism, as Ann McClintock calls it, from scientific racism, was its accessibility. As McClintock argues, whilst other cultural forms were relatively class bound 'imperial kitsch as consumer spectacle, by contrast, could package, market and distribute evolutionary racism on a hitherto unimagined scale' (1995: 209). It is worth adding here that in constructing a racially defined, yet popular, English national identity, such marketing techniques, advantageously for some, also inhibited the development of class consciousness.

The allegiance of the white European working classes to colonial expansionism was also facilitated by social reforms which were introduced across Europe, by Bismarck in Germany, under Giolitti in Italy and by Joseph Chamberlain in Britain in the late nineteenth and early twentieth century. These 'social imperialist' programmes (Semmel 1960) aimed to appease the working classes by throwing a few crumbs in their direction. The programmes were thus paid for out the spoils of empire and aimed at uniting the nation around the imperial project (ibid.: 23ff.). They were also interestingly supported by reformist socialists (or 'social chauvinists') like Sydney and Beatrice Webb (ibid.).

In the US, in contrast to England, nineteenth-century regimes of representation drew both on frontier relations with Native Americans and on the direct experience of plantation life. 'Indian Policy' was always a euphemism for an attack on communal property rights, an excuse and justification for the appropriation of land and the eviction and genocide of Native Americans. The fast-shooting, yet God-fearing, frontiersman emerged out of this context and I shall return to him below. On the other hand, whilst the mammy figure became a popular stereotype in the plantation context of the US, the idea of the 'black Venus', which was common in Europe, was virtually unknown in the US (Pieterse 1992: 129). Likewise, the 'brute nigger' stereotype reflected the anxieties surrounding the black presence in the US, whilst the 'savage' stereotype, as I have suggested, reflected a more distant geographical relationship between Europe and its African colonies (ibid.: 123). Again what is of interest here is not what the stereotypes tell us about the objectified 'other' but what they tell us about the objectifying coloniser. They were not just about controlling the other (e.g. the Sambo and Jim Crow characters as antidotes to the reality of slave rebels like Nat Turner (ibid.: 233)) but also about self-discipline: 'the images of others reflect the concerns of the image producers and consumers' (ibid.).

Toni Morrison elaborates some of these themes in her analysis of early American literature and the constitution of white masculinity. In the following she sees the development of white male settler ideology *in relationship to* the 'other'.

> I want to suggest that these concerns – autonomy, authority, newness and difference, absolute power – not only become the major themes and presumptions of American literature, but that each one is made possible by, shaped by, activated by a complex awareness and employment of a constituted Africanism.
>
> (Morrison 1992: 44)

Romantic fiction provided early American writers with a means of conquering fear through their imaginations, by expressing deep-seated anxieties 'of being outcast, of failing, of powerlessness, their fear of boundarylessness, of nature unbridled and crouched for attack; their fear of the absence of civilisation, in short the terror of human freedom' (ibid.: 37). Its narrative themes built around the search for self-validation and struggles with the 'natural world'. In literature, whiteness became the exnominated synonym for self-realisation through conquest, civilisation and enlightenment and the antonym for unbridled nature, savagery and darkness. In this context, racialised discourse became a metaphorical device for concealing forms of social degeneration and conflict potentially far more threatening than the racialised accounts around which the narratives were invariably spun (ibid.: 63).

Joel Harris's 'Uncle Remus' character illustrates the strategic role played by black stereotypes in the construction of whiteness. First published in the *Atlanta Constitution* and later in book form in 1880, the Remus stories depicted an idyllic ante-bellum south in which plantation owners and slaves happily co-existed. According to Silk and Silk, Remus was as quick to condemn freed black slaves for being lazy and greedy, as he was to love and respect white characters, notably the little white boy to whom he tells the stories (1990: 15). Not surprisingly, the Remus character emerged at a time of heightened tension in the US following the introduction of the punitive black codes in the post re-construction era. Moreover, Silk and Silk argue that Remus had an added advantage over whites: 'Apologies for racism proved to be far more effective, when its victims like Uncle Remus himself, were made to argue its cause' (ibid.: 14). I shall return to the significance of defending and expressing whiteness without necessarily 'being white', below, and in subsequent chapters.

The case of black minstrelsy is also illuminating since, as Saxton argues, it not only epitomised and concentrated the thrust of white racism (1990: 165), it also provided whites with an opportunity to articulate taboo topics behind a black mask. Minstrels were predominantly white males from northern cities who brought together themes of anti-elitism, frontierism, slavery, and homosexuality and masturbation (the latter 'veiled but not negated by the blackface convention') (1990: 171) and all to the backdrop of African music which was both 'exploited and suppressed' (ibid.: 168). Minstrelsy thus provided an important cultural medium for the articulation of whiteness. As Roediger comments, 'blacking up served to emphasise that those on stage were really white and that whiteness really mattered' (1991: 117). The latter had the advantage of being spoken by a 'black voice', thus making it possible to transfer white views on to 'others' and in so doing both reassured their predominantly white audiences as well as articulating their repressed sexuality. According to Roediger, 'the smearing of soot or blacking over the body represents the height of polymorphous perversity, an infantile playing with excrement or dirt. It is the polar opposite of the anal retentiveness usually associated with accumulating capitalist or Protestant cultures' (1991: 118–19).

bell hooks (1981), Angela Davis (1981) and Patricia Hill Collins (1990) trace the forms of representation of black women in the US back to slavery and their roles both as domestic workers and objects of sexual desire and fantasy. The 'mammy', 'Jemima', 'matriarch', 'Jezebel' and later the 'welfare queen/mother' images (what Collins calls 'controlling images') thus had their origins in specific historical circumstances, i.e. understandings of and rationalisations for life on the plantations and, in the case of the welfare queen, the economic recession of the post-World War II period. K. Sue Jewell (1993) also traces the origins of these cultural images to specific plantation work practices both in the fields and in the house. Popular depictions of the mammy (the 'antithesis of American womanhood') served to identify and regulate the limits of behaviour for white women. The more recent proliferation of images of black femininity for example in television situation comedies like *Good Times* and *The Jeffersons* help to shape decisions regarding, and reactions to, social policies affecting minority groups (ibid.).

Asebrit Sundquist's research also serves to illustrate the ways in which both white femininities and masculinities are implicated in constructions of Native American women in nineteenth-century literature (1987). She adopted both quantitative and qualitative methods to reveal different versions of Native American femininity of which the most common was what she calls 'the angel'. Sundquist illustrates this most dominant version with reference to the character of Pocahontas in John Esten Cooke's *My Lady Pocahontas* and Mary Mosby Webster's *Pocahontas, a Legend*. In both cases Pocahontas was portrayed to be both virtuous and vulnerable. In Cooke's version, this was achieved by drawing attention to her 'smallness' as well as shy, modest and pious demeanour (cited in Sundquist 1987: 97). In Webster's version, Matoa (alias Pocahontas) was of 'chiselled innocence', 'worthy of a shrine', 'spotless, guileless' and had a 'forehead (which was) sealed by the sign of the deity' (ibid.: 98). Not only was she virtuous but a victim too;[6] her mother and stepbrother both died, her father neglected her and then exiled her for not agreeing to marry the man of his choice (ibid.). The legend ends with the almost inevitable martyrdom but not before Pocahontas marries the white man of her dreams (ibid.: 99).

According to Sundquist, Native American women played other roles too; 'sybils' and 'witches', 'sirens' and 'furies', 'mothers' and 'drudges' (1989: 49). The reason for the dominance of the 'angel' character might ironically have to do with the white settlers' *lack* of contact with Native American women (ibid.). This resulted in characterisations which were more akin to those of white women or at least how white women were idealised in fiction. Both sets of characterisations had white masculinist origins and, for all their apparent virtues, ideas of female 'subjection' and 'self-renunciation' ultimately had more to do with male projection (ibid.: 203).

Towards the end of the century racial thought in both the US and England was influenced by adaptations of Charles Darwin's theory of evolution, including the work of another Englishman, Charles Pearson and other social Darwinists. At the time, (ironically, given the subsequent polarisation of the debate in the US) religion and natural selection were not only thought compatible but capable of being harnessed to an imperial project. The task of Anglo-Americans was spelt out in the following address to senate by Albert Beveridge who proclaimed

> God has not been preparing the English-speaking and Teutonic people
> for a thousand years for nothing but vain and idle self-admiration. No!

48

He has made us master organizers of the world to establish system where chaos reigns.

(cited in Hoffstadter 1955: 180)

There were important differences between Anglo-Saxon imperialists, like Beveridge, who wanted a global empire, and those who preferred to concentrate on securing white supremacy at home. Ideas of origins and stocks were clearly very important in these debates and formed the basis of differences and conflicts between white ethnic groups. For example, many Irish Americans in the nineteenth century were understandably less interested in appealing to a common heritage with their old colonial enemy than to their Celtic, European and nascent American identities.

Mercurial whiteness

The constitution of whiteness is never a once and for all; it has always been a process of becoming. This is in part because, as Toni Morrison argues, it has always been developed in relationship to otherness and otherness which changes according to different historical circumstance. I shall illustrate the general contingency of whiteness with reference to Tomas Almaguer's account of nineteenth-century ethnic and class relations in California before looking at changing white identities with reference to Irish and Jewish diasporas in the US and England.

In his persuasive re-construction of the historical origins of white supremacy in California in the nineteenth century, Almaguer examines the factors responsible for making some groups 'whiter' than others. Once again, class played an important role in shaping patterns of inclusion, so that in the period following the American/Mexican war in the mid nineteenth century, Mexicans were considered whiter than Native Americans, both because their numbers included some rancheros, i.e. members of a landowning class position, and because they had assimilated European culture, including its Catholic religion. Native Americans, on the other hand, were deemed non-white, partly because there were so few Native Americans left after the genocidal policies and practices of the white settlers and partly because those that were had been isolated in reservations.[7] African-Americans were likewise considered non-white because of their association with unfree labour systems. Moreover, groups which had been racialised in other contexts, namely the Irish and the Jews, were deemed white in California. According to Omi and Winant, 'the racial order drew a colour line around rather than within Europe' (cited in Almaguer 1994: 11).

The overriding thrust of policy at this time was, thus, to define Californians in racial terms. In its attempts to gain statehood California took its lead from the American Constitution and the Naturalisation Act of 1790 which entitled only free white persons to citizenship. Processes of racialisation also reflected the idea that economic development was tied to a Christian calling, an ethic associated with English Protestants who dominated the white settler population in the late eighteenth century. In line with numerous federal precedents, therefore, white male Californians took it upon themselves to oppose black immigration on the grounds that black labour had adapted to servitude and was incompatible with free labour (ibid.: 37) and that the extermination of the Indian race would continue until it was extinct. Such 'was the inevitable destiny of the (white) race' (cited in ibid.: 121). These views were reinforced by the local press in 1848, just two years before statehood was granted. The *Californian* wrote 'we desire only a white population in California' (cited in Almaguer 1994: 34). The ideas of manifest destiny and free white labour which Almaguer cites as key in the initial process of racial formation in the state are precisely those which have underscored the rhetoric of contemporary expressions of white politics in California, including both white supremacist groups as well as more mainstream campaigns around immigration and affirmative action.

The experience of the Irish in California reflected changing forms of identification and self-consciousness in the US in the nineteenth century. A growing body of writing has explored how, in Noel Ignatiev's terms, the Irish 'became white' during this period (Ignatiev 1995; see also Roediger 1991, 1994; Allen 1994). In the late eighteenth and early nineteenth centuries, the status of Irish immigrants was by no means assured. They were known as 'niggers turned inside out' and hence not automatically considered 'white' under the terms of the Naturalisation Act of 1790, referred to above, and passed by the First US Congress (Ignatiev 1995: 41). Moreover, their marginal status was compounded by the peaceful, amicable and, in some cases, intimate relations the Irish forged with African-American communities in northern cities. In Roediger's words, 'for some time there were strong signs that the Irish might not fully embrace white supremacy' (1991: 134).

Several factors encouraged the development of the Irish as a white ethnic category (Roediger 1991: 23). Firstly, there was the Catholic church and its hierarchy which, according to Roediger, offered 'at best . . . muted defences, and at worst racist defences, of slavery' (ibid.: 138). Kentucky Catholic newspapers, for example, carried advertisements for the return of runaway slaves (ibid.: 140). Secondly, the Irish gained considerable political advantage from their alliance with the southern planter class under the political auspices of Jackson's Democratic Party. The latter, in the period up to the Civil War, 'refurbished their party's traditional links with the people and offered political democracy and an inclusive patriotism to white male Americans' (ibid.).[8] Their common interests were thus forged around the notion of a 'white republic'. The results of this alliance were witnessed in the growing disaffection of Irish troops during the civil war as they became increasingly aware that they were fighting less for a union and more for the abolition of slavery (Ignatiev 1995). Their militant history, built on four hundred years of anti-colonial struggle against the English, was a third factor facilitating the development of a cohesive and distinctive form of consciousness.[9]

In the post-bellum period, these historical factors helped to secure a place for the Irish on the white side of the colour line. One important factor in this process was the way in which the Irish moved one step above African-Americans in the labour market. Numerous manual jobs, e.g. roads, railroads, canals, and textiles, became the preserve of Irish workers in many northern cities. Moreover, political patronage resulting from such organisations as the Tammany Club, also secured positions in politics and government bureaucracies, for example the newly created city police forces. Behind this labour market mobility was what Christine Sleeter calls 'white racial bonding' (1996: 261) between the Irish and white southern landowners, whose forged interests facilitated the 'whitening of the Irish' and their 'assimilation' into mainstream US culture. As Roediger points out, Irish racism against African-Americans was not about jobs *per se*. If it had been the Irish would have targeted other ethnic groups. Rather, the alliance between southern and northern class factions was what effectively incorporated the Irish into a newly formed 'white' constituency. Allen links this process back to England when he writes,

> the problem of job competition was cast in the mould of white supremacy as an integral part of the social control system instituted by the American slaveholders in the days of William of Orange and Queen Anne and the opening of the Penal Laws era in Ireland.
>
> (1994: 195)

The print media played an important role in the formation of this coalescence of white interests. For example, during the Civil War, the New York *Caucasian* (sic) attacked abolition, allegedly in defence of the interests of the white working class (ibid.: 143). The *Working Man's Advocate*, too, through its editor, George Evans, whilst ostensibly defending the interests of both white workers and black slaves, argued that African-Americans were better off being plantation slaves than competing on equal terms with white labour in the north. However, as Allen notes, 'his concern . . . was apt to be belied by the coupling of references to the "pride and delicacy of the Caucasians" with the most hateful white supremacist references to African-Americans' (1994: 164). The *Irish Citizen*, too, defended whiteness *vis-à-vis* other groups and not just African-Americans. In the following quote, the target was Chinese immigration. As the author pleaded, 'we want white people to enrich the country, not mongolians to degrade and disgrace it' (9 July 1870; cited in Lee 1996: 196).

Overall, the class position of Irish emigrants, their historic militancy and justified fears of wage labour, pressure from the Catholic hierarchy, their sheer weight of numbers in many northern cities in the US and the prospects of political representation through the Democratic Party constituted what Roediger terms an 'imperative to define themselves as white' (1991: 137) and, more than that, to 'treasure their whiteness as entitling them to both political rights and to jobs' (ibid.: 136). Their interests were not God-given or materially determined but politically and culturally constructed. An alliance with the African-Americans instead of Jacksonian Democrats would undoubtedly have thrown up spectacularly different political alignments, the outcome of which can only be speculated.

In developing this 'construction of whiteness' thesis, it should not be assumed that such trends coincided with the erasure of all forms of anti-Irish and anti-Catholic racism throughout this period. On the contrary, there are numerous examples, from the New Englanders who continued to burn an effigy of the Pope on Guy Fawkes day, to the 'Blood Tubs' used to 'dip' the Irish, to such comments as were made by an Oxford academic on a visit to the US, who suggested that 'the best remedy for whatever is amiss in America would be if every Irishman should kill a negro and be hanged for it' (cited in Hall Jamieson 1992: 79). Interestingly, on this occasion, the double-edged racist comment was an English import.

Indeed, the history of the English colonisation of Ireland provides an important historical context for understanding both subsequent Irish migrations to the US and England and representations of the Irish in English popular culture. In his account of the parallels in the histories of Anglo-Irish relations and the history of slavery in the US, Theodore Allen notes that at the very time the English were instigating their punitive penal laws in Ireland, southern states were enacting their slave codes. What he calls religio-racism (1994: 48) entailed severe curtailments of property rights, the banning of literacy which prevented Catholics from learning to read and write and the dismantling of family ties (ibid.: 81ff.). The shift from a racial to a national oppression occurred in the late eighteenth century when the English believed they needed to prop up their colonial regime in Ireland with the aid of a Catholic bourgeoisie. However, religio-racism by no means died out with this shift, rather it continued to form the basis of anti-Irish racism in the nineteenth and twentieth centuries.

In nineteenth-century England representations of the Irish ranged from the 'regular or even handsome features of the "wild Irishmen" (to the) monstrous Celtic Caliban capable of any crime known to man or beast' (Curtis 1971: 29). In the latter part of the century, the Irish, in contrast to their US counterparts, were anything but 'white', a condition not unrelated to a growth in the threat of Irish nationalism and the presence of Irish immigrants in English cities. The Irish were brutalised by the police (Hickman 1995: 78), attacked by fellow workers (ibid.: 90) and subject to the divide and rule tactics of the press and government (fearful of an alliance between Chartists and Irish nationalists) at this time. Hickman explains Irish 'visibility' in terms of religion, national identity and position in the labour market (ibid.: 78). Such differences as these were then simultaneously racialised in the popular press. In 1862, for example, *Punch* ran a cartoon under the title 'the missing link: a creature manifestly between the gorilla and the negro' (cited in Pieterse 1992: 214). The 'paddy joke' was an attempt to defuse the danger of an all-alien working-class alliance in the same way that the Sambo image sought to defuse the appeal of the slave rebel. Cohen maintains,

> his 'congenital stupidity' is . . . symbolised by his proverbial absence of family planning. His catholic tastes (in food and drink) are another sign that he does not fit in . . . it is in and through the figure of the paddy that racist theories of intelligence and moral degeneration were linked and relayed through popular culture to become common sense.
>
> (Cohen 1988: 74–5)

Whilst the concealment of ethnicity in response to religio-racism may appear easier than that built around skin, the consequences of 'assimilation' for the Irish or any ethnicity for that matter are by no means unproblematic. Becoming 'white' has not just been about not being racially marked as 'other' or 'appearing' white. On the contrary, it has provided an integral part of self-identification and a collective sense of belonging. Hence, studies of both anti-Irish racism and anti-Semitism have addressed the 'costs' of assimilation and the prospect that such strategies, in the long run, might prove counter-productive. The dilemmas facing Irish immigrants and their first and second generation descendants in Britain in the latter half of the twentieth century is a case in point. Against the background of conflict in Northern Ireland, collective ethnic denial might well have minimised racial tensions at the expense of more open forms of cultural expression. However, 'assimilation' did not protect the Irish from discrimination in employment and housing markets, the health service and education (Hickman 1995). Nor did it contain the routine patterns of harassment and discrimination meted out under the auspices of the Prevention of Terrorism Act (Hillyard 1993). The media's role in demonising the Irish and re-kindling nineteenth-century stereotypes has been well documented by Lewis Curtis (1971) and Liz Curtis (1984).

Conflicting, shifting strategies of concealment and expression also have been central to negotiations of Jewish identity which has been shaped by the long history of anti-Semitism. Furthermore, anti-Semitism played an important role in the construction of white Christian identity. Hence, the historical significance of mediaeval anti-Semitism, along with the Crusades and the Inquisition, lay partly in their role in forging the unity of Christendom (Trachtenberg 1993: 11). Anti-Semitism was thus about the construction of a Christian identity at a time when Christianity was perceived to be under threat from both Islam and Judaism. Christian values were thus defined in opposition to 'otherness'. According to Sartre,

> the Christian, the Aryan, feels his body in a special way . . . the messages and appeals that his body sends him come with certain coefficients of ideality, and are always more or less symbolic of vital values . . . the nonchalant or the elegant . . . the grace of women . . . *and to these values are naturally linked some anti-values*.
>
> (1962: 120, emphasis added)

From the seventeenth to the nineteenth centuries, not only were Jews widely believed to be black-skinned (Gilman 1991: 172) but they were also perceived to share other 'African' characteristics. According to Robert Knox, 'the African character of the Jew his muzzle shaped mouth . . . the whole physiognomy, when swarthy, as it often is, has an African look' (cited in ibid.: 174). Racial markings shifted over time as the emphasis switched to different physical characteristics. The nose was one such 'race' marker which also had important sexual connotations.

53

According to Wilhelm Fliess and Sigmund Freud, the nose was developmentally analogous to the genitalia. Accordingly, they argued, the cure for sexual dysfunction was to operate on the nose (ibid.: 188). In fact rhinoplasty (nose operations) became popular in the early part of the twentieth century as Jews sought to remove their racial markings and render their Jewishness invisible.

The background to such drastic cosmetic steps was the anti-Semitic climate in the US and England in the late nineteenth and early twentieth centuries. In England it was manifest in the establishment of anti-'aliens' organisations in the 1890s. Popular sentiment was fuelled by press coverage of such events as the 'Ripper' murders in Whitechapel (see Chapter 5) and the 'Dreyfuss Affair' in France.[10] Some newspapers not only supported the 'aliens out' campaign but appeared disappointed at the 'lacklustre response' to its call (Taylor 1993: 174). When the British Government did pass the Aliens Act of 1905 the absence of explicit reference to Jews could not conceal the fact that, as Robert Miles points out, 'it was formulated at a time when a negative, racialised, representation of Jews was widely reproduced . . . the formal definition of 'undesirable immigrant' in the Act was understood in the everyday world to refer to Jews' (Miles 1993: 145).

Whilst scholars have argued over the commitment of the Union in the US Civil War to the abolition of slavery, less has been said of the strategies used to exclude Jews from the Union cause and subsequently from dominant versions of Anglo-American identity. According to one newspaper of the period, the *Boston Investigator*, Jews were denounced as 'about the worst people of whom we have any account' and 'a troublesome people to live in proximity with' (cited in Dinnerstein 1994: 31).[11] The *Chicago Tribune* asserted that the Rothschilds and the whole tribe of Jews sympathised with the South (cited in Dinnerstein 1994: 31). A study of Baltimore's three Catholic newspapers in the period 1890–1924 found evidence of editorial anti-Semitism. Likewise, Henry Ford's *Dearborn Independent* published a series on the 'International Jew' including the forged Protocols of the Elders of Zion, which had been used to whip up anti-Semitism at the time of the Dreyfuss affair. In defence of the decision to publish this series, Ford was quoted as saying 'one is trying to awake the gentile world to an understanding of what is going on. The Jew is a mere huckster who doesn't want to produce, but to make something out of what somebody else produces' (cited in Dinnerstein 1994: 81).

The series was translated into several languages and circulated in Europe and Latin America. During the 1930s and 1940s the press in both countries jumped on the anti-Semitic bandwagon. In England, the prospect of being overrun by Jewish refugees was not lost on the *Sunday Pictorial* which reported the threat to the English countryside of a babble of waving palms of an eastern bazaar (cited in Kushner 1989: 127). Local newspapers like the *Hackney Gazette* went as far as to openly support discrimination against Jewish tenants (cited in Kushner 1989: 59). Moreover, wide sections of the media identified the black economy with 'immoral' Jewish enterprise. Tony Kushner maintains that, 'the identification continued, present in radio plays, house of commons, popular literature, comics . . . major attacks on Jewish involvement in black marketing in papers ranging from *Time and Tide* and the *Daily Mirror* to the *Spectator*' (Kushner 1989: 120).

According to Dinnerstein, since the 1940s, anti-Semitism has become less integral to US culture as Jewishness has become not so much assimilated but almost imperceptibly seen to feed off and into mainstream culture. In acknowledging its diminishing significance in mainstream culture, Dinnerstein does not deny the continuing prevalence of anti-Semitism in extreme right-wing organisations, as well as its more subtle presence in mainstream culture. The author cites the example of the 'Jewish American Princess' slur in the 1980s (and one which entailed both racial and sexual harassment) as an example of its continuing capacity to re-surface (Dinnerstein 1994: 136). However, if Dinnerstein is right about the general trend over the last forty years, then this is possibly an example of the capacity of whiteness to re-define itself through otherness, manifesting elements of cultural syncretism and interdependence much talked about in postmodern writings.[12] I shall come back to this in later chapters. Its contingent status, however, cuts both ways. In the past, whiteness has been adopted by Jews at great cost and with no guarantees. Likewise, in its striving for self-definition and regulation, whiteness might well attempt to play its anti-Semitic card at some point in the future with the aim of making Jewishness, once again, a significant racial marker within mainstream culture.

'Sexing the race'

> The 'white *man's* burden' thus becomes his sexuality and its control, and it is this which is transferred into the need to control the sexuality of the Other, the Other as sexualized female.
>
> (Gilman 1992: 194, emphasis in original)

The process described by Sander Gilman underpins much writing on race and sexuality. Racial and gendered stereotypes are seen, within this psychoanalytic framework as integral to the policing of whiteness. In particular, in Lola Young's words, stereotypes give whites 'a scapegoat and symbol into which various desires and longings can be injected with impunity' (1996: 23). In her discussion of white femininity Young argues that putting white women on a pedestal of sexual unattainability went hand in hand with the construction of white masculinity, that is to say, 'the idealization of white female sexual purity and the valorisation of "masculine" attributes such as courage, autonomous action and independence' (ibid.: 61). The elevated status accorded to middle-class white women was in marked contrast to women of lower social orders and to black women. Both the latter groups constituted objects of desire (transgression) and denial. Young reminds us how imperial literature made black women metaphors for the conquest of Africa and how the landscape of the latter was feminised and described in terms of 'penetration', 'conquering the interior' etc. (ibid.: 63). The monopoly of 'looking' belongs only to white men, whilst white women's virtue lay in their subordination to the reproduction of the white race. The sphere of popular representation was significant because of its capacity to valorise such deceptions through its pervasiveness and, relatedly, its capacity to tell the same stories using different media forms and genres. According to Lola Young,

> Newspapers, popular entertainment, postcards and comics in the first decade of the twentieth century constantly reinforced the idea of war as glamorous, character building and fascinating: an activity which occurred in far-off exotic places. These images and fantasies were inextricably linked to conceptualisations of masculinity, and the idea of what constitutes masculinity was a key site for confrontations springing from racial conflict.
>
> (1996: 60)

In her analysis of the part gender played in the construction of whiteness in orientalist discourse, Raina Lewis writes, 'the gender specificities that accrued to women *qua* women were always built on their difference as *white* women' (1996: 15). Her examples, drawn from literary and visual culture, confirm the need to think of race and gender not in hierarchical terms but 'reciprocally constituting each other through a kind of narrative invocation, a set of associative terms in a chain of meaning' (Cora Kaplin cited in Lewis 1996: 15). Zilah Eisenstein (1996), too, draws on a psychoanalytic framework to explore the subconscious processes involved in the multiple and fluid 'hatreds' characteristic of the last years of the twentieth century. How do we connect immigration, policing and hate crimes, along axes of gender, sexuality and race? Eisenstein begins with the notion of *fear*. Hatred embodies fear and racial and sexual markers are the mechanisms through which we 'see', 'speak' and/or 'deny' fear. It has been racialised along religious, ethnic or gendered lines. Once again what is at root here is fear, not of the other, but of the unbridled self. The ensuing struggle, which is invariably projected on to others, is more about the struggle to contain desire (Eisenstein 1996: 23). Mapping identities on to different bodies, white female, Jewish male, black female, black male, is more instructive in terms of what these mappings tell us about their source, white neuroses.

Psychoanalytic ideas have thus been particularly helpful in unravelling the claims and proposals of eugenicists whose main concern was white racial contamination. Although taboos surrounding interracial sex had been around since at least the sixteenth century, eugenics gave those ideas a spurious scientific rationale and a boost to burgeoning ideas of national socialism which came to fruition in Germany in the 1930s. It also extended the use of metaphors of disease, plague, infection etc. which became part of a common sense discourse around 'class, gender, "race", sexuality, and mental ability' (Young 1990: 51). Although eugenics has proved a source of inspiration for the extreme right in both the US and England, its early supporters were from the reformist left in Britain and included many Fabian Society members including Sydney and Beatrice Webb and Marie Stopes.

Joel Kovel, in his psycho-history of whiteness make a distinction between '*dominative* racists' who overtly and intentionally subjugate blacks and more common '*aversive* racists' who appear liberal until deep seated anxieties are put to the test (cited in Young 1990: 254). The heightened anxieties around interracial sex are one example of aversion and are explicable for reasons discussed above but, according to Kovel, there is a more widespread aversion to relate intimately to black people's knowledge and experiences (ibid.: 26).

I shall now illustrate some of the above themes with reference to the racialisation of the Chinese communities in England and the US in the late nineteenth and early twentieth centuries. Many of the ideas borrowed from psychoanalysis prompt us to consider not anti-Chinese racism *per se* but the implied version of whiteness which underscores it. During the nineteenth century, Chinese labourers were brought to the US to work on the railroads and in other parts of the construction sector of the economy. From the outset the print media invoked ideas of defilement and contamination to describe immigrants and their living conditions. For example, an editorial comment in the *New York Daily Tribune* 1854, alleged that the Chinese and the 'oriental' are,

> uncivilised, unclean, filthy beyond all conception, without any of the higher domestic or social relations; lustful and sensual in their dispositions; *every* female is a prostitute, and of the basest order . . . . Clannish in nature . . . pagan in religion they know not the virtues of honesty, integrity or good faith.
>
> (cited in Lee 1996: 184, emphasis in original)

The text thus plays on 'contamination' fears, i.e. the fear of interracial mixing and the degeneration of white Anglo-American stock and follows it up with characteristics which are less about the Chinese and more about constructions of white American identity. Moreover, popular discourse employed the trope of inundation (ibid.: 186) which Lee describes thus: 'the phobia of drowning in an unclean and alien fluid is invoked . . . the fear of contamination, the terror of being made unclean by the filthy and sick' (ibid.: 187). Inundation also implies lack of autonomy, as does the term 'dirt' in so far as it was used to evoke fears of the decay and submergence of white culture in a tide of 'waste' (ibid.: 188).

Such views provided a rationale for a series of legal measures designed to restrict entry of and contact with Chinese immigrants. In 1882, an Exclusion Act was passed which halted all new Chinese immigrants, to the US. It was not repealed until 1943 (ibid.: 197). Likewise, laws banning inter-marriage and miscegenation were not repealed until 1948 and 1967 respectively (ibid.: 198). The growth of interest in 'orientalism', sinology and Chinoiserie in American academic/research institutions foregrounded 'the splendour that *was* China' (ibid.: 195). This not only devalued contemporary China, it also meant that Chinese history became known and understood through western eyes and in western terms. Although Edward Said's *Orientalism* (1978) drew heavily on the 'near orient', his analysis can be used here to illustrate the process by which whiteness, through its control over knowledge-producing institutions, defining itself as subject/knower by constructing 'otherness' as the object to be known.

In England the settlement of Chinese communities in London's Limehouse, and other port cities (e.g. Liverpool) resulted from the employment of Chinese seamen in shipping and trading companies (Clegg 1994: 8). However, public discourses did not always converge in their thinking. On the one hand, the press reinforced recurrent and popular racist themes of contamination. In 1906, for example, the *Sunday Chronicle* talked about Liverpool as a 'yellow town not fitted to be part of civilized white society'. On the other hand a Liverpool Commission stated that Chinatown's Pitt Street was 'long noted as a street down which a woman might walk without molestation' (cited in Clegg 1994: 9). Six years later in 1912 Max Rohmer's Fu Manchu stories were published and later turned into a series of Hollywood films, the latest in 1968 was *The Blood of Fu Manchu* with Boris Karloff and Christopher Lee (ibid.: 3). These stories re-worked nineteenth-century stereotypes of sex, drugs, crime, ruined virgins and tenacious white police officers personified in the heroic Sir Denis Nayland-Smith (ibid.: 2).

Likewise, the English press used similar language and images to describe Chinese immigrants. For example the *Weekly Courier* of 8 December 1906, ran a headline YELLOW PERIL: PUBLIC INDIGNATION INCREASING. Likewise, in June 1911, *London Magazine* wrote, 'beneath its calm and dingy exterior there stir the same dark passions, instincts and racial tendencies which cause this mystic yellow people to be so misunderstood, feared and hated' (cited in Lee 1996: 200). The English press, too, were pre-occupied with contamination as the following quote from the *Weekly Courier* confirms. Under the headline TAINTING THE RACE the article spoke of interracial mixing in the following terms: 'the result of such unions (Chinese men and English women) is found in swarms of half-bred children to be seen in the district . . . (moreover) it is not only degraded women who mate with these men' (ibid.: 211).

The dilemma faced by both US and British governments was whether to bow to pressure from indigenous workers, their union representatives and from those anxious about the deterioration of the stock, or to support immigration for the sake of those employers whose interests lay in cheap immigrant labour. The mobilisation of such contradictory interests was invariably left to politicians with a little prodding from their press allies. So, for example, politicians like James Sexton, played the race card to build up electoral support. Sexton, a local labour councillor in Liverpool, attracted the support of white working-class voters by promoting anti-Chinese racism (ibid.: 205).

Post-colonial whiteness and strategies of resistance

I use the term 'post-colonial' loosely to refer to the period after 1945 which witnessed the formal independence of British colonies and the civil rights struggle in the US. For both the US and Britain, this period has brought a decline in sovereignty. Britain has lost almost all its remaining colonies (including India in the 1940s, Kenya, Cyprus, Malaysia and Nigeria in the 1960s and Hong Kong in 1997). Although the US did not have an empire to lose in this sense, its role in Korea in the 1950s, Vietnam in the 1960s and 1970s and the Middle East and Central America in the 1980s raised similar question marks over its sense of superiority and invincibility. This was compounded by the loss of other European colonies (Dutch, Portuguese, French) which left the west bereft of its one time control of 95 per cent of the world's surface.

National sovereignty, as I suggested in Chapter 1, was also increasingly undermined by the growth in importance of the transnational company (TNC) which owed its allegiance not to any one particular country of origin but to its global constituency of stockholders and consumers. As Masao Miyoshi points out, 'the "Buy American" drive is increasingly a hollow battle plan' (1996: 89). Does a car buyer loyal to the US auto industry buy a Dodge made in Japan by Mitsubishi or a Honda built in Ohio with parts largely manufactured in the US? Does a loyal Briton buy a Rover which is now owned the German company, BMW, or a Japanese Toyota made in Derby, England? The catch-phrases 'Buy British' and 'Buy American' have been important planks of advertising campaigns and national economic policy. Miyoshi links this to his argument that 'against the effective operation of TNCs, the nation states more and more look undefined and inoperable' (ibid.: 91).

The growth in significance of TNCs has had profound cultural implications. Consumer goods have global production processes and a myriad of markets (or micro-consumption units calculated by computer analysis) (Dirlik 1996: 33).[13] The de-coupling of industry and consumption from their national base has compounded the sense of loss which coincided with the end of empire and the certainties that went with a sense of imperial sovereignty. Popular culture, in turn, has provided an important repository for rendering such events intelligible and recognisable as well as opportunities for moral alignments and forms of identification. I will illustrate the significance of such cultural forms with reference to Hollywood film and popular fiction.

J. Williamson suggests that the upsurge in the 1950s in what he calls the 'coonskin characters' of Daniel Boone, Andrew Jackson and Davy Crockett had something to do with a growing crisis of masculinity brought about by shifts in employment patterns from traditional blue-collar to office jobs. Saxton has explored the origins of the Davy Crockett character back to the Tennessee frontiersman/congressman of the late nineteenth and early twentieth century whose defence of homesteaders and squatters became an icon of Whig/Republican publicists who popularised him first in theatre and subsequently in dime novels

(1995: 77ff.). A century later in the 1950s, cinema audiences were treated to six depictions of Davy Crockett in one decade (1995: 90). Davy Crockett, like Daniel Boone and Andrew Jackson, was the quintessential frontiersman who let no man (read Native American) or mountain stand in the way of his territorial goals.

In his essay on mid twentieth-century 'wilderness' novels (a combination of adventure and political romance genres, for example found in the work of Wilber Smith) Abena Busia argues that Africa was used as a vehicle for the peculiar private imaginations of white Englishmen (1985: 171). The 'buccaneer hero', as Busia refers to him, tired of his dull, uneventful, repressed middle-class life in England, turns to Africa for liberation and self-discovery. Dramatic narratives can be 'vehicles for the imaginations of white men' which can work around superficially anti-racist themes but remain tethered to a white problematic and an example of what I have referred to as 'progressive whiteness'. Silk and Silk give a further illustration of this in their discussion of Clarence Brown's *Intruder in the Dust* (1949), in which a black farmer Lucas Beauchamp is accused of the murder of a poor white. In the end, according to Silk and Silk, 'his white lawyer is allowed the final word, that "it depends on people like us" to safeguard Beauchamp – the latter is no more than "the keeper of our conscience"' (1990: 151).

The revived images of white masculinity built around the early settlers and adventurers has been significant in the consolidation of certain forms of white masculinity in the US. The psyche of the frontiersman, comprising the drive to 'go where no man has gone' and the commitment to violence and death, if necessary, in God's name, has helped to shape contemporary forms of masculinity in the US. Whether on film or the less fictional world of white politics, there has always been room to celebrate the rugged individualist who fought the establishment as much as he did enemies 'in the wild' (including that of the 'urban jungle'). Guns have always been an integral part of this culture, indispensable in the ongoing battle with corrupt officialdom and/or unwelcome intruders or outsiders. The 'frontiersman' has helped to shape a distinct white male consciousness in the US which, faced with decreasing options in employment and political representation, has often found sanctuary in local militia groups and/or organisations of the religious right.

Thirty or so years later, in the 1980s, the 'interracial buddy' movies arguably aimed to provide a cultural palliative to the kind of neurosis already referred to and, at the same time, to act as a comment on wider economic and political developments. The idea of interracial brotherhood has been used in 'wilderness' novels, as Abona Busia refers to them, which feature 'the white man seeking redemption through interracial comradeship' (1986: 172). The post civil-rights era had witnessed a growing black presence in government and business. Moreover, as Robyn Wiegman remarks, 'a proliferating inclusion of African-American characters and cultural contexts in mainstream film and television, at least from a 1950s perspective, could be heralded by some as evidence of a profound transformation of US culture' (1995: 116). However, the Reagan/Bush/Thatcher successes of the 1980s mobilised a backlash against their versions of the 1960s counter-culture.

This backlash was made up of four '-isms': nationalism, authoritarianism, individualism and populism, all of which were racially inflected. In popular culture enhanced visibility did not, by itself, challenge dominant discourse. For example, interracial buddy movies like *Lethal Weapon I, II* and *III*, *48 Hours* etc. depend, not on racial parity, but the privileging white masculinity. Moreover, according to Weigman, 'Implicit in this narrative (action genre) scenario, is the discourse of sexual difference, where the white male occupies the traditionally masculine position of rugged self-assertion while the African-American male assumes the emotional feminine sphere' (1995: 117–18).

The feminisation of black men, through representational devices such as these, draws on earlier gendered images, i.e. Uncle Tom, Jim Crow, Sambo and Uncle Remus. It also relates to more overtly brutalised expressions of white privilege, for example lynching and castration. Both physical and cultural strategies served to assuage white male fears (the black rapist myth and/or the black and female 'equal' of the post civil-rights era) and secure racial/sexual hierarchies. Interracial buddies were not sexually bonded, though at a subliminal level they could be read this way. Whatever interpretations of interracial male sexuality were offered, these relationships both served to dissipate fears of miscegenation and relatedly secure existing racial and patriarchal relations.

Films like Robert Mulligan's *To Kill a Mockingbird* (1962), and more recently Euzhan Palcy's *Dry White Season* (1989), Alan Parker's *Mississippi Burning* (1988) and Joel Schumacher's *A Time to Kill* (1996), explicitly decry racism, but nevertheless rely on white lawyers or reporters to defeat it. These characters become repositories of culturally loaded terms like decency, fairness, intelligence and good looks. It is not just that they are white skinned but also that they embody 'white' qualities; the powerful conjunction of ontological and 'liberal whiteness'. As Silk and Silk point out, 'the problem of racism is portrayed as one which liberal whites can solve; blacks are shown as completely passive' (1990: 151).

Liberal whiteness, like its more conservative counterparts, depends on defining others for its own self-definition. The liberal version of whiteness also depends on a definition of racism which exonerates itself. Arguably, it achieves this through a strategy of *containment*. In films like *Mississippi Burning* and *Dry White Season* such containment is achieved by distancing racism from the here and now, i.e. both geographically (South Africa) or historically (in the early 1960s). In films like Constantin Costa-Gavras's *Betrayed* (1988) and *A Time to Kill*, it does so by equating racism with the extreme right and thus setting it apart from the dominant white voice. These films develop white characters to the near exclusion of others. Films like *A Time to Kill* and Brian De Palma's *Bonfire of the Vanities* (1990) deploy another tactic which enables the voice of white reason to prevail, that of equating black politics with extremism and/or political corruption.

The strategy of containment is not confined to film. It can also be applied to the white consumption of ethnic cultures other than its own. Niching 'otherness', putting it behind glass, confining it to a street or a 'quarter' plays an important role in white consciousness in both the US and England. It serves to re-define whiteness in more inclusive terms, i.e. as both interested in, and tolerant of, difference as long at it is kept within limits and always understood through the white gaze. It gives whiteness its multicultural gloss whilst leaving hierarchies intact. The multicultural option does not exhaust resistance strategies *within* whiteness, as I shall argue in later chapters, but it does characterise much of what passes for white liberalism and as such pinpoints some of the dangers associated with contesting whiteness on its own terrain.

I have suggested in Chapter 1 that 'resistance' can also be understood through the ideas of discordant readings and diverse audiences; ideas inspired by the work of Foucault, Derrida and deconstructionists. This latter intellectual tradition, in turn, has coincided with the rapid movement of people and the circulation of ideas around the world, thus ensuring that cultural products, including films, are more likely to be interpreted differently and more complexly than before. Shohat and Stam use Fanon's example of black audiences in the Antilles who identified with Tarzan, in contrast to mainly white audiences in France who saw Tarzan as a savage 'other'. The emergence of conflicting readings of such films has raised new doubts and challenged old certainties. White audiences are beginning to contemplate what the first lines of Jonny Mercer's *Oklahoma* mean to Native Americans: 'we belong to the land and the land we belong to is grand' (cited in Shohat and Stam 1994: 353). The loss of certainty compounded by the possible inference of guilt has helped precipitate what Fiske has referred to as a white neurosis, symptomatic of what others have understood as the crisis of modernity. Intellectual projects to de-essentialise, or de-centre whiteness are thus part of an assault on the authority of the white male subject who is being called into question as never before. Attempts to defend its centredness have always been fraught and contradictory. As Gilroy has argued, the relationship between black and white intellectual traditions at the height of modernity was always one of syncretic interdependence (Gilroy 1993a: 1ff.). Now, new hybrid forms of identity are constantly serving to undermine attempts to essentialise whiteness.

Examples considered in this chapter have been re-interpreted in ways which confirm that what might be encoded in terms of dominant whiteness might be decoded in oppositional terms; hence the possibility of new meanings and identities and political agendas forged around different understandings. For example, *The Harem* can conjure up a turban-clad Elvis Presley 'off to where the harem girls dance' (cited in Shohat and Stam 1994: 161) or, alternatively, in the context of nineteenth-century art, provide a space for the 'fantastic promise of disobeying the phallic order' (Lewis 1996: 180). Lewis's analysis thus not only explores the formation of racialised genders, but also points to potential points of conflict within discourses which allow openings as points of resistance (ibid.: 19). Likewise, Sundquist's reading of the Pocahontas legend does not preclude other interpretations and Shohat and Stam refer to readings by some Native American 'interpretative communities' who have understood it more as a survivalist narrative than a love story (1994: 44). And even minstrelsy has been thought about in terms of the scope it provided for a more subtle class critique of both the white interlocutor and the dandified black. Its more overt forms of racism were taken for granted and/or ignored (cited in Roediger 1991: 123).

Interpretations or readings can also vary over time. Kobena Mercer's account of white gay photographer Robert Mapplethorpe's work is illuminating in this respect (1994). Increasingly he (Mercer) became dissatisfied with his initial dismissal of Mapplethorpe's work on grounds that it offered negative images of black men. Instead, he came to appreciate the complexity of the identities inscribed in Mapplethorpe's work. The background against which Mercer departed from his earlier reading was a wider critique of the positive/negative image debate and the shift to what has already been referred to as 'the politics of representation'. Whiteness has thus been historically resisted and transformed through political struggle and immortalised in accounts of slave revolts like Nat Turner's Virginia uprising in 1830, the accounts of industrial struggles of black trade unionists in England from the 1970s onwards and the representation of diverse forms of subaltern culture in both mainstream and quasi-autonomous sites of cultural production. These have included initiatives in print and electronic media, photography and art, music and new information technologies as well as their incorporation into the school curricula, exhibitions and via the establishment of specialist museums. Overall, post-liberation politics in both the US and England has spawned a new challenge to western intellectual and aesthetic canons, political and religious orthodoxies, and it is precisely this challenge and the alleged collusion of white liberals, which has, in turn, provoked the backlash which forms the focus of the next chapter.

Conclusions

Whiteness is neither a set of values nor a set of physical properties which we can apply with certainty to some groups and not others. This chapter has born witness to the problems of searching for exhaustive distinctions and definitions. The histories of so-called white ethnicities, e.g. Jewish and Irish, are just two examples of the shifts in formation and mobilisation of ethnic groups. To understand the transformations with respect to particular groups demands an analysis which draws heavily on changing class structures, political alliances and strategies, and the role of popular culture in rendering these events and developments both recognisable and legitimate.

For long periods whiteness has been inscribed in the unwritten normative structures of both the US and England. Its genealogies in both countries have reflected their reciprocal and intertwined histories as well as numerous internal specificities, for example narratives of the white settler and frontiersman in the US and traveller's tales, romantic fiction, and the popular press in England. In both countries, whiteness, like some slumbering beast, has stirred only in moments of apparent and imminent danger. A number of such moments have been identified in this chapter including the early political history of California which heralded the prospect of a culturally diverse and egalitarian (in formal political terms) state, early twentieth-century England which faced an influx of Jewish immigrants fleeing from persecution in eastern and central Europe and the more recent period in which the threat appears both economic (transnationals), political (e.g. the EU), cultural (e.g. the impact of global media) and demographic (e.g. migration). At these moments, whiteness has declared itself; the exnominated has named itself.

This chapter has explored the ways in which gendered and racialised identities have been constituted simultaneously both in terms of ideas of whiteness and femininity, for example in the novels of Jane Austin, and how it has relied on constructions of the 'other' to define both white femininity and masculinity. The traditional stereotypes from 'paddy' to 'Shylock' to 'mammy' and 'brute nigger' have all served to define and regulate whiteness. Discourses of contamination and inundation have also proved popular in their efforts to set limits to and discipline white sexual norms.

Several media and cultural forms have been discussed in terms of their role in cementing white identities and allegiances, including newspapers, novels and Hollywood film. Each has been shown to play a distinctive role defined by a particular period and genre, yet these forms have, in other ways, been shown to be reciprocal, intertextual and cumulative. However, the idea that such cultural texts are only open to one interpretation has been questioned and provides the basis for all-important deconstructions of unitary constructions of whiteness. Even iconic figures in the history of whiteness like the minstrel have been used both to negate blackness *and* to parody whiteness. Moreover, global diasporas and the political and cultural struggles of subaltern groups have forced whiteness to locate itself in relationship to those ethnicities around it. Diverse forms of representation, including new forms of literary, musical and cinematic expression, all stand in opposition to all-pervasive, conservative liberal and normative progressive forms of whiteness.

3

BACKLASH CULTURE AND THE DEFENCE OF WHITENESS

The attack on what became known as 'political correctness' (PC) originated on college campuses in the US in the 1980s. Initially, it stood for an attempt to remove terms from everyday discourse which were considered racially or sexually pejorative and discriminatory. The debate was largely confined to the campuses until the early 1990s when press articles began appearing, including one in January 1991 in *New York Magazine* entitled, 'Are You Politically Correct?'. The term quickly became appropriated, inflated and distorted in media reports as part of a wider attack on the principles and policies of multiculturalism, including affirmative action. Press columns were full of scare stories of fascist take-overs, thought police, censorship and white (male) victims (Neilson 1995). The origins of this wider backlash and the ideas which fuelled the attack on political correctness had been sown in the previous decade in a number of publications, one of the best known of which was Allan Bloom's *The Closing of the American Mind* in 1987.[1] As part of this broadside assault on multiculturalism, conservatives defended the maintenance of the white western literary canon and its epistemological assumptions against attempts to promote and reflect cultural diversity. In England the term PC caught on in the early 1990s but prior to this, from the mid 1980s onwards, a backlash of a somewhat different order had been waged, less on college campuses, but more against local authority anti-racist, anti-homophobic and anti-sexist initiatives.

The chapter will begin by placing these debates, principally shaped by the Reagan/Bush and Thatcher agendas, in their wider political context, the fall-out from which has continued to be felt throughout the 1990s. The chapter will begin with an examination of the dominant themes of backlash discourse in so far as it implied, and sometimes made explicit, a defence of white men and white values (i.e. ontological and normative whiteness). The capacity of whiteness to work through, and capitalise on, other discourses, notably that of sexuality, will then be explored. The articulation of racial *and* sexual demons has proved significant and effective in backlash discourse and I will illustrate these interconnections with reference to the Oregon's Measure 9 (Spearheaded by the Oregon Citizen's Alliance) in the US, and Section 28 of the UK's Local Government Act, 1988. This will be followed by a discussion of popular media representations of the backlash with particular reference to talk radio's attack on affirmative action in the US and the tabloid print media's attack on anti-racism and political correctness in Birmingham, England. The final section will examine different mobilisations against backlash culture with particular reference to Fairness and Accuracy in Reporting (FAIR), a New York-based media watch-dog/pressure group, and the 1996 California campaign to defend affirmative action. The overall aim of racialised backlash discourse on both sides of the Atlantic has been to discredit and marginalise opposition to prevailing white political norms, both liberal and conservative. As Teun van Dijk has argued with respect to the role of the media,

> More than any other form of public communication and discourse, the media have the ability to contribute the shared elements that define the ethnic situation and that develop or change the ideological framework used by white people to understand and control ethnic events and relations . . . if the press endorses the ideology that legitimates white group dominance, it may be expected that it will discredit, marginalise, or problematize anti racist positions and groups.

(Dijk 1991: 39)

Backlash: origins and themes

Michael Omi and Howard Winant distinguish three discourses of white supremacy in the US; the 'far right', the 'new right' and 'neo-conservatism' (1986) which serve as a useful, although not exact, point of departure for what follows. I will postpone a discussion of the 'far right' ('white pride' politics) until Chapter 6, bearing in mind that an important argument to be developed there will be to show the continuities between 'extreme' and 'mainstream' political discourses. According to Omi and Winant, the 'new right's' popularity, closely associated with the Reagan/Bush era, lay in its ability to *code* 'race' through an appeal to law and order and family values: in other words, hidden, sometimes barely so, beneath an authoritarian populist rhetoric. The television election commercial used by George Bush in 1988, depicting a convicted rapist Willie Horton, was nominally about criminality and law and order but subliminally all about 'race' (Horton was African-American) and sexuality. 'Neo-conservatism', on the other hand, laid stress on individualism over collectivism and group characteristics. The solution to 'racial problems', accordingly, was to ignore them. By allegedly treating everyone the same, universalism prevailed over particularism and difference (Omi and Winant 1980: ch. 7). It is worth adding here that ideas of universalism and 'race evasion' have also surfaced in more liberal and, indeed, socialist discourses, thus providing a shared set of assumptions across the political spectrum which have been commonly deployed in the defence of whiteness.[2]

The political successes of both Margaret Thatcher and Ronald Reagan in the 1980s have been widely attributed to their ability to identify and capitalise on a crisis which was widely perceived in both economic and moral terms. In the US, the most widely agreed economic indicators of the crisis were unemployment, foreign competition (Japanese in the US) and a budget deficit (Small 1994: 85). On top of unemployment, the UK economy was also widely claimed to be suffering from industrial unrest, inflation, low investment and unprofitable nationalised industries. Aside from the economy, however, both Republican and Conservative parties mobilised around a defence of the so-called moral fabric of their societies which, they claimed, was threatened by a declining commitment to family and nation, deteriorating educational standards, rising crime rates and, in the English case, immigration. In contrast to the liberal, permissive cultural attitudes associated with the 1960s, the electorates were offered, and took, a good dose of authoritarian populism; not once but three times in each country from the late 1970s to the early 1990s. In Anna Maria Smith's terms, the success of both political projects lay in their ability to create a 'social imaginary' in which all problems were addressed within its framework and where there was perceived to be the absence of an alternative (1994: 36). Rather than assuming the masses had been duped by the new right, Smith saw voters as cynics, who may not have agreed with the content, but liked the apparent order and stability that accompanied the package (ibid.: 38). However, this mis-identification of society as a stable order depended on 'alienation, transitivism and paranoid knowledge' as well as the stigmatisation of alternative political projects (ibid.: 39). The latter was achieved through a variety of representational strategies which, in the case of Thatcherism, were notably constructed around the demonisation of trade unions and racial and homosexual others (ibid.: 63).

The more immediate background to the English version of the backlash was the emergence of Labour-held local authorities in the 1980s, which seized the opportunity provided by the dominance of Thatcher on the national political stage to promote islands of socialism in an otherwise deep blue sea. Encouraged by Ken Livingstone's lead at the Greater London Council, local authorities elsewhere introduced equal opportunity and contract compliance policies. (The latter aimed to put pressure on the private companies with whom they did business to develop good equal opportunity practice or risk losing a contract.) Some of these local authorities also funded local community initiatives amongst marginal and socially excluded groups. The right hit back. 'Neo-liberals' attacked Labour for overspending, whilst 'neo-Conservatives' waged war on moral grounds, defending a version of individual freedom and attacking 'reverse racism'. In this highly effective campaign, the tabloids and local print media played an important role, but so too did the broadsheet press which disseminated the ideas of academics like Roger Scruton, Anthony Flew and Ferdinand Mount, thus reaching readerships far beyond those normally associated with their academic publications.

According to Michael Lemm in *Up From Conservatism* (1996), the origins of backlash culture in the US can be traced back to the early 1970s. Richard Nixon, according to Lemm, was the first President to see the political capital to be gained by waging a 'culture war' by courting the white working class Republican vote in both north and south. In the Reagan/Bush era, however, the backlash took a while to dig in. In the early 1980s the Supreme Court defended and, in some cases, extended affirmative action policies and practices. Moreover, black political influence at city hall level was increasing during the 1980s with the election of black mayors in major cities, including Philadelphia, New York and Chicago. Against this background, and faced by a Democratic Congress, Reagan, and later Bush, set out to veto and block civil rights legislation and to undermine affirmative action policies and practices through their 'strategic' appointments to the Supreme Court. Buttressed by populist-academic literature, talk radio and Hollywood cinema, growing credence and support were given to these political initiatives and the object of their concern: whiteness.

I turn now to the substantive themes of racialised backlash culture. As a whole, the latter has presented a relatively coherent account of the economic and moral 'crisis' referred to above. I have chosen to organise my account around three key ideas: 'white victims', 'relative knowledge' and 'rights and responsibilities'. I will suggest that some of the more specific lines of debate have developed unevenly, reflecting both a difference of emphasis, historical differences (e.g. of law and demography), and the distinct roles played by the media in the US and Britain. Debates around these themes have been more fully articulated in the US than in Britain and, as such, the chapter will draw more heavily on US examples. Ultimately, however, I will argue that the overall success of backlash culture, whatever its particularities or location, has been to hide its own dogma beneath a rhetoric of universal knowledge, old-fashioned rights, individual responsibility and freedom. Such rhetoric has consistently defended its objectivity but has not always successfully concealed its allegiance to one particular ethnic constituency.

White victims

On 26 February 1986, the *Sun* newspaper published an article under the headline: FREEBIE TRIP FOR BLACKS, BUT WHITE KIDS MUST PAY, which reported an exchange visit to Cuba for young people 'rehabilitating after being convicted' (cited in Searle 1987: 55). Six weeks later the *Caribbean Times* published a letter written by a group of young people in Brent, refuting the *Sun*'s story point by point. The trip was paid for out of funds raised by the young people themselves and their status was low waged or non-waged, not ex-convicts (cited in Searle 1987: 55). The appeal to reason was unlikely to make much headway, not just because the refutation appeared several weeks after the *Sun* article and in the letters' page of the minority press, but also because reason always had a tough job against a common-sense 'imaginary' in which whites were inscribed as victims of reverse racism.

'Reverse racism' was what had allegedly turned whites into victims. Efforts to promote multiracial and anti-racist practices in London and Berkshire were condemned as a racist attack on British institutions and values (Gordon 1990: 186). In the 'new right' publication, the *Salisbury Review*, in the output of The Social Affairs Unit, a right-wing think tank, and in the national tabloid press, notably the *Daily Mail* and the *Daily Express*, articles appeared accusing local authorities of 'apartheid' and 'reverse discrimination' (cited in Gordon 1990: 186). In a similar vein, when Bradford headteacher, Ray Honeyford, left his school with a twenty-two carrot-gold handshake after publishing articles in which he made racially offensive remarks about black parents and black culture, the *Sun* ran an editorial, TRUE RACISTS, in which it condemned 'the nasty actions of parents, councillors and race agitators' (Searle 1987: 65). It is worth noting that Honeyford, himself, had identified another group of white victims in his own writing. According to Russell Lewis, 'He (Honeyford) also drew attention to the unrecognised plight of white working-class children whose education was suffering in schools where they were hopelessly outnumbered by children of ethnic groups' (1988: 143). Such claims, boosted by Britain's 1988 Education Reform Act, inspired a succession of groups of white English parents in Cleveland, Dewsbury and Wakefield, to seek to remove their children from multi-ethnic schools (Gillborn 1995: 193).

In February 1996, a white teacher, whose application for a job was rejected, took her prospective employers to an industrial tribunal for alleged racial discrimination and won. The case was widely reported in the press. For example, the *Guardian*, a left/liberal broadsheet, ran an article under the headline WHITE TEACHER IN RACE BIAS VICTORY with the sub-heading 'prejudiced in favour of ethnic minorities'. Despite her own view that political correctness or backlash had nothing to do with her claim, the news worthiness of her case undoubtedly did. The assumed interest in this article was based on the widely held view that anti-racism and equal opportunity policies had gone too far. Inevitably, such reports never contextualise council decisions, which may or may not be justified, but which in this case may have reflected the potentially quite legitimate view that non-conventional selection criteria constituted a stronger measure of ability than just formal qualifications (which, in the case of the latter, are also easier to attain for some groups). The omission of this kind of discussion leaves the reader with little option but to see the case as one of reverse racial discrimination and evidence that PC had 'gone too far'.

During the 1980s in the US, expressions of white male anger, previously associated with skinheads and klansmen (see Chapter 6) were percolating the ranks of middle America. At this time, according to Omi and Winant, largely for reasons of political expedience, conservatives joined forces with the new right and began articulating and constructing white resentment around the impact of affirmative action. 'Unionized workers benefiting from *de facto* segregated seniority systems, for example, or white ethnic residents of urban enclaves who felt themselves to be an "endangered species" . . . became potential conservative constituencies' (1986: 132). The alliance of the new right and conservatives helped to forge a new class opposed to big government, public sector workers, and other 'pointy headed' professionals whose career interests were said to be served by such policies as affirmative action (ibid.: 126). The alleged impact of affirmative action was one source of anxiety. Another was demographic change. Darlene Kurier, one of the subjects of David Wellman's study, feared the prospect of a white minority. Apart from physical assault, 'working-class whites, in her (Kurier's) estimation, have other fears . . . . They are afraid that work will be given to coloured people instead of to whites' (1993: 133).

In February 1995 *US News* ran a cover story; does affirmative action mean NO WHITE MEN NEED APPLY? The graphic image accompanying the inside story showed a sleeve (with a stars and stripes print) from which a hand appeared, only the hand took the form of a ladder one half of which descended to one side of a ravine where a black man was already seen climbing up, whilst on the other the ladder fell well short of the ravine's edge where a white man waited in vain to reach it. The article was one of a growing number of publications which were suggestive of a social equilibrium under threat. The norms associated with the stable, taken-for-granted, privileged order of dominant white masculinity were being increasingly called into question. One of Feagin and Vera's respondents had this to say: 'As a white male, I feel like I'm the only subsection of the population that hasn't jumped on the victim bandwagon . . . I haven't oppressed anybody, but I've experienced being oppressed' (1995: 146). When Wellman's white students at Berkeley talked about their experience of affirmative action they did so in ways ('it benefits the wrong people' or 'it's reverse discrimination') which ignored the benefits of whiteness. According to Wellman, 'because they do not locate the speaker in the organization of racial privilege, whiteness need not be addressed' (1993: 232–3). Assumptions regarding employment, domesticity and gender relations, sexuality and the certainties associated with the dominance of western knowledge paradigms were being challenged and partially displaced, in both the private and public spheres. The comprehensiveness of this challenge prompted an ideological counter attack, or backlash, the overall aim of which was to maintain the *status quo* or, better still, to return to some idealised past.

In the above cases, whiteness was defended consciously and explicitly, as it was in Frederick Lynch's *Invisible Victims: white males and the crisis of affirmative action* (1989). His study reviewed thirty-four cases of white male victims of discrimination. His conclusion was that a counter-white male bias had been institutionalised and that worst of all there was a taboo surrounding affirmative action which constituted censorship (1989: 107) and served to generate alienation and tension amongst white men (ibid.: 91). In other studies, the defence of whiteness was more coded, for example, Charles Sykes' *A Nation of Victims: the decay of the American character* (1992). Sykes traced the rise of victim culture back to the 1950s, not uncoincidentally back to the early days of the Civil Rights movement. Although Sykes attacked therapy and the 'so sue me' culture in general, he was particularly concerned with the combined markers of skin and gender as a cue for victim status, e.g. African-Americans seeking reparations and women suffering from 'battered wife syndrome' (sic). Not so far beneath the surface of his account was the real object of Sykes' concern, the victim *par excellence*, who kept getting the blame for both racism and domestic violence: the white male.

Philip Howard (1994) also codes the problem of white male victimisation but in somewhat different terms, that is with respect to rights and responsibilities. He argues that 'new rights' unlike old, constitutional rights, may have been intended to bring excluded groups into society, but turned out to be the means of getting ahead (ibid.: 133). For example, 'gifted students, in contrast to disabled children, receive virtually no support or attention from America's school system' (ibid.: 151). Howard conceals the racial identity of his victims behind the reference to 'gifted students' and lumps all the beneficiaries of new rights behind the reference to 'disabled children'. In common with numerous other attacks on affirmative action and related policies, Howard conveniently forgets the numerous forms of invisible support and attention 'gifted students' receive, not just from the educational system but from parents, personal contacts, scholarship funders etc. Likewise, both Dinesh D'Souza (1995) and John Edwards (1995) critiqued the rationales behind and outcomes of affirmative action policies and in effect end up defending the white victim in racialised politics. What these examples also serve to illustrate are the ways in which the strands of backlash culture interrelate and how the status of a white male victim was constructed on the basis of a certain understanding of rights, responsibilities and, what I discuss now, knowledge.

Relative knowledge

One of the most significant features of both campus debates in the US and anti-racist education in Britain in the 1980s was their efforts to challenge taken-for-granted notions of what passed for knowledge. In the US the critique of the dominance of white, Eurocentric paradigms over others rested on the idea that knowledge could only be understood in terms of its historical context and that one system of knowledge could not claim superiority or dominance over another. As a result, backlash arguments invariably ended up defending the canon and the epistemological base of whiteness via a critique of the concepts of cultural relativism and historicism.[3] To illustrate these arguments, I will draw on an essay by Roger Scruton on cultural relativism (1986) and Allan Bloom's backlash classic, *The Closing of the American Mind* (1987).

Scruton's critique of cultural relativism was based on his rejection of the idea of England as a 'multicultural society'. The latter, he argued, was a fiction, so long as the English language and English law overrode all but the most superficial aspects of cultural difference, or what he called all but 'the shallow customs of social intercourse' (1986: 127). Furthermore, if Britain were to become a genuinely multicultural society (i.e. multi-lingual, multi-faith) Scruton argued that many people would be alienated and cut off from their surrounding culture. Implicit in Britain's adherence to a particular legal system and language, Scruton argued, was a critique of other systems or, put another way, it rested on the inevitable assumption that the British way was best. It followed, therefore, that the idea of giving equal weighting to different cultures and to pretend not to pass judgement on them, i.e. the cultural relativist view, ran counter to the British experience.

By way of illustrating this point Scruton invited cultural relativists to accommodate such practices as suttee and polygamy under the guise of multicul-turalism (1986: 128) or to argue that the British political system was just an alternative to, i.e. no better or worse than, say nazism or communism. According to Scruton, the only way to defend the British system is to use an absolute yardstick of comparison and hence to reject the idea of cultural relativism. Taking a some-what different context (i.e. London's educational policy for schools), but arguing the same point, Scruton posed the question, should reggae be taught in schools on a par with Shakespeare and, if not, why not? (cited in Gordon 1990:187).

Scruton's distinction between multiculturalism and monoculturalism is, arguably, false and untenable. Not only do many societies exist with devolved legis-latures and multi-lingual provision, but cultures are constantly evolving and responding to change. Like it or not, what once was the preserve of one culture has inevitably seeped, unwittingly, into another. The only myth here is that of cultural purity. In addition to those inevitable and informal cultural leakages, Scruton also ignores the legitimacy of the formal political terrain, not necessarily in order to claim absolute or relative 'truth', but merely as a site for either defending versions of cultural homogeneity or promoting cultural difference. Rather than open up this debate into the public realm, Scruton's attack on cultural relativism conceals a dogma, dressed in a pseudo-universalistic notion of standards and, arguably, an example of the very relativism he seeks to refute, i.e. the promotion of a particular version of monoculturalism expressing a white ethnic or class standpoint.

Although arguing from a broadly similar political perspective to Scruton, Bloom's objection to cultural relativism is less concerned, at least superficially, with the definitions and realities of multiculturalism, than with its (cultural relativism's) alleged intellectual dogmatism. He is particularly critical of those left academics who, having benefited from the intellectual openness which characterised campus debates in the 1960s, were now guilty of turning against the very knowledge foun-dations on which their careers had been built (1987: 39). According to Bloom, by questioning western literary and historiographical canons and engaging with other cultural (including popular) traditions, they were 'closing', not opening, American minds.

A closer reading of Bloom's argument suggests, however, that the author's real concern was not so much with cultural relativism, *per se*. In actual fact both it (rela-tivism) and historicism have been around for some time and, in some quarters at least, respected philosophical traditions. Rather, Bloom's anxieties were more 'local' and concrete, at least according to his account of the following incident.

> A group of black activists disrupted the class of an economics teacher, then proceeded to the chairman's office and held him and his secretary (who suffered from heart disease) hostage for thirteen hours. The charge of course was that the teacher was racist in using a western standard for judgement of the efficiency of African economic performance. The students were praised for calling the problem to the attention of the

authority . . . and the teacher disappeared miraculously from campus never to be seen again.

(1987: 354)

Mixing the academic with the anecdotal proved an effective marketing strategy for backlash literature, the 'academic' enhancing its credibility, the anecdotal making it more accessible and quotable. Bloom was not engaging with cultural relativism as a philosophical dispute now, but more with its inference that non-western economic indicators, in this case from an African perspective, would need to be taken seriously. The incident allowed Bloom to re-define cultural relativism as academic terrorism and to cast the white victim (with a heart condition) as 'hostage'. Bloom used the term hostage both in its literal sense in his description of this incident but also symbolically, i.e. intellectual hostages to accusations of racism and sexism. Under such circumstances, 'detached dispassionate study (is) impossible' (1987: 355).

Ultimately, Bloom's goal was an academy which legitimated and celebrated 'the United States as one of the highest and most extreme achievements of the rational quest for the good life according to nature' (ibid.: 39). Doing so went hand in hand with his need to assert what is good and evil, right and wrong. Such moral agendas were to be built, unashamedly, on Eurocentrism which, for Bloom, was a cultural imperative. Without it the west would collapse (ibid.). There may be the odd cost. Amongst the hundred flowers 'blooming' might be racism and other prejudices, but these Bloom would tolerate, as necessary pre-conditions for 'detached, dispassionate study'. The fact that such prejudices might assist one group whilst making study extremely difficult for others does not enter Bloom's argument because whiteness is treated throughout as the universal norm. In his view, affirmative action is all about lowering standards and should perish on the vine.[4] His proposals thus aimed to remove the threat (both physical and in terms of self-esteem) posed both to the individual (i.e. ontological whiteness) and, from an institutional standpoint, to an entire intellectual heritage (i.e. normative whiteness).

'Paranoid knowledge' here is not just rooted in the fact that long established 'authorities' and 'privileges' were being questioned, sources of legitimacy undermined and even career opportunities reduced, but in the removal of the epistemological means to answer back. The attack on western paradigms and the defence of affirmative action are related in this sense, forming part of an alternative social imaginary, in which affirmative action facilitates the expression and study of cultural difference and the challenging of the western canon. The idea that other cultures have, for example, literary and aesthetic traditions of equal merit to classical European literature means that the west can no longer be held up as a yardstick by which to judge other cultures. It becomes just one of many.

Dinesh D'Souza (1995) provides a final example of both the paranoias induced by the critique of cultural absolutism and the hidden political hand at work in its defence. His target on this occasion was the Guatemalan human rights activist and

Nobel Peace Prize winner, Rigoberta Menchú whose testimonial *I Rigoberta Menchú*, was a portrayal of the oppression of an indigenous people by a ruthless dictatorship. According to D'Souza the purpose of the testimony, irrespective of its authenticity and representativeness, which he doubts, was to provide the left with ammunition for a critique of western society. Regrettably for D'Souza his accusation not only flies in the face of considerable independent evidence to the contrary.[5] He also managed to match the alleged dogma of cultural relativism with his own assumption that who you are and the position from which you speak is an adequate measure of the validity of your claims.

Rights and responsibilities

Whilst cultural relativism has dominated the backlash debate within US universities, in public policy circles it has centred on the issue of rights. Philip Howard made a distinction between the old kind of rights associated with the Constitution which conferred protection on its citizens (1994: 116) and so-called 'new' rights, as he called them, which provided and subsidised rather than protected (ibid.: 117). The problem, according to Howard, was that granting new rights for some meant a curtailment of freedom for others (ibid.: 167). He took, as an example, the case of New York City's requirement to make public spaces open to all, including those requiring wheelchair access. The policy meant that amenities such as public toilets were denied to all because making them accessible to the disabled was deemed impracticable (ibid.: 117).

In England, the idea that one man's rights were another man's loss of liberty was illustrated in the 'Honeyford affair' examined in the previous section. The tabloid press and the Conservative broadsheets, i.e. *The Times* and *Sunday Telegraph* were unanimous in their condemnation of the treatment of Honeyford which they described as an 'inquisition', 'inverted McCarthyism' and 'censorship' (Gordon 1990: 178). In effect elements of the media seemed to imply that the rights of African Caribbean and south Asian pupils and parents to be free from racial harassment impinged on Honeyford's right to racially harass. As Smith comments,

> the dominant white British culture was thereby positioned as a beleaguered victim .... Through the inversion of power relations, racial otherness was constructed as a corrosive external force bent on the total destruction of the 'peaceful' (white) British way of life
>
> (Smith 1994: 115–16)

The fact that 'rights' have not been codified in Britain in the way that they were enshrined in the US Constitution has made them a less explicit, but none the less effective point of reference. Instead, appeals to old-fashioned common sense, embedded custom and practice, have been used to defend whiteness against its multicultural critics. Frank Palmer (1986), for example, has defended the idea of 'education for its own sake' against attempts to attach some moral imperative to it, notably a commitment to anti-racism. Whilst moral training, he argued was necessary for the young 'at the highest levels of moral understanding, virtue in this sense cannot be taught' (1986: 157). The correlate of this view was the idea of 'free autonomous agents with intentions, beliefs, desires and feelings' (ibid.: 159). The problem with Palmer's argument is that it rests on the assumption that education 'for its own sake' and ideas of 'agency', 'freedom' etc. are abstract universals rather than part of a very definite moral or philosophical position, i.e. humanism. Anti-racism, for all its flaws, merely attempts to question those taken-for-granted assumptions and practices on which normative whiteness has been built.

Russell Lewis (1988), like Palmer, has also defended a 'rights and responsibilities' position in terms of philosophically and morally informed notions of fairness, freedom, etc. Numerous examples are scattered throughout Lewis's book. For example, he cites the case of the Sikh boy who claimed racial discrimination for not being allowed to wear his turban to school. Lewis sees this as an example of 'special' privileges over general rights (ibid.: 51). Likewise, he questions the Commission for Racial Equality's monitoring of ethnic representation in the workforce as 'a mixture of deception and intimidation' (ibid.: 50). He also feared the impact of the welfare benefits on West Indians with their 'feebler family structure' (ibid.: 116), and berates the librarians and teachers who sought to remove racist books thus curbing what Lewis saw as important freedoms (ibid.: 147). Running through these examples is an implicit defence of common-sense notions of individual freedoms and rights as well as pathological assumptions regarding black families. Lewis's argument treats existing moral norms as given, i.e. natural and universal, when in fact they are highly particular in terms of the interests, freedoms and rights they have served and protected. Any attempt to challenge the *status quo*, i.e. to promote and secure cultural diversity, is thus tarred with a 'special interests' brush and attacked for denying what were, in effect, the rights and freedoms of the white majority.

Backlash arguments of this ilk view rights as problematic for other reasons. According to Charles Sykes (1992) they absolve individual responsibility. Rights, he argues, are based on the premise that someone else is to blame. No one is responsible and/or guilty, just dependent or sick. The removal of individual responsibility reflected other trends in US society, according to Sykes; notably the proliferation of therapies and litigation. By accusing everyone, including presumably numerous white males, of victim status, Sykes has escaped accusations of bias against particular groups, although many women and some men may take issue with the suggestion of 'red carpet' treatment. Sykes's canvas was broader, one which portrayed a society of whiners, compulsive shoppers, gamblers and drinkers all of whom found a couch to lie on to avoid personal blame. He illustrated the alleged absurdities of the 'so sue me' culture with reference to a convicted flasher who was fired by his employer, the local parks department. In his defence, the flasher protested that his previous convictions had been for flashing in laundromats and that he had never actually exposed himself in a park. The court found in his favour.

In a C-Span television interview, which gave him the opportunity to publicise his views to a wider audience, Sykes cited the case of ' battered wife syndrome' which he dismissed as both fashionable and dangerous. In two instances he knew of (once again a reliance on anecdote) it was cooked up to cover deaths under suspicious circumstances. New rights (as opposed to old but legitimate constitutional rights) he argued, had turned people into victims. Women, for example, despite massive changes to the contrary, remained 'yoked to (a) victim status . . . even when the world is rolling out a red carpet for you'.[6] D'Souza takes this further in his analysis of the problem facing African-Americans which he attributes to their own 'destructive and pathological patterns of behaviour: excessive reliance on government, conspiratorial paranoia about racism, a resistance to academic achievement as "acting white", a celebration of the criminal and outlaw as authentically black and the normalization on illegitimacy and dependency' (1995: 24).[7]

Similarly, John Edwards has argued that respect and dignity cannot come from the assumption that minorities are always the victims of discrimination and oppression (1995: 228). Indeed 'oppression talk will turn out to be more functional for white liberals in need of a cause than for equality of opportunity and respect for all' (ibid.). For Edwards and others, rights are also highly suspect when they are based on the principle of compensation for past injustices. In the following, he critiques this argument and seeks to absolve white men in the process. Edwards begins by asking,

> How can a white person avoid complicity in the harm doing? . . . Are all white males guilty or only those who gain or already hold positions that ought rightfully to be held by minority group members? If all white [males] are guilty, does that mean that none of them should now be in the positions they hold? Surely this cannot be what is intended. But if not this, then *which* white [male] position holders and gainers should not by rights be where they are? These questions must be posed because they are the logical extension of guilt-by-benefit and they point up, because of their unanswerability, the fatal flaws in the argument.
>
> (1995: 188, emphasis in original)

What has compounded a sense of paranoia within backlash writing is a perception on the part of its authors that there has been no space, until recently, to talk about the impact of rights conferred on so called 'minority', white men. According to Lynch, it was the taboo status of these arguments which turned the climate surrounding affirmative action into one resembling the earlier McCarthy era. Hence, 'there is no denying the official bullying, the baiting and the labelling, the manipulation of guilt and fear, the complicity of the media and institutional paral-

ysis produced by both McCarthyism and affirmative action' (ibid.: 115). To make
matters worse, the defence of new rights has, in Edwards' words, not only given
white liberals a cause to fight, it has also feathered the nests of a growing black
middle class who, like their white liberal counterparts have grown fat on the backs
of a black underclass (D' Souza 1995). In fact, D'Souza has argued that the black
middle class needed a black underclass to legitimise subsidies (e.g. in the form of
affirmative action programmes) to itself (ibid.: 23). Similarly, he argued, organisations like the National Association for the Advancement of Colored People
(NAACP) benefited from a system of reward allocation which depended on
patronage from organisations like theirs, rather than on the basis of merit (ibid.:
317). Once again, the irony of this judgement about patronage is the way in which
it renders white patronage systems as either invisible or normal and fair. We could,
for example, ask about the patronage embedded in powerful corporate, political,
publishing and media networks which rewarded these authors handsomely, just for
legitimating and fuelling the backlash.

The fact that backlash writing includes intellectuals of south Asian origin like
Dinesh D'Souza within its ranks, enhances its universal claims and, according to
D'Souza himself, disproves the idea that racism remains a significant shaper of
destinies. On the contrary, according to D'Souza, racism 'no longer has the
power to thwart blacks or any other group in achieving their economic, political
and social aspirations' (ibid.: 525). A common ploy in both England and the US
is to cite individual success stories, e.g. Colin Powell, Clarence Thomas and
Douglas Wilder, as illustrative of the opportunities open to everyone, regardless
of ethnicity or racialised status. Furthermore, these prominent figures are often
the most effective voices in backlash discourses. D'Souza is a case in point,
according to Smith when she writes, 'the new racism therefore borrows the legitimating structure of "identity politics" discourse and finds itself a Clarence
Thomas to dismantle affirmative action or a Dinesh D'Souza to denounce "political correctness" and an Asian–Briton to support anti-Asian remarks about
immigration' (1994: 109).

Interconnecting backlash themes

I have argued that the defence of whiteness has been linked to a broader political
agenda which has zealously defended and policed established institutions against
attempts to re-present and re-work white ideologies and institutional practices in
more ethnically diverse, equable and equitable ways. In doing so, it has proved
expedient, within the discourse of whiteness, to work through other discourses, for
example, sexuality. It has also proved adept at linking various 'demon groups' and
underpinning its attacks on one group with a morality which equally condemns all
'others'. The issue of homosexual rights is one example of this and to illustrate it I
will look at Oregon's Measure 9 in the US, the same issue of lesbian and gay rights
in Britain, in the 1988 Local Government Act and, thirdly, the talk radio polemics
of Rush Limbaugh, again in the US.

In the late 1980s and 1990s Oregon became the battleground for a series of attempts to legislate against gay and lesbian rights. Lon Mabon, the leader of the Oregon Citizen's Alliance (OCA), was the chief architect of these political campaigns. The aims of both state Measures 9 (1992) and 13 (1994) was to make it illegal for Oregon to use categories like 'sexual orientation', etc. in state policies, the assumption being that the use of such terms helped to promote homosexuality. On the contrary, the OCA proposed that efforts should be made to promote the view that homosexuality, like paedophilia, sadism and masochism was perverse, wrong and unnatural. Campaigns against Measures 9 and 13 contributed to the defeat of both at a state-wide level, although the OCA's efforts were instrumental in passing 25 local anti-gay rights measures in 1993 and 1994. Similar attempts had been tried elsewhere in the US with more success, although in 1996 a Supreme Court ruling rendered illegal an amendment to Colorado's Constitution which forbade laws aimed at protecting homosexuals. The Supreme Court voted by 6 to 3 against Colorado, arguing that it was unconstitutional to deny rights to homosexuals to which other groups were eligible (*Oregonian*, 21 May 1996). The case was important because it challenged a core assumption and plank of the OCA campaign and one borrowed from a wider backlash discourse. The OCA had argued that, in recognising gay rights, Oregon would be conferring something special and privileged on homosexuals over and above the rights of white heterosexuals. The Supreme Court, on the contrary, argued that legislating for gay and lesbian rights was necessary to ensure equal rights.

The OCA's focus on special rights was evident in its campaign publicity [8] which in turn was part of a wider attack on the 'liberal establishment'. In one letter to friends and supporters of the OCA, Lon Mabon wrote, 'every day, the liberals, new agers, and secular humanists are tightening their grip upon the most powerful institutions in our society . . . we know the opportunity to turn the tide is fleeting' (OCA correspondence, 12 March 1994). This tactic enabled the Alliance to broaden its political base to include not only the anti-gay rights lobby, but also anti-affirmative action interests therefore extending the OCA target beyond gays to include white women and 'minority' groups. The initiative campaigns were thus able to play on racial and sexual fears simultaneously. Reported beatings and arson attacks on black gays and lesbians[9] were thus rationalised by an integrated anti-rights discourse. Graffiti, spray-painted on the walls of churches (which were also arsoned) included anti-gay, anti-Semitic and anti-Latino slogans (*Oregonian*, 12 October 1992).

The OCA itself went further than this in its campaign video 'Dangerous Behaviour: a hidden pattern of abuse'. The film's narrator linked homosexuality to paedophilia, sado-masochism and serial murder, 'the video flashes pictures of nude boys, . . . bondage scenes and serial killer Jeffrey Dahmer. Measure 9 is held up as a salvation' (*Oregonian*, 8 October 1992). The pre-occupation and fascination with child sex, bondage and various anal practices invites the question, do they protest too much? Should we be considering the subliminal motives for making such a video and the unconscious desires and pleasures as well as the fears that enabled OCA supporters to make such connections?

The flexibility of the anti-rights discourse enabled the OCA to turn its attention to illegal immigration in 1996, when it gave support to the Oregonians for Immigration Reform (OIR). The issue had received a boost with the success of California's 187, other similar state initiatives (e.g. Florida) and federal debates on immigrant welfare eligibility. Although OIR failed in its attempts to deny benefits to illegal immigrants, it none the less fanned the backlash discourse with its emphasis on the so-called rights extended to immigrants who, according to OIR founder Sharon Shepperd were 'uneducated, unskilled workers coming in who put a pressure on the infrastructure' (*Oregonian*, 15 March 1996). The success of the OCA and kindred groups may not have been in their success at the ballot box, but more in their capacity to generate and satisfy popular fears and fascinations as well as to seek to impose moral standards and regulate behaviour. Proof of the dynamic interplay between discourses of race and sexuality was evident in the OCA's ability to both play on and forge common-sense links between serial killers, paedophiles, gays and Latino immigrants.

Religion played an important ideological role in OCA campaigns. Not only did the OCA attract strong support from evangelical Christians, it sought biblical sanction for its homophobia, i.e. on the grounds that homosexuality was unnatural and immoral. Such claims to a higher spiritual authority also enabled the OCA to add other religiously sensitive political issues, notably abortion, to its platform. Hence, when Mabon ran for Senate in 1996, he campaigned (unsuccessfully) on the abortion issue as part of a wider Christian/Republican campaign to forge connections between homosexuality, abortion, affirmative action and immigration. Ironically, however, in expanding its scope and increasing its range of demons, the OCA sowed the seeds of its own electoral failure by provoking a wide and extremely successful campaign of opposition.

A very similar measure to those being advocated by such groups as the OCA was passed in England as part of the UK's Local Government Act, 1988. Section 28 of that Act made it illegal for local authorities to 'promote homosexuality' through publishing material with the intention of promoting homosexuality or promoting the teaching of homosexuality as a 'pretended family relationship' or providing financial support for either of the above. The right's ability to mobilise in support of Section 28 has been understood as part of a wider defence of norms of heterosexuality and nuclear family life. In so doing the pro-28 lobby sought to capitalise on anxieties around AIDS, the reported imminent collapse of the family and the perception of profligate and undemocratic 'socialist' local authorities. Gender, sexual and anti-racist politics were central to such local authorities and, as Jackie Stacey has observed, 'the appearance of Section 28 in the Local Government Act, then, is no coincidence, since the attacks on "loony lefties" in local government were fuelled by their association with lesbian and gay rights and used to discredit their position' (1991: 285).

The relationship between the different strands of identity politics was thus made complex not just by internal differences but by the efforts of the Thatcherite state throughout the 1980s to confer a common moral pariah identity on feminists, blacks, anti-racists and lesbians and gays alike. The relationships each had with the state also impacted, for better or worse, on relationships with the others. According to Stacey, for example, the fact that sexual politics was being debated as an object of political/public rather than private concern was in part due to the agenda set by feminists (1991: 297). At the same time, Section 28 took its lead from older racial arguments. According to Anna Maria Smith,

> Discourse on Section 28 reiterates the Powellian–Thatcherite racial logic. The Powellian version of the new racism helped to prepare the place for the self-promoting homosexual in the long list of 'enemies within', black immigrants, radical students, Irish activists, socialist school teachers, critical journalists, progressive intellectuals and so on.
>
> (1994: 217)

An important aspect of media coverage of Section 28 was the way in which lesbian and gay sexuality was opposed to family values. But what was more interesting was the use of what Stacey has termed 'discursive reversals' in which lesbian and gays were cast as powerful in contrast to the powerless and threatened nuclear family. Such reversals added urgency and legitimacy to institutionalised homophobia (1991: 288). In another 'reversal', both tabloids and even liberal broadsheets blamed homosexuals for the anticipated backlash against them. One even talked about a homosexual conspiracy, thus echoing an important ideological strand of anti-Semitism (ibid.: 289).

The Conservative's attack on the public sector throughout the 1980s thus forged a link between multiculturalism and homosexuality. The local state, particularly in Labour's hands, was allegedly both inefficient and interfering. Instead what was proposed was to devolve both multiculturalism and homosexuality to the 'private' domain. The success of Thatcherism throughout the decade of the 1980s lay in its ability to capitalise on the success of one campaign by applying its underlying ideological themes elsewhere. So it was with anti-rights politics which fed into and off a wider attack on the public sector, including its leftwardly inclined professionals, and other collective interest groups, notably trade unions. In the case of Section 28, however, whilst the government passed the law, the effect of the 'Stop the Clause' campaigns had been to mobilise and empower groups in defence of lesbian and gay rights, heighten their visibility and consolidate rather than undermine their sense of community/ies (Stacey 1991: 301).

Finally, in this section, I will discuss the views of the US talk show broadcaster and writer Rush Limbaugh in order to illustrate the ways in which connections between the above discourses have been forged at a popular media level. Like the OCA Limbaugh's 'world view' has been, first and foremost, Christian and he has used religion both to underpin and legitimate his moral message. He once wrote, for example, that 'The founders knew (the political system) would only work . . . if the society was girded on a bedrock of solid values and Judeo-Christian principles' (1993: 76). Those values were brought over on the Mayflower and were quickly inscribed in both the moral and economic conduct of the early settlers. Religion thus created *and* sanctioned the American Dream, a moral enterprise of which Limbaugh argues he has been contemporary living proof. He made this point when he wrote, 'I have learnt that it is still possible to succeed, not by relying on government handouts and affirmative-action programmes, but through self reliance, risk taking, hard work and the courage to believe in yourself' (ibid.: 25).

Welfare intervention, so reviled by Limbaugh, had poisoned the nation's soul (ibid.: 76–7). According to Limbaugh, not only did welfare discourage the kind of self-reliance which brought him his own success, but was also an example of the elimination of all but 'politically correct' ideas or viewpoints, a practice he provocatively called 'political cleansing'. 'Thought control' was rife in Limbaugh's America. For example, he has referred to a case of a student, Eden Jacobowitz who was allegedly working in his room in January 1993 when he was disturbed by a group of female students making a noise outside. He called them 'water buffalo' and suggested they might want to party down at a nearby zoo. The student was subsequently charged with racial harassment by campus authorities at the University of Pennsylvania. It was only when Limbaugh and the *Wall Street Journal* took up the case that charges were dropped (ibid.: 234). The impact of the student's remarks on the women concerned, not to mention the wider implications of Limbaugh's message on other would-be harassers up and down the US, was of little or no interest to Limbaugh. Instead, the rights and freedoms of the white male were not only paramount but universalised, i.e. made to stand for everyone's rights and freedoms. In reality, the combined effects of the student's action and Limbaugh's intervention not only threatened the rights of the women students but legitimated other similar acts of harassment.

Limbaugh's stance on sexual harassment was again borne out in his defence of Oregon's Senator Bob Packwood, who had been accused of sexual harassment on numerous occasions. Limbaugh retorted, 'what's the big deal? He's clumsy with women' (*Radio Flush Lush*, cited in Rendell *et al.* 1996: 51). His attempt to deploy humour, of sorts, to undermine the seriousness of issues, in this case allegations of sexual harassment, has been a common Limbaugh tactic on gender differences. Elsewhere, for example, he argued that higher male SAT scores, could only be due to superior intelligence and/or hard work (Radio 7, February 1994, cited in ibid.: 57).

Sexuality has also proved an important plank in Limbaugh's anti-PC polemics. In the following, Limbaugh defended the ban on gays in the military. He wrote, 'It is not just another employer whose imposition of social experiments can be harmlessly effected. There will be consequences to a lifting of the ban in the form of harm to the military and thus, arguably, to national security' (1993: 259) and elsewhere,

> What is the whole purpose of the armed forces? It is designed to kill people and break things . . . the best army in the world is the one that kills the most enemy soldiers and razes the most strategic targets.
>
> (ibid.: 258–9)

This is important to remember if we want to continue to be a great nation – the world's only superpower . . . our only standard must be excellence – no matter whose feelings are hurt, including heterosexual men who can't meet the physical or mental requirements.

(ibid.: 79)

In many ways these extracts go to the heart of 'Limbaughism'. The military were seen as the last line of defence, policing both national borders and national identity. For Limbaugh, gays in the military formed part of his wider dystopian vision of a nation under siege. And who better to personify that dystopia than homosexuals? As to the solution, Limbaugh predictably turned to the much maligned, yet physically fit, heterosexual male and a version of masculinity which, he claimed, encapsulated the US 'super-power' status.

Popular media and the white backlash

Birmingham City Council: the 'PC madhouse'

In 1993, television viewers across the world woke up to learn that Birmingham, England, had banned Christmas. According to the City's then Principal Race Relations Officer, Kurshid Ahmed, the story arose when the Leader of the Council went to switch on a set of hanging lights; a reporter from the *Mail on Sunday* asked her what their purpose was. She told the reporter that they were festive lights which were used for Diwali, Eid and other festive occasions, to which he put it to her that they were not Christmas lights. The Leader insisted that since they were 'festive' lights and the festival was, then, Christmas, they were therefore, Christmas lights! She went on to explain that the decision to use the lights on multiple occasions was meant to save money and cut out wastage and, moreover, that more 'tailored' decorations (Father Christmas, angels, etc.) were to be added later. The consequences of this seemingly innocuous exchange were, that, according to Kurshid Ahmed, 'Next day you had television and printed media throughout the world, not just Birmingham England but Birmingham Alabama, Los Angeles and São Paulo, Brazil, saying that Birmingham, that PC authority, had gone too far and banned Xmas' (interview, 10 October 1996).

This was one of many instances in which sections of the print media targeted Birmingham City Council's equality initiatives throughout the 1980s and into the 1990s. In 1994, the *Mail on Sunday* (23 January) ran a NEWS SPECIAL ON BIRMINGHAM, THE MOST POLITICALLY CORRECT CITY IN THE COUNTRY with the banner headline, IS THIS BRITAIN'S CRAZIEST COUNCIL? The article incorporated many of the themes associated with PC and loony leftism discussed above. It began with the Christmas ban story, attacking the Council's efforts to make the city's Christmas decorations relevant to other faiths in the city by replacing models of the three wise men and angels with stars and rainbows. It also criticised the use of interpreters to translate English into Caribbean

Creole, referring to the latter as 'pidgin English'. What appeared two extremely marginal and symbolic gestures were turned into threats against the cornerstones of national culture: Christmas and standard English.

The article took up a second popular theme of anti-PC tabloid rhetoric. Not only was national culture under threat but taxpayers money was being frittered away on 'irrelevant' and 'petty' projects, not to mention the harm allegedly being done to the image of the city. The idea that some projects, some groups and some salaries were economically and morally questionable has been a recurrent theme of much of print media coverage. Hence in the *Mail on Sunday* article, the caption, alongside photographs of two black members of the Women's Unit, described the latter as the '£470,000' a year women's unit. Likewise, under a photo of three black dancers the piece referred to the '£100,000' women's festival. Elsewhere it referred to the '£42,000' salary of the Chief Officer of the Women's Unit, the '£800,000' budget of the Race Relations Unit and the '£150,000' budget for the 'Festival of Racial Tolerance' which were all implicitly questioned simply by having their price tags attached. All these figures would look innocuous on a council balance sheet, particularly alongside much greater items of council expenditure, but their use in the context of an article about a 'crazy madhouse' council and against a backdrop of accusations of 'petty' and 'irrelevant' expenditure, helped to orchestrate a hostile public response. The mocking tone of the article ('the Women's Officer has achieved such break-throughs as demanding that all females aged 50–70 be referred to as "women elders" in council documents') served to undermine the role of the Unit in its efforts to counter ageist language. It also illustrates a common theme of such attacks: censorship and the denial of free speech through the imposition of a preferred language.

Finally, the *Mail on Sunday* report illustrates the ways in which backlash discourse makes connections between marginal groups, in this case the elderly, disabled, ethnic minorities, gays and lesbians, in order to marginalise them still further. With reference to the Women's Festival, for example, it stated that 'last year the event included "workshops bringing together lesbians with disabilities", screen printing for "women with special needs" and "oral history for black lesbians"'. There is an implied joke here which relies on listing the possible criteria for politically correct status in different combinations. The press report, in contrast to the festival programme, trivialised the multiple social disadvantages experienced by these groups as well as undermining the legitimacy of the festival as a positive, community-based intervention.

In contrast and almost inevitably so, the story's central characters/victims were a white able-bodied couple who wanted planning permission to build a garage and lower the kerb for easier access and who were asked to think through the equal opportunity implications of the change. Instead of acknowledging the failure of designers to think about wheelchair access, etc. the report went for a more newsworthy option, i.e. the local authority's infringement of white rights. Small wonder, under these circumstances, that the last word was given to the

Conservative leader of the council, who reiterated the voice of 'reasoned modera-tion' or normative whiteness. His reaction was thus: 'Scrap them (the equality units) straight away. We should treat everyone as human beings and stop treating some people as if they constantly need hand-outs. It is insulting and [has] created division where none existed' (ibid.).

There are a number of possible reasons why the local and the Conservative tabloid press have remained on a constant state of alert over Birmingham's equality initiatives. Since the abolition of the Greater London Council in the 1980s, Birmingham has been the largest urban authority in the country and sees itself and has been seen more widely as the country's heartland. Politicians of all parties thus see the city as politically significant in its own right as well as an impor-tant barometer of national trends. Whilst the Labour Party has remained in control in the city since 1984, there have been some closely called city-wide elec-tions in which the votes of the middle ring wards, for example Yardley and Selly Oak, have proved decisive. A widely held view is that control of the city's council has turned on the electoral results in these middle ring wards and that in turn the presentation of equality issues has been decisive in influencing the vote. According to Kurshid Ahmed,

a small racist fringe of *Evening Mail* [a local Birmingham newspaper] readers have held Birmingham Equality issues to ransom . . . the media picks on race as the most volatile issue when other problems go unno-ticed. Relatively minor issues in terms of expenditure like Punjabi lessons which are held after school in pupils' own time provoke stories under headlines 'who is to pay the heating bills for Punjabi lessons?'

(interview, 10 October 1996)

Arguably, the level and pitch of backlash hysteria has waned in England in the 1990s, at least in terms of national press coverage. However, Birmingham's experi-ence and that of some London boroughs suggests that paranoias remain latent, ready to surface if and when the opportunity arises. Whilst the number of anti-racist scares may have declined in absolute terms this may be as much a function of effective media policing as of a change in climate. In 1992 and 1993, for example, a number of articles appeared in the British press attacking the anti-racist policies of the Central Council for Education and Training in Social Work (CCETSW). In an article in the right-wing *Freedom Today*, Barbara Amiel argued that social work was only for the politically correct, i.e. for 'Marxist feminists' and 'anti-racists'. Likewise, the *Daily Mail* (14 December 1992) reported social services minister Timothy Yeo who accused social work of being in a 1960s time warp with too many 'isms' and 'ologies'.[10] And in an article in the *Guardian* Melanie Phillips also attacked anti-racist training for its authoritarian tendencies and argued that it was counter to principles of freedom of thought and speech. This and other Phillips' articles on similar themes proved significant in the backlash against political correctness because they were written by someone previously noted for her liberal views and because they arguably appeared in one of the few remaining organs/custodians of liberal values, the *Guardian* (Phillips 1994). Despite initial refutations of the allegations, CCETSW subsequently abolished its Black Perspectives Committee which had been responsible for developing anti-racist practice in social work and its new Chairperson went on to criticise the organisation's anti racist statement (*Runnymede Bulletin*, no. 272, February 1994).

Nevertheless, whilst the Conservative Party and its allies in the tabloid press have continued to make political hay from such scare stories, their reduction in terms of frequency and intensity since the height of such attacks on 'loony leftism' and anti-racism in the mid to late 1980s requires some explanation. It may have been due, in part, as I have suggested, to a retreat from high profile 'race' initiatives, for example, Birmingham's decision to abolish its Race Relations committee and subsequently streamline its equality structures.[11] This retreat may reflect not just effective media policing but also sensitivity to criticisms from the left and/or black intellectuals who have argued that municipal anti-racism has dogmatically reduced black people to passive victims and constructed them as a homogeneous group (Modood 1988; Gilroy 1990) and that, furthermore, anti-racism has been imposed on an unwilling, disadvantaged, white working-class community with sometimes tragic consequences. The incident at Burnage School near Manchester in which Mohammed Ullah was killed by a white pupil against a background of growing resentment on the part of white parents and pupils over the imposition of an anti-racist policy without adequate negotiation and consultation is arguably an example of anti-racism which was both misunderstood and misdirected.[12] It might have been an instance of the kind of strategy Stuart Hall was thinking of when he wrote,

> the whole PC strategy depends on a conception of politics as the unmasking of false ideas and meanings and replacing them by true ones. It is erected in the image of 'politics as truth' – a substitution of false racist or sexist or homophobic consciousness by a 'true consciousness'. It refuses to take on board the profound observation . . . that the 'truth' of knowledge is always contextual.
>
> (1994: 181)

Hall's comments undoubtedly reflect a shift to a new political terrain in England, one less fixated on unmasking and/or refuting backlash arguments or attacking homogeneous versions of whiteness through a unitary anti-racist politics, and more concerned with pursuing a politics built around particular issues and campaigns. It also attacks the absolutism of whiteness by default through challenging dominant versions of white Englishness with alternative, more complex, fractured and diverse representations. Parallel to these more overtly political trends has been a greater use of entertainment media to articulate and contest PC-related issues. This has happened, for example, through talk shows featuring interracial couples, television soaps and series running story lines and episodes on racial harassment, the casting of black actors in peak-time dramas, e.g. ITV's *London's Burning* and BBC's *Casualty*, and nightly broadcasts of the O.J. Simpson trial.[13] Alongside these developments has been the ongoing debate between those who reject specialist programming as ghettoising and those who see it as a way into, and complementary to, the mainstream media (Phillips 1995: 18).

Affirmative action and the case of the California Civil Rights Initiative, 1996

In November 1996, a majority of Californians voted yes to an electoral proposition to end affirmative action. The latter traditionally stood for policies aimed at increasing numbers of under-represented groups in employment and higher education. Sometimes this has entailed the establishment of quotas or set-asides where it has been shown that some groups, notably white women and minorities, have been hitherto under-represented. It has also entailed contract compliance, i.e. those contractors, both public and private, with whom federal government has done business have had to comply with government requirements or jeopardise the contract. Proposition 209 was the latest in a series of attempts to backtrack on the principle of affirmative action.[14] In July 1995 the Regents of the University of California had already voted by fifteen to ten to abolish the University's affirmative action programmes. Ten years earlier, in 1985, the Supreme Court opposed efforts to recruit minorities to government positions in Indianapolis, via the use of goals and quotas (Omi and Winant 1986: 134). By the 1990s the climate had shifted again. No longer was the electorate willing to let the Supreme Court alone take its decisions on affirmative action. It demanded a public debate and referendum, fuelled in part by the success of the referendum on benefits for undocumented immigrants (Proposition 187), which was passed in 1994 and which spawned similar proposals across the country.

As it transpired, whilst 209 was successful in California, affirmative action did not prove to be a major presidential election issue in 1996 as many had predicted. California's governor Pete Wilson, whose candidacy for the presidential election was largely based on his platform on immigration and affirmative action, dropped out early in the race for the Republican nomination.[15] Proposition 209's success was due to a peculiar configuration of economic and political circumstances which will be discussed in more detail in Chapter 4. It also happened against a historical background analysed by Tomas Almaguer (see Chapter 2) and California's status as a border state with Mexico. In this section I will look at the role played by talk radio in helping to mobilise popular opposition to affirmative action and to lay the groundwork for the success of the California Civil Rights Initiative (sic), as proposition 209 was known. Whilst it is inevitable that the 'converted' amongst listeners tune into these programmes, the ratings of such syndicated hosts as Rush Limbaugh and Bob Grant confirm that such programmes appeal to a mass audience. Moreover, the themes taken up by hosts and callers, which form the basis of this discussion, will be seen to resonate with the arguments of the backlash intellectuals discussed above. These themes include: angry white men; 'affirmative action is racist'; 'affirmative action feeds the dependency culture'; and 'liberal politics is obsolete'. I will then look at campaigns to defend affirmative action, which may have failed in the short term and on a local state level, but which may have contained this particular manifestation of backlash culture and built a political base for future struggles.

The theme of 'white victim' has already been discussed in general terms, but the specific role played by 'talk radio' hosts in the formation and confirmation of this dimension of white identity was illustrated in the shows devoted to affirmative action during 1995. Radio talk show hosts in the US are notoriously adept agenda setters. Not only do they choose the topic for discussion but, equally importantly, they encourage certain responses and pre-empt others by the way they introduce the topic and, subsequently, by their ability to cajole, incite and bully audiences to agree with their point of view. Joe Crummey, a white male, who hosted a show on KMPC, was no exception. The day immediately following the UC Regent's decision to end affirmative action at the University of California (21 July), Crummey 'steered' his audience with the following opening remarks: 'the tide has changed . . . people just don't want affirmative action . . . it makes white men mad . . . who are the minorities now . . . let's re-visit that one?' He then somewhat provocatively invited those would-be beneficiaries of affirmative action to call in to express their fears arising from the University's decision. Predictably, no beneficiaries telephoned the show. Perhaps they found his offer more of a dare than an invitation, particularly after he had used his introduction to the topic to whip up and sanction white male anger. And, as if those opening remarks were not sufficiently pre-emptive in themselves, he added, 'you'll be surprised how many minority people will be happy it's over'. Crummey was also amongst those who spoke about affirmative action as if it were a policy exclusively for African-Americans and Latino/as. Only subsequent campaigning ensured that white women were also seen as beneficiaries of such policies.

When the occasional caller did offer an alternative point of view, Crummey used it as an opportunity to put forward the 'reasoned' white male perspective. For example, one caller gave his interpretation of the University's decision in the following terms: 'I am fearful . . . whites have a phobia about their security . . . it's linked to the Republican agenda of keeping women as second class citizens . . . the Republicans are playing on white fears'. In his reply, Crummey defended the beleaguered yet, in his view, justifiably angry, white male. He said, 'whites are reacting to the feeling that they are being discriminated against now . . . the angry white man . . . it was cool to be angry in the 1960s but not in the 1990s'.

Crummey's stance on the topic inevitably prompted calls from those hostile to affirmative action. For example, Vanessa called to complain about affirmative action in the following terms: 'I don't want anyone to give me a push up . . . it's a lot to do with dignity . . . let's make it a level playing field'. This reaction reflected the widespread interpretation in which affirmative action = quotas = lowering standards = discriminating against whites = racism. Crummey did not dissuade the caller from this viewpoint. On the contrary, he took this common-sense interpretation to its conclusion when he replied, 'Jesse Jackson said the Regent's decision was racist . . . well it's not racist . . . it's just about giving people an equal shot . . . what he said was racist . . . what is racist is considerations based on race . . . he had it backwards'.

Another white male talk show host, Royal Oaks, also chose to discuss affirmative action the day after the University of California's decision to end it. He, too, defined the policy exclusively in terms of its significance for African-Americans and callers were asked whether they approved of 'race-based' affirmative action or not. One caller, who identified herself as an African-American woman, compared her husband's Jewish experience with that of African-Americans. She believed that Jewish success in general was down to education which provided the means to overcome the barriers erected by racism. She went on, '(Jewish) parents didn't bellyache or complain . . . blacks should stop saying gimme gimme . . . educated black children don't get dependent on the system . . . you've got to get beyond this and say instead what can I do to help myself?' (KABC, 21 July 1995).

The caller's African-American status undoubtedly lent credence to the backlash point of view. Her opinion could not, after all, be dismissed as white prejudice, however it served to bolster white male interests. In fact it echoed the sentiments of one of Proposition 209's principal supporters, Ward Connerly, an African-American self-made businessman and Regent of the University of California. His staunch defence of self-help and opposition to government intervention proved decisive in the University's decision to end affirmative action and in the wider 209 campaign. In particular, his high media profile suggested that it was not just a black versus white issue and that white campaigners were not just arguing on behalf of their own narrow self-interests but on behalf of everyone. The public airing of views such as those of this caller and indeed Ward Connerly thus served to deflect attention away from whiteness through universalising its point of view. It also shifted the focus away from the networks and informal channels which have facilitated entry into universities and subsequently sections of the labour market for some and not for others and the construction of these practices as the norm. Ironically, it was whiteness which had become dependent on a system of (white) preferential treatment. Yet as a result of such media discursive strategies as those described here, it was able to project its own state of dependency on to others and to dismiss dissenters as 'belly-achers' who had abdicated individual responsibility in favour of dependency. This is linked to another very important strategy.

The very invisibility of whiteness and its associated privileges, serves to *de-ethnicise* its beneficiaries and turn them into *individuals* who achieve, not as a result of their collective ethnic status, but because of individual merit. Such a view coincides with the widely held belief that American democracy is built on the principle of individual opportunity. This view was taken to its conclusion by Jo Klein, white Jewish writer and talk show host, when he argued that national identity was at stake and that to judge people according to group was un-American. He went on, 'what I object to most is the idea that groups have rights' (KCWR, 25 July 1995).

Klein's comment is testimony to the extraordinary capacity of whiteness to hide its own group status and on the contrary to build an illusory version of American identity which is based on its opposite, i.e. on individualism.

Attempts to marginalise and discredit your opponents is a common political ploy and Joe Crummey was not above it when he described the pro-affirmative action demonstration, in which Jesse Jackson participated, in the following terms,

> (Those protests in support of affirmative action) look obsolete . . . participants who stopped living in the 1970s . . . Jesse Jackson says they weren't arrested because they were too strong . . . they weren't arrested because they don't matter when they all sang 'we shall overcome' . . . it sounds hollow.

The tactic of undermining opposition by seeking to dispatch it to the historical dustbin, is not new or peculiar to the US. The grain of truth in Crummey's remarks lay more in the inference that politics have been increasingly waged elsewhere and in particular through the media, including, of course, talk radio. The problem with the new political terrain is its unevennesss which, I shall argue, played a decisive role in the success of Proposition 209. The seeds for an assault on affirmative action had been sown in individual court decisions in the 1980s which served to undermine the principle of legitimate opposition and the groundwork done by politicians of the extreme right like David Duke, who had campaigned on the issue in the late 1980s and early 1990s (see Chapter 6). By mid 1995, the issue had moved out from behind the closed doors of the Supreme Court and in from the margins to the mainstream of political and media debate. The tangible political result of this groundswell of opposition was Proposition 209, the purpose of which was to: end affirmative action on education, public employment, and government contracting and cut the budget for magnet schools, counselling, outreach and tutoring programmes, and target financial aid for universities (Los Angeles Metropolitan Alliance 1996, campaign publicity leaflet).

Mobilising against the backlash

Correcting media bias: the case of FAIR (Fairness and Accuracy in Reporting)

FAIR's first issue of their bi-monthly publication EXTRA was published in June 1986. It describes itself as 'national media watchdog offering well-documented criticism in an effort to correct media bias and imbalance' (Editorial statement reproduced in each issue of EXTRA). Apart from EXTRA and EXTRA UPDATE which comes out alternate months, FAIR has a weekly half-hour radio programme Counterspin on PACIFICA Radio. Jeff Cohen (Director) and Norman Solomon (Associate) have written regularly for progressive magazines and published books based on collections of their pieces (1993, 1995). Its advisory board membership includes Toni Morrison, Alice Walker, Susan Sarandon, Noam Chomsky, Studs Terkel, Tim Robbins and Jackson Browne.

The organisation has increasingly relied on subscriptions and donations to support its activities, but it also receives foundation grants, including one from the Veatch Foundation, the Unitarian Universal Church based in Long Island, which has a long record on funding and supporting civil rights issues, etc. and which has donated regularly to FAIR, including $30,000 to run an anti-racism desk for one year. FAIR also receives grants from other bodies including the McArthur and Streisand Foundations. Hollywood has raised the profile of the organisation partly through its star sponsorship and financial backing. So, for example, Tim Robbins donated proceeds from *Bob Roberts* (1992) to FAIR and Nirvana gave the takings from what turned out to be one of their last concerts. In 1996, there were plans to cut an album produced by award-winning producer Don Waz with tracks from well known bands and using Noam Chomsky's ideas as a thematic link. The band X, for example, had agreed to record a track 'Your Domestic Enemy'.

The organisation's strategy relied heavily on 'myth debunking'. For example, Janine Jackson in her article 'White Man's Burden', sought to counter media coverage of affirmative action. For example, she argued that the latter was *not*, as the media had suggested, primarily about preference or quotas. On the contrary, she argued, it had been more about promoting diversity through proactive recruitment drives including outreach work. Quotas have only been used where evidence of discrimination has been proved. On a second point, Jackson countered the view that discrimination was a thing of the past. In doing so she cited evidence from The Glass Ceiling Commission, a body initiated by Elizabeth Dole (sic), which found that 97 per cent of the top managers in the biggest corporations were white men.

Jackson's tactic of 'counter pointing' was endorsed by Steve Rendell, FAIR's Senior Analyst. Although he admitted that all of FAIR's staff support affirmative action, the organisation is more concerned with,

> looking at coverage of affirmative action . . . to point out all kinds of myths, not least spread by liberals who claim that discrimination is a thing of the past and that blacks are chief beneficiaries. In fact, most of elite schools have legacies. What is that if not affirmative action? The fact is that white women are the largest group to benefit from affirmative action and let's not forget the veterans who also benefit. What this means is that affirmative action is a code – for race . . . so you can read between the lines and tell what our position is [and] my point is but I won't come out and say it – and it isn't in our mission statement.
>
> (interview, 31 July 1996)

The analysis of media in terms of myths and distortions raises an important question of strategy for those groups mobilising against the politics of whiteness. It relates both to the possibilities of objectivity and truth and to the appeal to reason as a tactic of persuasion. FAIR's statement of aims and its approach to affirmative action suggests that there is 'a truth' about discrimination, the benefits of affirmative action and a 'fair', i.e. neutral, undistorted way to present the issue. FAIR's output would appear to confirm this view, which has also been endorsed by Noam Chomsky, an eminent member of its advisory board. On the other hand, FAIR do not pretend to be objective in the sense of giving equal weight to both sides of a debate. On the contrary, it seeks to redress the bias of mainstream media with its own version of events and issues.

The effectiveness of the tactic of appealing to 'reason' is also open to question. Many would say that the power of whiteness lies precisely in its capacity to disguise itself, project its fears on to others and to say one thing and mean another. In other words its irrationality is a source of imperviousness and strength, not a key to its undoing. Moreover, FAIR, for all its efforts to utilise media openings only reaches an audience of mainly converts and its success in capitalising on media celebrity sponsorships has inevitably been of symbolic and gestural value, as FAIR staff themselves have conceded (interview, 31 July 1996). This is not to dismiss the role of such organisations. On the contrary, it is very difficult to predict the climate *were it not* for their interventions. It is, however, to recognise their limitations, thus confirming the overall thrust of Chomsky's propaganda model and its filters vis. organisations like FAIR and to which Chomsky himself is affiliated.

The campaign against California's Civil Rights Initiative (Proposition 209)

The decision to call the anti-affirmative action initiative (Proposition 209) the 'California *Civil Rights* Initiative' (emphasis added) was politically astute and, of course, extremely misleading. In fact, it has been suggested that 209's eventual success was because many people mistakenly voted for it thinking it was a pro-civil rights measure. This section, rather than look at the CCRI itself, will examine the role of the campaigns set up to defend affirmative action. In Los Angeles, in 1996, local groups, under the umbrella of the Metropolitan Alliance, mobilised against Proposition 209. The Alliance produced an organising kit which contained: a list of neighbourhood networks and progressive organisations opposed to 209; a leaflet listing the benefits of affirmative action and debunking some of the myths surrounding it; a pledge card inviting individuals to participate in the campaign and donate at least $1, and an outline of forthcoming events. Local organisations involved in the campaign included labour unions, churches and neighbourhood block clubs. The campaign involved educational work (meetings, forums), making and distributing publicity (including yard signs, window stickers, buttons etc.) and house to house, meetings and rallies to increase voter registration and 'getting the vote out'. Materials were in Spanish and English to maximise support in both English and Spanish speaking communities in Los Angeles.

The issue of white women's rights was important to the campaign for a number of reasons. Firstly, affirmative action had been predominantly associated with

African-Americans, Latino/as etc., despite evidence that white women were the main beneficiaries of such programmes. This proved important both in mobilising against proposition 209 and also in discouraging Republicans, keen to increase their share of the female vote, from making affirmative action a front line election issue. Secondly, it provided the campaign against 209 with a chance to build an alliance of 'interests' of white women, African-Americans, Latino/as, Asian-Americans, etc. In an interview on Pacifica Radio's *Democracy Now* Patricia Ireland of the National Association of Women, located the specific attack on affirmative action in the context of the wider 'war on women'. The latter, she argued, was part of a wider backlash targeting minorities and in defence of the new victim category: white men. She went on to say,

> there's a very distinct effort to roll back those rights (won over the last thirty years). Not only has there been substance to it but there's been an edge to it as we've heard poor women analogised to alligators and wolves . . . that effort to make women independent, to make us empowered is resented.
>
> (22 July 1996)

She linked this to Governor Pete Wilson's attack on affirmative action as she continued,

> He is in favour of many restrictions that would injure women especially young women and poor women in their ability to receive necessary medical services not only abortion but birth control as well. When he was trying to decrease welfare benefits for poor women and their children he argued at one point that this would only mean that poor women would have to buy one less six pack of beer a week – he has been particularly vicious in portraying stereotypes of women as undeserving welfare mothers, unqualified workers who get jobs through affirmative action.
>
> (ibid.)

Over 400 national, state, civic and community organisations mobilised under the umbrella of the 'No on 209 Campaign'. Such groups included the Feminist Majority, the Black Business Association and the NAACP Legal Defence Fund. The aims of the umbrella campaign were both short and long term; to defeat 209 and to change the debate around affirmative action. It was hoped that working with individual groups and organisations to build a coalition was the most effective way of achieving these aims (interview Teri Stein, 6 September 1996). The aim of defeating 209 at times called for a more expedient strategy which was not always compatible with the longer-term goal of changing the terms of the debate. For example, the foregrounding of gender was agreed for reasons already cited and because pragmatically, women were an important electoral constituency to mobilise in the run up to the vote. But this tactic also opened the door to persuade white men to vote no on 209, not because of any new-found conversion to affirmative action but because of the potential implications of its abolition for their daughter's educational opportunities. These tactics might have secured a no vote but what about the less instrumentally motivated, internalisation of the principle? The campaign literature attempted to address affirmative action as it affected women *and* minority groups, but it nevertheless retained a strong emphasis on gender, i.e. clause C, which proposed allowing employers to use gender as a reason to deny opportunities for women on any ground deemed 'normal' by the employer (campaign leaflet). The attempt to broaden the campaign to include white women was in part a response to the oversimplified language of the proposition's advocates whose terminology dominated the print media's early coverage of the debate. According to Kim Deterline, who developed the Campaign's Media Action Kit,

> Terms like affirmative action, racial preference, civil rights were used as if they were neutral terms. On the contrary, the couching of the debate effectively elicited a common (intended) response: 'this issue is about race and the unfairness of policies based on racial preference . . . affirmative action programmes . . . give jobs to unqualified people of colour over qualified white people.'[16]
>
> (interview, 6 September 1996)

The decision to call the campaign the 'California Civil Rights Initiative' was, as I have suggested, an astute ploy by the campaign's architects. The intention, apart from to mislead, was also presumably to emphasise that 'race preferences' worked against the rights of white men. The fact that there had been a historic consensus in the US in favour of civil rights thus made it hard to vote against an initiative which both described itself and which was described uncritically in the media as a 'civil rights' initiative. Likewise, the idea of racial preferences implied that individuals were given jobs on racial criteria alone instead of seeing affirmative action as an attempt to devise polices and practices which increased opportunities for people of all ethnic and gender backgrounds to be more fairly represented throughout the workforce.

The ways in which the mainstream media were presenting the debate and popular understandings of the issues encouraged campaigners to develop a media strategy including a Media Action Kit. The kit was intended to provide a coherent platform against 209. It evolved out of both research and training groups of young volunteers and gave advice on writing letters to the editor, phone trees which encouraged ever increasing numbers of people to take a specific action and to encourage a more critical debate on terms like racial preferences which framed the terms of the proposition and media coverage of the debate. The researchers and authors of the Media Action Kit argued that supporters of affirmative action lacked a cohesive message and they often presented the argument in a legalese which was inappropriate to challenge common-sense thinking.[17] Moreover, a review of the Proposition 187 campaign around immigration highlighted the need for a more reflective approach to the media. According to Kim Deterline,

> 187 had some media consultants with views similar to those on the right (who) were telling the 187 campaign that the message should be 'if we cut services to illegal immigrants then those sick and dirty immigrants come and get all our children sick'. Well – that's not a helpful message.
>
> (interview, 6 September 1996)

Instead, the alternative interpretation of affirmative action put the responsibility on the conservatives and their economic policies. Again, according to Kim Deterline,

> the reason why people don't have jobs isn't because of illegal immigrants [or] affirmative action [or] because of women on welfare down the street pulling $300 on welfare. It's because of corporate downsizing and the economic policies of the very people behind the initiative.
>
> (interview, 6 September 1996)

Conclusions

The success of both talk radio and the tabloid press in mobilising backlash values can only be understood in terms of a wider understanding of historical developments in both the US and England. Neither radio nor the press worked in isolation and hence neither can be held solely responsible for the political success of 209 or the marginalisation of anti-racism in England. Their effectiveness cannot be understood outside of well-oiled publicity machines with their networks which have comprised wealthy conservative foundations, newspapers and the Republican Party in the US and right-wing think-tanks, publishers, the Conservative Party and the tabloid press in England. These machines gave new right intellectuals outlets to disseminate their ideas which both enhanced the respectability of such ideas as well as serving to complement the more 'grass roots' expressions of backlash culture articulated in the tabloids and on the radio. In fact, the political successes of backlash, in both the US and England, have invariably been 'local', targeting the perceived ineffectiveness of federal/central government as much as their more global racial 'demons'. I have also looked at ways in which the latter have been present in homophobic discourses. The OCA invoked racial demons both as a tactic to compound white heterosexual anger and as part of a wider ideological ploy to build a broad-based anti-government, anti-'special interests' bloc.

Backlash arguments critically entailed the 'outing' of 'whiteness' in mainstream English and US culture. Both academic and more popular media interventions broke the alleged taboo of silence and began speaking publicly and widely about 'white victims', 'reverse racism', etc. for the first time. Talk radio hosts like Joe

94

Crummey in California, and the tabloid press in England, complemented the quasi-intellectual contributions of white authors like Frederick Lynch and Russell Lewis. However, this did not mean the end of efforts to code whiteness in universal norms and bury it in everyday routines, customs and practices. On the contrary, the examples from this chapter confirm the importance of maintaining both strategies simultaneously. In other words, the mention of white victims not only helped forge a greater consciousness of white identity, it also facilitated a common-sense deciphering of more coded versions.

The role of figures like Dinesh D'Souza, Ward Connerly and as we shall see later, John Taylor, has been pivotal in the consolidation of whiteness. They have helped to make universal principles like 'self help', 'individual responsibility' (and 'rights') and absolute standards/knowledge, which have undoubtedly secured the privileges of dominant white ethnics. The enhanced profile afforded these figures by the mainstream media has lent credence to the argument that whiteness is not just in the interests of whites but can appeal to everyone. The exceptional case of ontological blackness (not to mention the occasional subaltern 'white') has thus been used to bolster dominant normative whiteness. Moreover, the latter has counterbalanced its accommodation of the odd African-American espousing white discourse by demonising other African-Americans who express an Afrocentric perspective. The cases of Al Sharpton, Leonard Jeffries and Louis Farrakhan spring immediately to mind.

What is evident is that neither effective, yet traditional political campaigning, or close media monitoring, or anti-racism done 'on the quiet' or 'in the open' has been a match for the backlash roller-coaster. It is very probable that such campaigns and political interventions may well have stemmed the tide or contained the worst excesses of the backlash but to what extent is only a matter of speculation. My aim has not been to pass judgement on these different strategies but to identify them and to leave their spokespeople to explain their respective strategies. Nevertheless, much politics which has aimed at challenging ascendant forms of whiteness, including the strategies of FAIR, has been premised on the assumption that appeals to reason and spotting the bias, negative image or distortion forms an important and integral part of the process of dismantling or abolishing these forms. Such tactics were an important feature of the broad-based campaign in support of affirmative action and against Proposition 209. The absence of alternatives makes such options appear all the more attractive, but not necessarily more effective. In England there has been a marked shift away from one version of PC, municipal anti-racism, towards a more fragmented politics partly played out in the sphere of representation, partly in grass roots, often single-issue community campaigns. In policy terms there has been a corresponding shift towards policies which have sought to subsume equality measures under 'quality' initiatives, thus pre-empting the former's 'special' status and the associated strategies of marginalisation of which I have given examples throughout this chapter. The re-vamped equality structures in Birmingham's City Council in England represent this latest phase in municipal efforts to undermine whiteness from within.

At root the backlash has been a response to a perceived crisis of white masculinity. The last two decades of the twentieth century have proved a key historical moment in the history of whiteness; its moment of 'truth'. In rushing to its defence its advocates have sought sanction in the Bible and the Constitution (witness the case of Rush Limbaugh) and in notions of liberalism and justice. The effectiveness of whiteness has in the past been to pass itself off as the norm. Yet this has become progressively more problematic as the norm is increasingly called into question by political or cultural developments such as 'post'-colonialism, multiculturalism, anti-racism, new ethnic alignments and the politics of representation. Somewhat unevenly, whiteness has been strategically made visible to its adversaries. Much of the time it has remained hidden, occasionally outing itself to become both visible and self-conscious. This latter strategy might be thought of as a politics of last resort since, ironically, it can only help to displace whiteness as the norm. In such a scenario, it becomes just another ethnicity, privileged but certainly not prized. Whiteness has made great play of taboos, speaking the allegedly unspeakable, putting into words what has been in people's hearts. Its alternating tactics of concealment and 'admission', often with different media playing the respective roles of 'good cop'/'bad cop', have worked to great effect in forging its common-sense beliefs. In the next chapter I will turn attention to a racial taboo *par excellence*. Immigration provides the site for possibly the most paranoid expression and assertion of backlash culture and is one in which the metaphors of borders and bodies have been freely exchanged in an all-out, last-ditch effort to police both.

4

BORDER GUARDS, BODYGUARDS, LIFEGUARDS

Historically, immigration discourse has proved a most effective site for the construction of whiteness in both the US and England. In this chapter, I am particularly interested in exploring the ways in which immigration debates have helped to forge 'white interests' and thus served to consolidate white identities. Rather than assuming that interests are straightforward expressions of different social locations (class, gender, ethnicity), the assumption here is that those locations themselves are internally diverse and always changing and that interests, too, are ever in the process of being constructed. The ideology of 'white interests' has been built around and harnessed to ideas of economic security, prosperity, ontological security, and a sense of local and/or national belonging. Such interests and identities will be shown to have been formed in opposition to subaltern white ethnicities as well as those more commonly associated with processes of white racialisation. In the main part of the chapter I will draw on two case studies, one from either side of the Atlantic, to analyse the formation of whiteness through political discourse and the media .

The backdrop against which such processes have become significant has been analysed by Cornel West who has distinguished three features of the contemporary period (1990). The first is the displacement of European models of high culture, the second is the emergence of the US as a world power and the third is decolonisation. The end of European cultural hegemony has had a profound impact on the US since it has been a particular version of its European ancestry which has given white America its sense of history and origins. Decolonisation, in so far as it has empowered the margins in the south/periphery and moreover the margins within the north and centre (via migration), has exacerbated this fear and imminent sense of loss. Immigration thus has provided both Anglo-America and Anglo-England with 'too-good-to-be-missed' opportunities to re-assert themselves, although as Howard Winant has suggested, we should not expect these particular expressions of white absolutism to be the last (Winant 1994).

A recurrent theme of immigration discourse, and one which I want to tie to my analysis of whiteness, is what David Sibley has called spatial purification (1995: 77). He has linked the latter to deep-seated paranoias around defilement and pollution which, he has argued, have formed the basis of dominant understandings of homosexual, female, mentally ill and minority identities, i.e. to alterity in general. Not only are different 'alterities' linked laterally but ideas of sexuality have provided important deeper, psychic dimensions to the fears and anxieties associated with the loss of employment, livelihood and 'roots'. Historically, the manifestation of such fears has varied but representations and codifications of immigration have remained amongst the most enduring in the racialisation of whiteness. This has been in no small part due to the capacity of such fears, e.g. defilement, purification, to work at a number of levels, including the personal or local, national and the global. Paranoias around the body *and* the nation state have freely exchanged metaphors to the mutual enhancement of both. For example, the term 'leaking' has been applied to both bodies and borders. The capacity of immigration discourse to forge links between bodies, both politic and personal, has proved decisive in the construction of whiteness. According to Sibley, 'Local encounters or the fear of encounters with an other are informed by images of alien other worlds and these local/global connections . . . need to be teased out' (1995: 112). The media has played an important symbolic role in 'energising and charging' this paranoia from representations in detergent advertising to those in popular film (ibid.).

My aim in this chapter is to explore these local and global connections and the images and fears they have generated through a discussion of two recent mobilisations around immigration, the UK's Immigration and Asylum Act and California's Proposition 187. The latter was a ballot initiative passed in 1994 which was aimed at eliminating the state's 'illegal' immigration by denying undocumented immigrants access to basic services (health education and social services). Bob Carter, Marci Green and Rick Halpern have compared the periods 1900–25 and 1948–71 in which immense social change profoundly challenged older versions of national identity, forcing re-evaluations of what it meant 'to be British' or 'to be American' (1996: 139). Shifting notions of national identity thus served to resolve the contradictions thrown up by need for labour *and* the urge towards homogeneity (ibid.). Many of the themes uncovered by these authors throughout their investigation of political records remain relevant to a discussion of political discourse in the 1990s. Both the UK's Immigration and Asylum Act 1996 and California's Proposition 187 will serve to illustrate ways in which immigration has helped secure dominant versions of white identity.

The backdrop against which the US and England have encountered immigration has been the successive phases of globalisation discussed in Chapters 1 and 2. Mercantilism, slavery, colonialism and post-modern forms of globalisation have each brought new migrations and diasporas in their wake. I will begin by examining some of these earlier migrations. In the case of the English experience this is in order to illustrate the ways in which subaltern forms of whiteness were racialised as part of a process of constructing and anchoring a more dominant version set of white interests and identities. My aim here, as in my discussion of the post-1945 period when 'skin' reputedly became the dominant, through not exclusive, object of racialised discourse, is not so much to explore the specific reasons for migration or the impact of migration on diasporic communities. Rather, the argument will focus on the strategic importance of immigration in the construction of dominant versions of Anglo and Anglo-American culture and identity and the related role of the media. I am also interested in how such monolithic conceptions have been resisted and re-worked, particularly through anti-racist campaign politics.

Immigration in the history of white Englishness

I have already referred to Elizabeth I's Royal Proclamation in 1601 to expel all 'Negroes and blackamoors' from her kingdom, an order which distinguished bona fide subjects from groups of undesirables and was made against a background of widespread poverty. The Proclamation made what became a 'common-sense' argument, namely that immigration was costing jobs and threatening living standards. It defined and distinguished 'natural' subjects whose interests, it argued, would be protected by repatriating those it defined as undesirable, thus forging what Stuart Hall has called a 'racist chain of meaning' (1990). Immigration rhetoric has not only thrown up sets of institutional regulations and directions but has formed part of what Goldberg has referred to as racism's ethical choices. These choices are informed by 'rights and expectations' which are attached to immigration and which in turn etch a sense of self-belief in the ontological status of white Englishness (1993). The means by which such ethical choices have been created is an important concern of this chapter.

Elizabeth I's reasoning has subsequently been applied to a succession of immigrant groups, including subaltern white ethnicities. The stereotypical characteristics varied from group to group but the role in defining who did and did not belong in England and what was and was not in the 'national interest' promoted historically specific but none the less important continuities in the construction of white identities and interests. Phil Cohen has argued that such interests crystallised around ideas of codes of breeding which initially targeted 'insiders', i.e. the working class, and subsequently applied to waves of 'outsiders' (1988). Ideas of contamination and pollution were woven into a discourse in which policing the body became synonymous with policing the body politic, i.e. the nation state. Such themes were taken up in the press and popular fiction, invariably in ways which explained and sanctioned government policies and practices. The seeds of white Englishness were thus sown.

A number of writers have commented that whilst anti-Semitism and anti-Irish racism were both prevalent in the nineteenth and early twentieth centuries, no entry restrictions were applied to the Irish in the way that aliens' legislation was effectively aimed at Jewish and Gypsy populations from 1905 onwards (e.g. Solomos 1993: 42). This might in part be due to the peculiarity of England's historical relationship with Ireland. During this period, successive British Governments defended the Union against pressure for 'Home Rule'. Under these circumstances, demands for immigration control (of those same union subjects) would have appeared somewhat anomalous. In any event, whilst the violence against Irish Catholics in Wolverhampton and Stockport did not provoke demands for immigration control, they did lead to arrests and some deportations in Stockport (Millward 1985: 209). The local press had played an important role in whipping up anti-Catholic sentiment, the *Stockport Advertiser* publishing five anti-Catholic editorials in 1852 in the build up to the uprising (ibid.: 210). Although it has been suggested that there was less ethnic tension in Wolverhampton, there were Irish protests against anti-Catholic speakers in the town in the late 1850s and clashes with the police did centre around Irish drinking houses. Moreover, whiteness was, in part, defined (and perhaps regulated too) by the manner in which the local press reported such incidents. According to Roger Swift, 'by concentrating on purely "Irish rows" (*The Wolverhampton Chronicle*) highlighted the relative orderliness of the non-Irish population' (Swift 1985: 198).

One enduring and recurring feature of immigration discourses has been their capacity to simultaneously present racially defined groups as both capable *and* incapable of assimilating into the dominant culture. This ambivalence has served a number of ends. The 'good Jew'/'bad Jew' distinction which ran through nineteenth-century discourse, is an early example of what I mean here. Like its successors, the distinction allowed whiteness to project its ideal characteristics and values on to one and, *at the same time*, their worst fears and desires on to the other. In terms of practical outcomes, a minority of Jews were rewarded with 'co-opted status' for their allegiance to normative whiteness whilst the majority were subject to institutionalised forms of exclusion.

Brian Cheyette gives the example of George Eliot's *Daniel Deronda* which contains both good (the Derondas) and the bad Jewish stereotype (the Cohens) (1989: 16). Likewise, John Buchan's admiration for Jews and Kipling's 'Imperial Jew' in *The Army and the Dream* can be contrasted with the novels of Anthony Trollope, for whom the Jew symbolised the crisis of modernity and Whig liberalism. H.G. Wells also used Jews to represent his vision of a disease-ridden England (1989: 22). Cheyette puts the relationship between literature and politics this way: 'Trollope's disillusionment with liberal progress in the 1870s anticipated and perhaps made thinkable racial anti-semitism' (1989: 15). The British Brothers' League (BBL), which was formed in 1901, leafleted and lobbied the support of MPs as part of a campaign against alien immigration. Propaganda suggested that alien paupers were 'driving English people out of their native parishes and literally taking the bread out of English mouths' (cited in Holmes 1979: 90).[1] Legislation, introduced in 1905 and again in 1914 and 1919, culminated in the Aliens Order 1920 which gave the Home Secretary the power to deport aliens whose presence was not conducive to the public good (Solomos 1993: 47).

In 1906, an article on Chinese immigration in Liverpool appeared in the *Sunday Chronicle*. After allegations of crime, underage sex, opium, gambling, squalor and of turning the city into a 'yellow town' which was 'not fitted to be a part of civilised white society', the article went on,

> Is this open sore to be allowed to fester in a white community? Remember this, the Chinese are in close touch with one another all over the world, and when they hear from their countrymen that England is a good place where they are allowed to do as they like, they will come here in droves.
>
> (cited in Clegg 1994: 9)

The common threat of 'alien ethnicities' to the national stock was a common theme of Fabian socialist eugenicists, Sydney and Beatrice Webb. According to Holmes, 'Sydney Webb could turn his attention to the prospect of "degeneration of type", "race deterioration if not race suicide" and contemplated the country falling into the hands of the Irish, the Jews or even the Chinese' (1979: 47).

Immigration to the UK in the post-1945 period has been seen largely in terms of 'black' immigration from the New Commonwealth countries of the Caribbean, the Indian sub-continent and Africa. Much that has been written on the racialisation of immigration during this period has been focused on immigration from these areas. In fact there have been other, less newsworthy, migrations from Eastern Europe, Hong Kong and the European Union, including Ireland. Research evidence has confirmed that discussions of immigration control began in cabinet discussions from the late 1940s onwards and began to seep into the public realm (both Parliament and the media) in the 1950s (Carter *et al.* 1993). The Notting Hill and Nottingham 'riots' 'helped to bring to national prominence issues which had previously been discussed either locally or within government departments' (Solomos 1989: 48). In contrast to the uprisings in the 1980s, which were widely discussed in terms of black criminality, the 1950s riots, which were racist attacks by young whites on black immigrants, were *not* equated with white criminality but rather turned into a discussion of the impact of immigration on housing, employment and sexual norms. The following extract illustrates the way in which the press helped to construct and reinforce this 'white viewpoint':

> There are three main charges of resentment against coloured inhabitants of the district. They are alleged to do no work and to collect a rich sum from the Assistance Board. They are said to find housing when white residents cannot. And they are charged with all kinds of misbehaviour, especially sexual.
>
> (*The Times*, 3 December 1958, cited in Solomos 1989: 49)

Over the next few years parliamentary debates on immigration and the creation of a campaign for immigration control culminated in the 1962 Commonwealth Immigrants Act. Although the term 'Commonwealth Immigrants' applied equally to Canada, New Zealand and Australia as well as to India and Commonwealth countries of the Caribbean and Africa, Government Minister at the time, William Deedes, admitted that the intention of the law was to restrict black immigrants (cited in Solomos 1989: 50). Attempts to disguise the law's main preoccupation, i.e. immigrants from the Caribbean and Indian sub-continent, were at best half-hearted and for good reason. Immigration laws had already proved a sound political investment in their capacity to construct and mobilise white interests.

According to Smith (1994), Enoch Powell's stance on the loss of empire and his subsequent contribution to immigration discourse typifies a psychoanalytic state of trauma, what Barnor Hesse has referred to as 'white amnesia' (1997: 92). In Powell's case he sought to 'forget' or repress Britain's imperial role by appealing to a sense of Englishness that transcended empire (ibid.: 132). This loss of historical memory and the pretence that Englishness was unaffected by its dependence on its colonies is a peculiar characteristic of British racism and one which Powell helped to foster (ibid.). Powell grew to public prominence in the mid to late 1960s, rather later than he might have done, according to Paul Foot (1969). When he did eventually speak out in the late 1960s he used the national media to appeal directly to, and on behalf of, his local white Wolverhampton constituents. This is evident in the following extract from the *Daily Telegraph* in which Powell claims,

> bombs from the sky, they (his constituents) could understand; but now, for reasons quite inexplicable, they might be driven from their homes and their property deprived of value by an invasion which the Government apparently approved . . . Those were the years when a 'For Sale' notice going up in a street struck terror into all its inhabitants. I know; for I live within the proverbial stone's throw of a street which 'went black'.
>
> (7 February 1967, cited in Foot 1969: 62)

Powell's belated interest in immigration might well have been influenced by the 1964 election campaign in Smethwick in the West Midlands which was fought on the immigration issue. There, voters had been encouraged by the Conservative candidate, Peter Griffiths, to vote Labour if they wanted a 'nigger for a neighbour'. The majority of electors took him at his word and Griffiths defeated Labour's then Foreign Secretary, Patrick Gordon-Walker, in an electoral swing against the national trend. Such were the shock waves within the Labour Government that they subsequently published a white paper in 1965 supporting tough immigration controls and subsequently passed their own immigration law in 1968 (Ben-Tovim and Gabriel 1979: 6). In the months preceding Powell's infamous Birmingham speech of 20 April 1968, immigration had been kept in the headlines thanks to speeches given by Powell and other politicians (Foot 1969: 107–9).

According to Foot unsubstantiated gossip about immigrant sexuality, violence, eating habits, noise and hygiene were circulating in the British National Party organ *Combat* and via the local branches of the Immigration Control Association which was particularly strong in the West Midlands. What Powell did in his Birmingham speech, and with the assistance of the media, was to bring those rumours out into the public sphere through an account of excrement allegedly pushed through the letter box of a Wolverhampton constituent who was never subsequently found and of whom Powell was unable to give further details (ibid.: 116). A gallup poll taken a week after the speech (which had been to an audience of

85 people) found that 96 per cent of those surveyed were aware of Powell's views (Seymour-Ure 1974). In the weeks following the speech Powell received 180,000 letters of which only 2000 disapproved of his views (ibid.: 105). Powell's speech received blanket coverage for the following ten days. London dockers led a one day 'We Back Powell' strike (Cashmore and Troyna 1983: 216). Sections of the press condemned it, whilst others objected to the manner of its presentation. Yet it was not so much what the press thought about his speech, but rather the 'sheer intensity and duration of the coverage' that counted (Braham 1982: 281).

Whilst Powell's career as a minister was over from that date (he was dismissed from the Shadow Cabinet by the then Conservative Party leader, Edward Heath, as a result of the speech) his influence in public debates on race was assured from that time on.[2] The years following his speech witnessed a tightening of immigration legislation. The 1968 Commonwealth Immigrants Act excluded Kenyans with British passports unless their father or grandfather held British citizenship. Reminiscent of the grandfather clause in the US, the patriality clause was extended to cover all new Commonwealth citizens in the 1971 Immigration Act and incorporated into the Nationality Act of 1981. British citizenship was thus formally racialised and the coincidence of national and racial identities 'made official'. The legal position could not affect those already settled in the UK. Whiteness was, by and large, a national, and now a racial, credential, although individual cases, like the Pereiras, whose threatened deportation was challenged by local white village residents, proved that whiteness was not just a matter of skin but of values and social relations.[3]

The immigration control argument won 'hearts and minds' because it could be simultaneously linked to cultural and economic arguments *and* play on unconscious sexual fears and fantasies. The economic argument on its own was built around very real trends, i.e. a decline in manufacturing, capital flight, unemployment (disproportionately concentrated in some sectors and regions) and a combination of rising expectations and deteriorating standards in areas of social expenditure (e.g. education, health, housing). However, an embedded white neurosis, historically primed to project its fears and anxieties on to a racialised object, begged the common-sense connection between economic trends and immigration control and the black presence in England.

As immigration became associated with ideas of 'trauma' and loss, so its control offered the possibility of temporal re-location to an imagined, purged and purified past. But immigration control *per se* was never enough to evoke such emotive imaginaries. What was needed was an immigrant group with a history of racialisation. Why else was the patriality or 'significant ties' clause built into immigration law whilst EU membership opened the door to potentially millions of white immigrants? The racialisation of immigration varied between different ethnic groups but always drew on histories of racist thought inscribed with notions of superiority, civilisation and culture. Of particular concern remained the prospect of interracial mixing which always succeeded in touching the nerve ends of colonial and post-colonial sensibilities. Ideas of racial contamination of pure English stock and the deflowering of English white femininity fuelled a peculiarly English response to black immigration and served to bolster notions of whiteness, however hidden or coded they remained. Moreover, the racialisation of popular explanations of alleged national 'decline', which embraced both economic and cultural or moral aspects, made it subsequently possible to shift attention from first to second and third generation immigrants, as the 1960s and 70s gave way to the 1980s and 90s. It was never just about immigration but always about race.

Twenty-five years after Enoch Powell's speech, in 1993, Winston Churchill, grandson of *the* Winston Churchill, made a speech on immigration in which he called for an end to the 'relentless flow' of immigrants in order to preserve the British way of life. He claimed that the population of some British cities was over 50 per cent immigrant and that allegations of social security fraud were 'but the tip of a gigantic iceberg. The long-suffering British taxpayer is being taken for the biggest ride of his lifetimes. The rot must be stopped and if it takes photo-identity cards to do it – so be it' (*The Times*, 29 May 1993). Like Powell's speech, it was widely reported, although not with the same intensity or duration. Most national newspapers criticised his speech for its factual inaccuracies, and reported both the Prime Minister's endorsement of the Home Secretary's rebuke of the speech and Labour's condemnation of Churchill's racist and putrid remarks (ibid.). Other newspapers, for example the *Daily Express* and the *Mail on Sunday*, were sympathetic. In the case of the *Daily Express,* Robert Kilroy-Silk asked, 'is Britain the only country in the world where we not only have to assimilate all other cultures at our expense but where we can't even discuss the damage to our own identity without being racist?' (*Daily Express*, 31 May 1993). The *Mail on Sunday* echoed a widespread response to Powell's speech by praising Churchill for his courage and willingness to mention the unmentionable (30 May 1993). The significance of Churchill's speech was fourfold. Firstly, it provoked an enthusiastic and exaggerated media reporting of remarks (many of which were widely regarded as inaccurate) which had, after all, only been made to a handful of the local party faithful. Secondly, although a number of journalists acknowledged the inaccuracies, such 'balanced' reporting is hardly proof of media neutrality. On the contrary, it begs the question as to why his speech was reported in the first place. Winston Churchill, in effect, was allowed to set the agenda and discussions were focused on whether journalists were for or against him. In other words, they were forced to respond on his terms. Thirdly, the *Daily Express* and the *Mail on Sunday* used the speech to peddle two more general arguments integral to the construction of whiteness. Namely, they put forward the notions that 'black cultures' were not part of British cultural identity and that anti-racism, in it efforts to defend ethnic and cultural pluralism, was illiberal and dogmatic (in contrast, presumably, to Kilroy-Silk's monocultural version of Britishness). Finally, whilst Churchill's speech failed to catch the public mood as Powell's had done a quarter of a century before, the idea that rigorous monitoring and surveillance of ethnic minorities was necessary to protect the taxpayer and the welfare state has been taken up in more recent legislation on asylum seekers and refugees.

The Immigration and Asylum Act, 1996

An analysis of the press coverage of the Immigration and Asylum Act underlines Foucault's insight that language constructs the people who use it, in this case, the white English. The debate surrounding the Act is testimony, once more, to the amenability and profitability of race to political campaigning and the strategic use of the idea of 'ethical choices' (Goldberg 1993). The latter have been built around in-group/out-group distinctions which in turn have shaped notions of entitlement and restriction, disrespect and abuse (ibid.). In immigration discourse, the media, and the tabloid press in particular, have compounded such choices through the criminalisation and tainting of the out-group with socially constructed notions of the unnatural. Within the media and political discourse, the deployment of what Goldberg has called 'conceptual errors' and 'category mistakes' have effectively absolved the in-group whilst simultaneously finding quick-fix, easy-to-grasp, gestural solutions to alleged problems. This has been combined with a rhetoric which has integrated the public and private domains, bringing seemingly remote and abstract news items into the realm of daily experience (Edelman 1988; Hall 1992). The representation of the political debate surrounding the bill in the mainstream press thus served to endorse a sense of whiteness in the private sphere.

In 1995, when the Conservative Government announced in the Queen's speech its intention to legislate further on immigration and asylum, the result of which was the Immigration and Asylum Act 1996, many Government opponents asked why it was necessary. After all, an Asylum and Immigration Appeals Act had already been passed in 1993 which curtailed the rights of asylum seekers. It reduced the time allowed to appeal, removed housing rights for asylum seekers, allowed finger printing of all asylum applicants (and for these to be kept on computer data bases for ten years) and removed all rights of appeal for some categories of people seeking entry (e.g. visitors, prospective students). Why, it might be asked, was more restrictive legislation felt necessary? Several factors have been suggested here which encompass local, national and global factors. The first and perhaps most persuasive on the basis of the above historical overview, not to mention news of California's successful Proposition 187 Campaign, was the possibly unrivalled success of immigration control as a potential vote winner and, hence, vote loser for your opponents. The view within Conservative circles was that the bill would win votes for the Party in the upcoming general election, partly by 'flushing out' Labour's soft policy on immigration. The gestural nature of the law itself, in terms of reducing both numbers of immigrants and expenditure, is irrelevant here. As Murray Edelman points out, 'the enactment of a law that promises to solve or ameliorate the problem even if there is little likelihood it will accomplish its purpose . . . is perennially effective in achieving quiescence from the discontented and legitimation for the regime' (1988: 24).

Secondly, deep divisions within the Conservative Party over European unity and the erosion of national sovereignty provided an important backdrop to the bill. During the 1990s European issues had provided important opportunities within political and media discourse to re-assert dominant versions of white Englishness, of which John Major's talk of warm beer, village greens and cricket, was one example. At first glance, then, the bill appeared to appease Euro-sceptics who feared 'leakages' and 'contaminations' from many directions, including Europe. The bill actually served to harmonise EU policies on refugees and asylum (for example with respect to lists of safe countries and rights to appeal), a consequence which evidently did not prevent the bill's rhetoric from serving other, contradictory, ends.

On a global scale, a growing number of authoritarian political regimes, which had been supported by multinational or transnational companies and/or arms, often supplied by western governments, created a class of displaced refugees who have fled persecution. In 1996 Nigeria was a case in point. Shell's investments in oil-rich Ogoniland had been the object of numerous environmental protests, including those which led to the murder of Ken Saro-Wiwa and other human rights activists. Despite the circumstances in which the dictator, Abacha, seized power from a democratically elected government, the British weapons company Vickers supplied rubber bullets and CS gas to the regime with an export licence from the British Government (The 1990 Trust 1996: 14). Meanwhile, Nigerians fleeing their country and seeking refugee status in Britain were informed that Nigeria was one of those countries deemed 'safe' by the government and that any asylum claims would be assumed to be bogus.

Interestingly, interests appeared divided by the bill as it progressed through parliament in the period 1995–6. On the one hand, neo-Conservatives, who supported the bill, saw it as a chance to code their defence of whiteness in seemingly more general narratives of crime and terrorism, metaphors of collapse and tropes of water. The tabloid press, notably the *Daily Mail, Daily Express* and *Sun* took this line. On the other hand, the broadsheet press, including papers and magazines which had hitherto been generally supportive of the Conservative Party, for example *The Times, The Economist* and, to a lesser extent, *Daily Telegraph,* all opposed the bill. Such a split suggests that business interests were not necessarily compatible, at least for some employers, with the idea of cutting off a potentially cheap, if illegal labour supply and that for all employers, the responsibility to police immigration would inevitably interfere with their primary preoccupation – profits. The split also reflected what was by the mid 1990s a growing lack of confidence in Conservative policies by some of the Party's allies in business and the mainstream press. In any event, the division also underlines the idea that white interests were not simply 'out there' waiting to be turned into laws, policies, etc. by the Government, but were the object of divided opinion.

A common tactic of the Conservative tabloid press was to conceal its whiteness through seemingly 'neutral' discourses. For example, in response to the allegation that the bill was racist, a *Sun* leader responded: 'The Government's crackdown on bogus asylum seekers is surely motivated only by a desire to make sure your money isn't wasted. Britain cannot have an open door for all' (21 November 1995). In an article in the same edition under the headline SMASH THE IMMIGRANT

SMUGGLERS the bill's proposals were couched in terms of stopping 'racke-teering' and 'gang masters who arrange bogus marriages'. The *Sun* thus had its proverbial cake *and* was able to eat it. The article seemingly distanced itself from racist motives in one breath only to code its racialised constituencies in seemingly universal terms like 'taxpayers' and 'law abiding citizens' on the one hand and 'fraudsters', 'smugglers', 'racketeers' and 'bogus marriage partners' on the other. Set in the context of a debate about immigration control, the article inevitably encouraged interpretations which drew on dominant constructions of white and black identities. In so doing it served to polarise such identities and forge 'white interests'. There was no need to historicise or even mention groups by name, since there already existed a common-sense knowledge in which groups had been racialised in both economic and moral terms. The 'race card' had been put away with one hand only to be played face down ('ex-nominated') with the other.

In a similar vein, the *Daily Telegraph* ran a fuller piece under the headline BOGUS MARRIAGE RACKETEERS FACE SEVEN YEARS IN JAIL (21 November 1995). The piece took its lead from Michael Howard's speech and Labour spokesperson Jack Straw who agreed that 'procedures for asylum seekers needed to be speeded up and for fraudulent asylum seekers to be weeded out' (ibid.). The *Daily Mail* ran an article under banner headline DOOR SLAMS ON ASYLUM CHEATS with references to 'bogus' applicants and 'abuse' of the asylum procedures, suggesting that all asylum seekers are rightly assumed to be guilty until proved innocent (with the proviso that the new bill would reduce and, in some cases, remove the right of appeal). The fact that both political major parties, Conservative and Labour, resorted to the coded discourse of law and order, merely reinforced the legitimacy of a white consensus across the political spectrum and left little room for a popular, mainstream alternative.

Another strategy used by the *Daily Mail* to conceal the bill's intentions was to refer readers to the so-called 'white list' of countries assumed to be safe and hence unlikely to give rise to genuine asylum cases. This list included not only India, Pakistan and Ghana but also Bulgaria, Poland and Romania. The inclusion of European countries on the list was another tactic designed to clear the government of any imputed racist motives. Revealingly, however, the above front page article was followed on page two by an inset article under the headline OUR ETHNIC POPULATION IS ABOUT TO EXPLODE which made explicit reference to those of 'Afro-Caribbean' and (south) 'Asian' background. This second article is of interest not just because of the way it tries to take the ethnicity out of whiteness; only some populations are 'ethnic'. Equally important is the way it uses the bill to trigger fears, not of asylum or illegal immigrants, but of the high birth rates of British African Caribbeans and south Asians, i.e. those with full citizenship rights.

'Water' has been a popular trope in immigration debates with recurrent refer-ences to 'tides', 'drowning', 'flushing' and 'swamping' familiar themes of immigration discourse, of which Margaret Thatcher's now much cited interview in 1978 is probably the most famous.[4] An early report that the Government was considering a further immigration bill appeared in the *Daily Telegraph* (13 March

1995) under the headline NEW PURGE ON MIGRANTS CONSIDERED. It sought to justify the proposals in terms of 'a rising *tide* of illegal immigration into Britain following a National Audit Office report which claimed that the true level was unknown' (emphasis added) and a plan 'where people not at risk from persecution would not be allowed political asylum'. The aim of the proposals, which would make employers responsible for carrying out ID checks using social security or national insurance numbers would be to '*flush out* thousands of illegal immigrants' (13 March 1995, emphasis added). 'Water'-related tropes have proved particularly apt in an island context. Their use has built powerful imaginary around common-sense understandings of immigration and has helped to 're-configure reality' in ways more commonly associated with more visual media (Hall Jamieson 1992). In such a 'reality', politicians have become lifeguards and immigration controls provide another way of describing land reclamation schemes.

In the following example, the *Daily Mail* (12 December 1996) juxtaposed its leader entitled BRINGING SOME SANITY TO THE ASYLUM LAWS alongside an article by Lord Hanson berating the EU for forcing the British to change their passports. The leader's defence of the Asylum Bill was couched in terms of anxieties around numbers (more images of drowning) with the claim that the Asian and African Caribbean population of London would increase by 40 per cent over the next twenty years. The article referred to the interest of all Britons not to allow any influx of illegal immigrants and sham asylum seekers. We see here how British interests are being defined in opposition to 'Asian and Afro-Caribbean populations of London', i.e. British citizens, who are then conflated with illegal immigrants and asylum seekers and lumped together under the catch-alls, 'outsider' and/or 'undesirable'. The theme of safeguarding white English identity was also taken up by Lord Hanson ('the chairman of Hanson PLC, Britain's biggest company') who complained,

> On the one hand we have a solid, reliable document [the old British passport] stiff in texture and significant in size. On the front it proudly advertises its owner and his or her full title. By its distinctive colour – its dignified shade of dark blue – it also proclaims its owner as British, a member of a nation with a long and equally dignified history. (On the other hand) the new passport looks more like a driving licence or building society cash book . . . anonymous in colour and appearance, flimsy in make-up . . . it is . . . in the style favoured by the bureaucrats.
>
> (*Daily Mail*, 12 December 1996)

Hanson's article, which was ostensibly about the Europeanisation of the British passport, was equally about the loss of British/English identity. Its juxtaposition alongside the above leader served to fuel and compound a sense of loss, both real and imminent, of white English identity. It served to resurrect and re-define the symbolic contours of whiteness.

As I have suggested, the economic rationale for and consequences of the bill were by no means voiced with unanimity, reflecting the potential diversity of white interests at stake. On the one hand, the bill's advocates argued that 'flushing out' illegal immigrants etc. would be a saving to the taxpayer as benefits would end. On the other hand, the bill was seen as a way of coercing the immigrant underclass to accept its lot. In the words of the *Sun*, 'ministers fear up to 100,000 go unnoticed. They do cleaning jobs, vegetable picking and packing or work in sweat-shop clothes factories . . . they are warned they will be booted out if they complain about pay or conditions' (21 November 1996). The article not only alluded to the general benefits of immigrant labour but in particular to the potential effects of the asylum law which would help to hold down the price of that labour. Interestingly, the article appeared alongside one which reported the threat of Asian tiger economies and the prospect of Europe being besieged by China and other Asian traders. The solution was to make Europe more competitive and stop wrangling over monetary and political union (*Sun*, 21 November 1996). Both articles shared a concern for Britain's economic wellbeing and the alleged threat posed by immigrant labour and/or tiger economies. The solution appeared to be an interesting defence of national sovereignty, a free market economy and an acquiescence in the use of illegal labour as long as the latter remained cheap and quiet.

Related to this last point was the extent of opposition to the bill within sections of the English establishment, voices the Conservative press could hardly ignore. For example, the *Daily Telegraph* reported Gillian Shepherd, the Education and Employment Secretary's concerns that employers would be discouraged from hiring ethnic minority staff (6 October 1995). This was taken up by a coalition of business leaders, opposition MPs, Unions and ethnic minority groups who were reported to be mustering to 'oppose Government plans to fine employers who hire illegals' in an article under the headline, ANGER GROWS OVER ILLEGAL WORKER CURBS (*Daily Telegraph* 25 October 1995).

Whilst the tabloids took leading government spokespeople as their principal source of opinion, the broadsheets took representatives from pressure groups and victims of current procedures to define the terms of their response. For example, Claud Moras's opinion, as Director of the Joint Council for the Welfare of Immigrants was quoted in the *Daily Telegraph*: 'Immigration is a touchstone for the Conservatives. When they are in trouble they bring out the immigration card. It is a very cynical move' (25 March 1995). In a leader which followed the first reading of the bill in Parliament, the *Guardian* posed the question, 'why do we need another Act (the 1993 Immigration and Asylum Act had already "overhauled and tightened" procedures)? We don't but the Tories remain 20 points plus behind in the polls and in such a desperate political position' (21 November 1995). The leader described the bill as 'a snooper's charter', and in so doing borrowed a jibe from the repertoire of Conservative tabloid press 'anti-big brother/anti-Labour' rhetoric and turned it back on the Government.

Whilst the broadsheet press opposed the bill, they were unable, with the exception of some human interest stories to wage the kind of campaign evident in the

Conservative tabloid coverage. Their objections were sensible, rational, and just, but in the main they were not 'news'. A good example of this is the coverage of demonstrations against the bill. According to Jude Woodward, of the National Assembly Against Racism and the Campaign against the Immigration and Asylum Bill,

> We were doing a lot of press work in the run up to the first demonstration – the bill was in committee at the time – we were trying to drum up support for the demonstration and we approached the *Guardian* and we asked the reporter whether the paper was going to cover the demonstration to which he replied 'is it going to be peaceful?' and when we said 'yes' he told us that 'well, that's not really news then'. We said 'so if a part of the demonstration breaks away and starts a fight you would cover it?' 'yes' he said.
>
> (interview, 18 October 1996)

In fact it was particularly important that the demonstrations remained peaceful given the precarious immigration status of many refugees and asylum seekers. In February, a march against the bill attracted 25,000–30,000 people (Campaign against the Immigration and Asylum Bill). Apart from local radio coverage, a photograph in the *Observer* and the odd short television news item, the media were noticeably silent. When another anti-racist demonstration attracted about a hundred supporters and the police insisted that it was small enough to march on the pavements, not the streets, the *Guardian* ran a story suggesting that demonstrations were a thing of the past (25 March 1996). Moreover, when the Campaign Against the Immigration and Asylum Bill wrote a letter to the Editor pointing out that there had been a highly successful demonstration the previous month, the paper declined to publish it (Jude Woodward, interview 18 October 1996).

Aside from their reasoned yet sporadically expressed objections, liberal broadsheets were left with 'human interest' stories to mobilise a more affective or emotion-led opposition to the bill. Hence there were a number of articles which concentrated on case histories of those facing deportation. Articles included cases such as that involving a Zairian woman who had been gang-raped by soldiers who shot dead her brothers-in-law, beat her family and kidnapped her husband. After arriving in this country the Home Secretary decided that she was at no more risk than other Zairians and set a date for her deportation at which point she went into hiding in a women's refuge (*Independent*, 9 December 1996). Then of course there was the case of Bernat Hecht who fled Romania in the 1930s in the face of anti-Semitism and fascism and settled in Britain as a refugee. His son, born Michael Hecht, became better known as Michael Howard, Home Secretary and chief architect of the government's proposals.

The Immigration and Asylum Bill became an important site for anti-racist campaign activity. In the case of the West Midlands, it was organised by black community activists, including those who had or were at the time facing deportation themselves. Such groups organised their own community-based meetings, pickets, demonstrations and publicity. The National Campaign Against Immigration and Asylum, a body which was officially launched in June 1995 at the House of Commons, attempted to co-ordinate national opposition. According to Jude Woodward, the meeting at the House of Commons included:

> churches, Liberty, the Campaign for Racial Justice, the Refugee Forum and other refugee support groups . . . we took it from there . . . We were able to put publicity out through other people's mailings and by February and March [1996] we had over 1000 affiliations, including Trade Unions, nationally, regionally and locally, refugee support organisations, churches, anti-racist groups, resident black community organisations, civil liberties groups.
>
> (interview, 18 October 1996)

The Campaign thus mobilised opposition through mailing to affiliated organisations who then disseminated it to members. This took the message to would-be supporters but wider media coverage was necessary to build a popular opposition beyond the campaign's activist base. Many established figures, including the Archbishop of Canterbury and Cardinal Hume (head of the Catholic Church) publicly opposed the bill and celebrities like former Iran hostage John McCarthy attended and spoke at lobbies and held press calls. However, press coverage was limited and local groups were critical of the Campaign's use of well-known, invariably white, establishment figures to front the opposition, instead of asking lesser known activists, including those facing deportation to represent the Campaign.

Local radio did prove the exception to widespread media indifference to the Campaign. According to Jude Woodward,

> local radio, black and ethnic minority radio have been fantastic – *Sunrise*, *Choice FM*, *Spectra*, *Kiss* and all main radio stations covered the legislation and the activities against it . . . radio used campaign spokespeople – I did some – to put the opposition point of view, although they often balanced it with a spokesperson supporting the bill . . . there were phone-ins too with people from the Campaign on the panel . . . people were not totally hostile . . . but at the same time there was not huge public interest.
>
> (interview, 18 October 1996)

The campaign thus relied heavily on national demonstrations and parliamentary pickets which were held to coincide with parliamentary debates on the bill. Meanwhile local anti-deportation campaigns continued to take up individual cases of those threatened with deportation and organise local protests against changes to asylum rules. The West Midlands Anti-Deportation Campaign, for example, organised a soup kitchen outside the Department of Social Security to highlight the implications of the proposed elimination of benefits. Despite their human interest potential, such demonstrations received minimal coverage in the national and local press and television. As far as new technologies were concerned, local organisations were just beginning to utilise their potential but, as regards this Campaign, the use of the Internet was still in its infancy. According to Jude Woodward,

> we've only just started getting into 'the net' since the campaign . . . we're working with black organisations which are setting up a black internet link and our home page (which we're just beginning to work on) will be linked into that . . . in other words we didn't use that technology but other groups which did have net sites – the TUC has its own web page – put stuff through publicising campaign activities as did various networks throughout Europe.

(interview, 18 October 1996)

In the end, grass roots opposition to the bill, a nationally co-ordinated campaign, dissent expressed by both church leaders and welfare representatives, who pointed out the implications of loss of benefits, and the CBI, which concentrated on the implications of yet more regulations and responsibilities for employers, proved no match for the tabloid press. You cannot beat a good story about cheats, terrorists, 'free lunches' and swamping. Human interest stories apart, there was little to sustain a concerted mainstream, media-led campaign against the bill and resource constraints made it impossible for the organised opposition to mount one. The Government managed to fend off unanimous establishment opposition against the bill, even from its own business lobby. Despite a very small majority in the House of Commons, it was able to ride this criticism thanks in large part to the ability of its allies in the tabloid press to exhort their readers to side with the law-abiding, taxpaying British against the bogus, terrorist, culture-threatening hordes of asylum seekers. To oppose the bill was to betray those British virtues and a much coveted sense of British identity.

Although the level and intensity of press coverage of the bill was under-whelming when put alongside immigration coverage in the late 1960s through to mid 1970s and opposition to punitive immigration curbs was more unanimous and wide-ranging than it had been before, the bill, nevertheless, became law in the summer of 1996. The relative absence of media debate and reaction may reflect a shift away from the battle-fatigued issue of immigration control to 'sexier' themes and genres, some of which were made to work in analogous ways. Such stories competed successfully with the bill to grab the headlines and cover the front pages during the passage of the bill through parliament. For example, Princess Diana's revelations about an affair with James Hewitt[5] took priority over the introduction of the bill in Parliament in November and the gruesome revelations of the mass murders in Cromwell Street[6] captivated readers around the time of the first reading of the bill in December. As I have suggested, the media's relative lack of interest in the bill also worked against the opposition groups since it meant that the detailed implications of the bill, including its breach of UN and European

112

Charters, Declarations and Conventions, the views of campaign organisations and the experiences of asylum seekers themselves, were all largely kept from the public realm.

Recoding and recording racialised discourse: the case of California's Proposition 187

The relationship between the ideological rationale to curb immigration along racial lines and the formation of whiteness can be explored in general terms with reference to Brimelow's *Alien Nation* (1995)[7] and Auster's *The Path to National Suicide* (1990). Brimelow himself has acknowledged his debt to Enoch Powell both for mentioning the unmentionable (although, as I have argued, taboos often speak louder than words) and for suggesting that 'numbers are of the essence' (1995: 264).[8] According to Brimelow, the critical population figures in the US are those which foresee the *imminence of a white minority* around the years 2060 or 2069, depending on which demographic data is more accurate (ibid.: 64).

A recurring point of discussion throughout this book has been the extent to which discourses outwardly display and defend whiteness or alternatively 'code' it by promoting a particular understanding of the world built around ideas of natural hierarchies and a social order in which white Christian male values dominate. Used together, the coded and the un-coded, buttress each other. Both Brimelow and Auster trace a white genealogy, purged of its hybridity and diversity. According to Auster,

> it would be a mistake to infer . . . that the American's image of himself . . . . is a composite or synthesis of the ethnic elements that have gone into the making of the American. It is nothing of the kind: the American's image of himself is still the Anglo-American ideal it was at the beginning of our independent existence . . . . It is the Mayflower, John Smith, Davy Crockett, George Washington, and Abraham Lincoln that define the American's self image.
>
> (Herberg cited in Auster 1990: 39)

Moreover, the defence and pursuit of values associated with these white icons has been used to excuse the oppression of minorities. For example, Brimelow attributed (to the point of justifying) the persecution of Catholics in the nineteenth century perpetrated by the Order of the Star Spangled Banner to the Church's hierarchical structure (1995: 13). According to Brimelow, whites were making the current situation even more indefensible, by not defending traditional Anglo-American values. They were thus colluding in their own demise, for example, by supporting policies on affirmative action and multiculturalism.

Brimelow used his son to illustrate the new class of white male victims: 'my son Alexander is a white male with blue eyes and blond hair. He has never discriminated against anyone in his little life. But public policy now discriminates against him' (ibid.: 9). Thus 'white' values, as well as 'white', blond, Aryan features, were also threatened by the new commitment to cultural diversity. Furthermore, capitalist values, rooted in the psyches of early white settlers, were under threat, Brimelow maintained, since capitalism depended on both 'a defined system of private property rights' (ibid.: 174) and 'ethnic and cultural coherence' (ibid.: 175).

Auster associated what he alleged to be the degeneracy of the Anglo-American stock with two indices of social decay: crime and disease, both of which he attributed to immigrants. Unsurprisingly for Auster, accusations of racism constituted an attack on freedom of thought ('thought control'), as well as an assault on the humanity of white people (1990: 69). He argued that there were several new mafias, each with its own specialities: Colombians (cocaine), Mexicans (marijuana, auto theft, alien smuggling), south Koreans (prostitution) and Russian émigrés who he claims are replacing 'costa nostra' as the largest criminal syndicate in the world (1990: 185). Moreover, he argued, immigration brought cholera, leprosy, measles and other diseases not associated with the contemporary US (ibid.: 187). The idea of 'disease' in racial thought has worked at both a literal and metaphorical level. The narrative of the physical decay of whiteness has been extrapolated from the individual to the nation as a whole and back again to the individual.

Finally, in common with many advocates of immigration control and the reclamation of Anglo-American identity, Auster has defended the promotion and monopolistic use of the English language. Interestingly, if predictably, he has done so, not in order to promote global communication and the consumption of fast food and designer clothes. On the contrary, English language is the key to the maintenance of old national values not to facilitate new global ones. Hence,

> we should not defend English on utilitarian grounds, rather on the ground of the survival of a distinctive American civilization . . . the answers to our current problems lie within the still-living but neglected roots of our own civilization – not in giving up that civilization for the sake of some utopian global order.
>
> (1990: 52)

The following discussion of California's 1994 Proposition 187 which was well served, in ideological terms, by the kind of rationale offered by Brimelow and Auster, has two broad aims. 187's success depended on the ability of its advocates (mobilised around the 'Save Our State' campaign) to draw on a wider commonsense discourse around which I have identified the following themes: 'defending national identity', 'taxpayers versus special interests', 'not enough whites' and 'the cost of illegals'. The second, related, aim will be to examine media coverage of the campaign. Talk radio shows, Rush Limbaugh's television and radio polemics and political advertising were the most prominent outlets for propagandist versions of 187's arguments. My aim is to show how these media forms employed a range of populist techniques to elicit a highly charged, emotional attachment to 187.

Whilst the more detached and dispassionate liberal media often came out in opposition to 187, their outward protestations coincided with coverage which legitimated the assumptions underpinning 187 by taking them (e.g. overpopulation and economic decline) as starting points for debate. Moreover, since the 'liberal media establishment' was, itself, already perceived to be part of the problem by the campaign's supporters, its opposition to 187 merely served to confirm this. Claims to hold a monopoly on 'truth' have become a common feature of political campaigns. However, in the US, levels of disaffection with mainstream parties have been such that 'truth claims' are often seen as more believable when made *outside* the context of political parties and special interests, both of which have been tarnished with a succession of major scandals. Against this background, proposition politics have proved an attractive and credible populist alternative in the US in the mid 1990s.

Despite the specifically US flavour to the discursive themes explored here, 187 can be placed in a context which transcends national boundaries. In particular, the re-assertion of certain versions of American national identity can be situated against a background of the diminution of US national power. This, as I have already suggested, has been attributed to the expansion of global electronic communications, the emergence of transnational companies and blocs, such as the European Union and the Pacific Rim, and a new world order where fragmentation and conflicts have become increasingly difficult to control and broker, as events in Africa and the Balkans in the 1990s have testified. These processes have also entailed the migration of capital and people which have, in turn, helped to create third world conditions in the west and first world conditions in parts of the third world. Overall, these global factors, which have played a significant part in shaping the incipient crisis of whiteness, fuelled more of the argument for Proposition 187.

National identity threatened

I will take three symbols of national identity by way of illustration here: the Statue of Liberty, the US Constitution and 'outsiders'. The Statue of Liberty, iconographically both feminine and national and bearing the inscription 'give us your huddled masses', featured prominently in pro-187 propaganda. In one cartoon, sent out with the publicity put out by Save Our State[9] (which was the organisation behind the 187 campaign) the words 'children of illegal immigrants' were written across Liberty's pregnant body, to which she replied, 'give me a break'. The symbolic mother of the nation, whose compassion had been expressed over the years in her open invitation to the world's poor and persecuted, was protesting, 'enough is enough'. Liberty also featured in campaign advertising. In one television commercial, for example,[10] carefully shot at night and taken from the base of the statue looking up, Liberty looked serenely majestic with beams of light trained on her upper body and head. Her saintly, celestial aura was heightened by a soft, choral soundtrack. The overall effect was to create a mood of reflective reverence, as the narrator began:

115

> It's how most of us got here
> It's how our country was built
> It's a treasure beyond measure

at which point the choir was interrupted by a loud, dissonant drum beat. The narrator continues:

> But now it's been broken
> there's a right way (shot of group swearing allegiance)
> and a wrong way (illegals running across the Mexican border)
> . . . To reward the wrong way is not the American way
>
> (KABC, 25 October 1994)

Of course, New York harbour, Ellis Island and the Statue of Liberty were not the routes by which African-American and Latino/a immigrants came to the US. The 'most of us' thus refers to US citizens of white European ancestry who were significantly linked to the 'American way' of entering the country.

Meanwhile, the US Constitution[11] was invoked, both in letter and spirit, as a rationale for opposing immigration and relatedly multiculturalism. John O'Sullivan wrote a piece in the *National Review*, in which he referred to one of 'the founding fathers',[12] Thomas Jefferson, in order to launch a direct assault on immigration and multiculturalism:

> It is a reasonable hypothesis, to borrow from Jefferson, that twenty million Asians and Latin Americans 'thrown all of a sudden into' America would make this Republic 'more turbulent, less happy, less strong'. In the past, these consequences were averted by two policies: restricting immigration to enable the immigrants already here to be absorbed into the national culture, and deliberately accomplishing this by a process frankly called 'Americanisation'. Today, however, we are pursuing exactly opposite policies – namely keeping the level of immigration high, and keeping the immigrants insulated from the rest of us through bilingual and multiculturalist programs.
>
> (*National Review*, 21 February 1994: 38)

Like the narrator in the Liberty advert, O'Sullivan adopted a mode of address in the above which was implicitly racialised. The 'us' referred to in the penultimate and last lines can be deduced by a process of elimination. Since O'Sullivan could not have been referring to those who were either recipients of bilingual or multicultural education or to recently arrived immigrants, it follows that his intended readers were descendants of old, white, European stock. African-Americans may not have recently arrived but they were closely associated with multiculturalism. Furthermore, 'Americanness'[13] is constructed as a unitary rather than a multicultural identity. O'Sullivan achieves this through his allusion to a single national culture and the process of Americanisation, which is taken to be a synonym for assimilation. The reference to Jefferson lends authority to the argument as a whole and suggests that what follows is rooted in the aspirations of founding fathers and embodied in the spirit of the constitution.

An analysis of talk radio calls provides further evidence of common-sense links between support for 187, attacks on multiculturalism[14] and the defence of the Constitution. For example, 'Jeff' from Van Nyess, who called white talk show host, Ray Briem, in the aftermath of the success of the ballot initiative had this to say:

> I have a son in LA Unified School District. This afternoon he was sent home with a paper from the members of the Board and it mentioned how they . . . pretty much are not going to abide by laws that the state of California just passed (i.e. 187). (Ray Briem interjected at this point with a dismissive, condemnatory grunt.) At the end of the letter there's a small print statement – the mission statement – and it says 'we are an urban public school system that will effectively educate all students so that each will contribute to and benefit from our diverse society' and I'd like to say that I think they stopped doing effective education a long time ago and it kinda went hand in hand with their diversity. When diversity as I see it arrived it seemed effective education went out of the window.
>
> (KABC, 11 October 1994)

In the wake of 187's success it was not only immigrants who were criminalised but also those 'special interest' groups for failing to implement the initiative. Prop 187 was used to forge common-sense links between an imminent apocalypse on the one hand, and immigration, professional unlawfulness or incompetence and cultural diversity, on the other. The above extract also illustrates a point made earlier. Sometimes subtle but more often crude strategies are used in which talk show hosts exploit conversational strategies to make explicit their views, thus directing and encouraging their callers to organise their views as well as channel their aggression around particular themes. In the above case, Briem, simply by the manner of his interruption, made clear his particular interest in the legality of the school district's actions.

SOS campaigners were also able to capitalise on 'local' anxieties induced by California's border with Mexico. Ron Prince, one of Save Our State's founders, illustrated these fears in ways which combined an outward sense of detachment with an inward sense of paranoia. He said,

> We've always accepted other cultures and been altered by that. There is a unique situation with regard to Mexico. I think you'll find that most second and third generation Mexicans do not want California to be part of Mexico. But there are new immigrants from Mexico who propose

117

exactly that and think that if they become a majority in the state that this will become a Mexican state; that the US will coolly allow them to be re-united with Mexico. I don't think this is realistic. The worst that could happen is that if they became strong enough we will have a civil war on this issue – if we do I expect the US will win.

(interview, 5 January 1995)

One dilemma faced by 187 supporters was to isolate 'acceptable' from 'unacceptable' immigration, made necessary, of course, because the Constitution, which they so zealously defended, was itself the product of an immigrant population.[15] Accordingly, Mexicans became what Goldberg would term a 'category mistake' in the racist discourse of 187. Immigration and the problems it allegedly caused thus became associated with Mexico and Mexicans and the idea of the territorial and numerical threat became an important weapon in the campaign. For example, SOS sent out a copy of an article which appeared in the Mexican newspaper, *Excelsior* in 1982 in which it was reported that 'The American Southwest seems to be slowly returning to the jurisdiction of Mexico without the firing of a single shot, nor requiring the least diplomatic action, by means of a steady, spontaneous and uninterrupted occupation'. Likewise, the widely reported waving of Mexican flags at an anti-187 demonstration was exploited by those who sought to inflate this sense of threat. Callers to Ray Briem's talk radio programme, including 'Dave' from Eagle Rock described the demonstration as anti-American and likened the demonstrators to traitors.

Criminalising the Mexican community in the US added weight to these claims. The period up to the 1994 vote on 187 was marked by a number of reported incidents involving Mexican and Latino communities in the US. In April 1994 the president of the League of United Latin American Citizens, Jose Velez, was charged with creating and supplying false documents to illegal immigrants (*Los Angeles Times*, 9 April 1994). In May 1994 the *San Diego Union-Tribune* ran an article reporting the 'kidnapping' of cars from San Diego which were driven across the border into Mexico and ended up being used by Mexican authorities including the police (8 May 1994). In April, the *San Diego Chronicle* reported that smuggling cigarettes out of and then back into the US to be sold cheaper (without tax) by small markets, mom and mop places and 'street vendors', was 'robbing the state of millions of dollars in revenue each year'. Finally, the *Orange County World* (15 May 1994) reported the case of a Mexican (whom the Mexican authorities refused to extradite) who had been convicted of raping a four-year-old girl in the US. The case was used to delay the signing of an extradition treaty between the US and Mexico.

The Mexican threat was posed as external as well as internal. The reporting of the Mexican authorities' opposition to 187 and the vandalising of a McDonald's restaurant in Mexico City, again in opposition to 187, reinforced the idea of an enemy without as well as within. The latter incident, in which a masked group 'trashed' a McDonald's, was reported in the *Wall Street Journal*. By way of reminding its readers where their loyalties should lie, McDonald's was described as an 'American symbol':

> The choice of McDonald's as a target was clearly meant to send a message. Not only are McDonald's Corp's restaurants so clearly identified with American pop culture, but the one attacked is in the middle of this city's trendy Zona Rosa, a favourite of American tourists.
>
> (9 November 1994)

Taxpayers and the truth versus special interests

In the run-up to the November election, various interest groups came out against 187, in common with their professional/elite counterparts in the UK over the Asylum Act. The LA police (unlike their British counterparts) also declared their opposition when the Vice-President of the LA Police Commission was quoted as saying, 'it's going to make it almost unbearable for the police to do their job in the city' and described 187 as 'racist and divisive' (*Los Angeles Times*, 19 October 1994). Consequently, in attacking these interests, including 'big government' and defending the supporters of 187 against accusations of racism, Rush Limbaugh said in November 1994 on his TV show,

> And I want to tell you one more time what Proposition 187 is about. It's about responsibility; it's about accountability; its about law and order. The word is 'illegal.' Words mean things and the people of California are not only sick and tired of having [the] federal government tell them they've got to provide social services for a whole bunch of citizens of the United States as well, not just illegals.
>
> But 'illegal' is the operative word, and the people of California are simply reflecting the national mood. It is time to end the welfare state. We can't afford it any more, and it hasn't worked. And we are not going to be called racists and bigots because this has nothing to do with race; it has nothing to do with bigotry. It has to do with law and order, responsibility and accountability.
>
> (Multimedia entertainment, 1994)

In a matter of a few hundred words Limbaugh pulled together the threads of neo-conservatism and the new right in the US. Taxes were linked to the problem of a dependency culture and the welfare state, which in turn were associated with unlawfulness and the need for people to be held responsible and accountable for their actions. What was at stake here was a populist, authoritarian, unitary, anti-immigrant version of whiteness, over that which espoused multiculturalism, social expenditure and welfarism.

The particular sections of the 'establishment' targeted by SOS varied. Like Limbaugh, at times it appealed directly to 'locals'/ Californians, invariably in order to challenge Washington and the Federal Government. In one television advertisement the sound of a relentless drum beat and scenes of illegals crossing the Mexican/Californian border at Interstate 5 was complemented and reinforced by the voice over: 'they keep on coming. Two million illegals in California. The Federal Government won't stop them at the border' (KNBC, CH4, 7.29pm, 13 May 1994).[16]

The anti-establishment thrust of the campaign was underlined in an article in *Heterodoxy*, the monthly magazine devoted to attacking multiculturalism, affirmative action and liberal foreign policy (it referred to the US policy in Haiti as affirmative action!).[17] One of the grass roots organisers of 187 was quoted as saying 'It's the taxpayers and the truth, versus the special interests' (*Heterodoxy* 2 (11) October 1994: 13).

By way of illustrating this widespread cynicism towards big government and special interests, *Heterodoxy* ran a cartoon in September 1994 in which President Clinton was being warned about illegal immigration: 'Voters feel good ol' uncle Sam is being suckered by a rising tide of illegals clamouring for quotas, bilingualism and revised history books' to which Clinton replied, 'you mean slam the door on those cute little Latinos that look like Cesar Chavez?' When the Clintons were told a tough line will mean a jump in his popularity, Hillary ordered Colin Powell to use tanks and mines on the border 'and whatever else will make prime time'. The cartoon thus forged common-sense links between immigration, multiculturalism, bilingualism and quotas, couched in an unashamed exploitation of 'comic' racial and sexual stereotypes.

The other aspect of the anti-establishment debate referred to above relates to the new right (referred to as 'Newt' right, after Newt Gingrich) backlash against social expenditure. In 1985 the *New York Times* ran a leader which suggested that Charles Murray's book *Losing Ground* provided Reagan with the perfect rationale for cutting social programmes. Murray, along with George Gilder and James Wilson all expressed the same view: anti-poverty programmes actually created poverty, crime, drug abuse, unemployment. The arguments put forward varied but essentially their assumption was that social programmes took away the incentive to take responsibility for one's own actions and created the basis of a dependent subculture. The attack on illegal immigrants thus became linked to a wider attack on government spending and regulation. The loss of Democratic majorities in both Houses of Congress in the November 1994 elections was tantamount to a popular endorsement of this view.

As a not insignificant footnote to the above, and just a week before the elections, Richard Herrnstein and Charles Murray published extracts of their book *The Bell Curve* (1994). The overall effect of this intervention, whatever their or their publisher's/editor's intentions, was to re-kindle the race/ IQ debate and to question public expenditure on education programmes aimed at redressing inequalities of attainment. Despite their own protestations that 'the fascination with race, IQ and genes is misbegotten' (*New Republic*, 31 October 1994: 27), their work undoubtedly, and not surprisingly, helped revive this very controversy. Moreover, the timing of the publication coincided with the wider political backlash discussed in Chapter

3; a backlash, like it or not, which the authors undoubtedly helped to fuel. 'We have been asked whether the question of racial genetic differences in intelligence should even be raised in polite society. We believe there's no alternative . . . It is essential that people begin to talk about this in the open' (ibid.: 27).

The precise detailed conclusions drawn by the authors are less important than the overriding impression left by the controversy: that African-Americans and Latino/as were less intelligent than whites; that genes played a large part in determining intelligence, and that even if environments, alone, determined intelligence, it would still be very difficult to improve IQ performance (an argument allegedly endorsed by the failure of numerous educational initiatives). These ideas, alongside immigration figures etc. served to enhance a sense of national decline and the deterioration of the white 'racial' gene pool. This is evident in the following extract taken from the *National Review*:

> America had once been a wonderful place . . . surviving . . . wave after wave of immigration – until sometime in the recent past . . . (now) America was losing the qualities that made it great . . . these values (a society needs to be at peace with itself) we no longer have . . . when the barbarians come, as they always do upon the collapse of a civilization, they will find that we have already sacked ourselves.
>
> (11 July 1995: 31)

At stake here was white, Mayflower culture. The analogy with the old Greek and Roman empires is implicit in the references to 'barbarians', 'sacked' and 'civilisation'. Moreover, the source of the problem is perceived as internal and, specifically, to do with immigration and the consequent loss of core values. The reference to 'recent' was important. It enabled the author to code his argument and, in case it might be suggested that African-Americans had been around for longer, the reference to 'qualities that made it great' excludes all but early white settlers.

There are just not enough whites

Chesterton's epigram 'America is a melting pot but the melting pot itself must not melt' was invoked at the Philadelphia Society's conference to justify immigration control as well to sanction attacks on multiculturalism: 'Only by restricting immigration sharply could we permit three decades of immigrants to assimilate – to become Americans' (*National Review*, 11 July 1995: 31). The report of the conference proceedings went on to trace an important lineage in thinking about national identity:

> Chesterton grew almost poetic in describing parts of America, notably in his portrait of an idyllic small-town and rural Middle-West, where he saw the same virtues that Timothy Dwight had seen earlier in New England.

121

And it was from that small-town . . . that Ronald Reagan derived his compelling vision of America.

(ibid.)[18]

Implicit in the above is a call to defend traditional American values against cultural diversity. More to the point, those traditional values are inextricably bound up with the founding fathers, and with some rural, white idyll.

The racial undercurrents evident in some population debates within the environmental movement have been explored elsewhere (see for example Young 1994). In the US, pressure groups like the Federation for American Immigration Reform[19] have tied their demands for a moratorium on immigration (except spouses, children and a limited number of refugees) to environmental arguments. So, for example, the case for immigration control in Los Angeles was expressed in the following terms: 'traffic congestion, noise, pollution, a deteriorating standard of living, growing violence and generally crowded conditions have replaced the irrigated orange groves that prevailed just one lifetime ago' (Fox and Mehlman 1992: 42). Alongside this romanticised rural nostalgia was the more practical threat to region in terms of resources and, in particular, water. Referred to as the 'life blood of the southwestern United States' (ibid.), the Federation argued that the future of the state depends on the preservation of habitat, only sustainable through population control. In a fuller account of the environmental costs of immigration, Leon Bouvier also referred to air pollution causing, amongst other things, a '10 percent to 15 percent erosion in the lung function of children born and raised in crowded southern California' (Federation for American Immigration Reform 1992: 82), waste disposal with the consequent 'spills of raw sewage into the ocean of southern California' (ibid.: 84) and climatic changes, including the greenhouse effect, one remedy for which is the reduction of population (ibid.: 86–7). The 'environment' thus provided an array of metaphors ('pollution', 'overheating', 'toxicity' and 'contamination') to use in connection with 'recent' immigrant populations.

More explicitly racialised themes were evident in population discourse in the context of discussions of fertility, crime and disease. The Federation predictably called for a lowering of fertility, but with particular reference to black and Latino/a Californians (Bouvier 1991: 100) as well as a call for television soap operas to promote the desirability of small families. Lower birth rates amongst Latino/as, in addition to immigration control, would allow immigrants to adapt to, and progress in, society's mainstream (ibid.: 102). Bouvier thus confirmed that whiteness was indeed an attainable state for a select few, to be exacted at the price of a drop in fertility and conformity to dominant norms.

Criminalisation was a recurrent theme in pro-187 arguments and continued to be in the post-1994 election period. In another full page advertisement taken out in the *National Review* which, at first glance, looked like another article on immigration, the Federation suggested that, whilst there had been nothing wrong with immigration in the past, 'all that changed in the face of the Haitian boats, the World Trade Center bombing, Chinese boats, international immigrant smuggling and crime syndicates, persistent illegal immigration from Mexico, and high profile tales of immigrant-related welfare rip-offs' (11 July 1994).

In the aftermath of 187's success, another pressure group, the American Immigration Control sent out a questionnaire containing possibly some of the most leading questions in the history of survey research. In one question, for example, respondents were asked:

Which of the following problems associated with illegal aliens are most personally disturbing to you? (tick all that apply)

i)   terrorism;
ii) taxpayer cost;
iii) welfare fraud/social security fraud;
iv) bring in diseases like AIDS;
v)   aliens voting in US elections;
vi) rising health care costs and overcrowded hospitals;
vii) bilingual public education;
viii) loss of jobs for American citizens;
ix) drug trafficking, crime, riots.

(American Immigration Control questionnaire, 1995)

The question was thus phrased so as to leave no room for doubt. The wording assumed the undisputed fact that illegal aliens were linked to all of the above. Far from being allowed to question its implicit racism, respondents were invited to state which they found most disturbing. Moreover, the poll's 'authority' was enhanced by its official appearance, including the recipient's poll registration number, their voting district and an attached list of advisors which included retired Brigadiers, Major Generals, former Governors and PhD's.

The state of our economy . . . and the costs of illegals

There was a broad consensus throughout the 1980s and 1990s, both popular and academic, concerning the state of the Californian economy. In terms of conventional economic indicators, e.g. gross national product, California was said to rank in the top fifteen *countries* in the world. It was also widely accepted that during the 1960s and 1970s whilst some sectors of manufacturing were effectively collapsing (automobiles, steel) with numerous plant closures and lay-offs, other sectors were booming (high technology, defence and aerospace and garment). The impact of these changes was a reduction in a skilled blue-collar unionised workforce with the result that the remaining workforce was split between a highly skilled white-collar workforce at one end and a low skill service class at the other. The two labour forces were polarised both in class terms and along ethnic lines, too, with whites 'and Latinos disproportionately represented at the top and bottom ends of the labour market respectively. More recently federal cutbacks in defence have led to the elimination of tens of thousands of jobs' (Valle and Torres 1994: 3).

Since the 1980s, however, attention has been drawn by commentators to four other developments. First has been the influx of foreign capital into the Los Angeles region especially from Canada and Japan which were responsible for 90 per cent of the high-rise building construction in the 1980s (Soja 1989: 305). Secondly, there has been an expansion of the banking and finance sectors of the economy with the increasing internationalisation of capital. Thirdly, and the focus of the previous section, the region has been the destination of growing numbers of immigrants, primarily from Korea, south-east Asia, Pacific islands, El Salvador and Mexico.

The fourth factor, the emergence of a Californian Latino working class, is worth elaborating. The large Latino/a settlement in east Los Angeles coincided with the displacement of white working-class labour associated with the automobile and steel industries in the late 1970s. A central concern in this process of restructuring was corporate competitiveness and, relatedly, the disciplining of labour. The growth of the garment industry discussed in Chapter 1 is relevant here. As Soja points out, alongside the high technocracy which has settled in Los Angeles,

> so too [LA] has what is probably the largest pool of low-wage, weakly organized, easily disciplined immigrant labour in the country . . . its imprint has been most visible, however, in the production of garments . . . which tends to be highly labour-intensive, difficult to mechanize, and organized around small shops to adapt more efficiently to rapidly changing fashion trends.
>
> (Soja 1989: 207)

The growth in both unionisation and political representation amongst Latinos has been one consequence of the displacement of white working-class labour. According to Valle and Torres (1994) 'the nation's largest manufacturing center is about to become completely Latinized, a dramatic transformation that has only recently received glib commentary'. One important political implication of these developments has been acknowledged by Valle and Torres: 'Two weeks before the April–May 1992 riots, Los Angeles County supervisor Gloria Molina . . . said she understood (that) local African American political leadership had become a prime obstacle to continued Latino political and economic empowerment' (ibid.: 22).

The riots subsequently provided a space for such differences to be exploited by the media. As a result, and partly due to the efforts of Latino leadership to secure rights through affirmative action programmes, divisions emerged between the Latino working class and African-Americans who were seeking to maintain their economic and political position *vis-à-vis* the white establishment. The white middle classes, who were already reeling from massive job losses in defence and related industries, aimed to backtrack on, not expand, affirmative action policies, and this position was supported by a business sector which was threatened by the growing unionisation and militancy of California's working-class Latino/a community. The linking of immigration, affirmative action and white unemployment helped to build a powerful alliance against that group who appeared to have most to gain from recent changes, including their own growing numerical strength, the Latino community.

The economic arguments for 187 exploited these divisions and the underlying assumption that the economic costs of immigration outweighed the benefits. Or, to put it in the words of the SOS campaign, illegal immigrants were costing state taxpayers billions and that states were now 'screaming for federal reimbursement' (Stein, executive director of the Federation for American Immigration Reform, in SOS publicity). The 'liberal' press, although often opposed to 187 in its leader columns, often supported the Campaign's assumptions by taking numbers of immigrants and costs as its starting point for debate. For example, in the run up to the ballot, the *Wall Street Journal* maintained that $4.3 billion was spent in services for illegal residents in 1994 compared to a figure of $780 which illegals allegedly paid in tax revenue over the same period (4 November 1994).

A further economic argument against immigration was succinctly put by Dan Stein of the Federation:

> The profile of today's immigrants simply does not match our needs as a nation. Faced with the already daunting task of making the transition to the high-tech, highly competitive global economy of the 21st Century, an immigration policy that admits more than a million people a year, without regard for their skills, is a luxury we can no longer afford.
>
> (Stein in SOS publicity press article)

Stein's argument was not just about numbers but skills and aptitudes and the implied link between inferiority and 'recent', and, in particular, Latino immigrants. There was also the unfounded assumption that immigrants are a net economic cost and that immigration is a non-affordable 'luxury'.

Proposition 187 was astutely fought by its proponents. It managed to secure a large non-white vote, whilst appealing to white values.[20] It secured the support of Latinos and African-Americans in three ways. In common with many examples throughout this book, the SOS campaign recruited African-American and Latino spokespeople to its cause. For example, James Coleman of the Black Education Commission in Los Angeles distinguished those, irrespective of colour, who had legal status in California, from the rest: '187 will allow us to regain our strength as a state' (*Los Angeles Times*, 12 September 1994). His support lent weight to the idea that 187 was not racist and that it was in everyone's interests to support Proposition 187 (i.e. he universalised it). His African-American status aimed to take the 'whiteness' out of the debate. Secondly, SOS sought to play up divisions between African-American and Latino/a populations. The use of Latino spokespeople to deny the charge of racism brought against 187 and its opponents was the third manoeuvre designed to win a non-white vote for 187. A good example appeared in the *Los Angeles Times* (10 January 1995) which featured on the front page of the 'Life and Style' section of the paper an 11" by 6" colour photograph of Harold Ezell, another SOS founder, pictured at home with his wife both seemingly at work on the campaign. The Latino spokesperson from Buenos Aires was quoted as saying that Ezell 'doesn't have a racist bone in his body'. The point served to confirm Ezell's own defence that 'he has friends of all ethnic backgrounds . . . including several friends who are Latinos'. Such tactics illustrate what Frankenberg calls 'race-evasiveness'. At one level, then, racialised discourse was re-coded in the vocabularies of national identity, economic recession, population and the environment. At another level, Save our State (SOS) went out of its way to establish its credentials by having an African-American amongst its founders and leaders.

The success of Proposition 187 lay largely in its capacity to weave the above discursive themes into an apparently seamless whole. National identity, anti-statism, anti-special interests, economic decline, overpopulation and anti-political correctness have all been prominent and popular themes of late twentieth-century neo-conservatism and the new right. What gave Proposition 187 its edge was the ability of its supporters to valorise these themes in the context of a single campaign. The discourses were of course racialised. The cultural traditions appealed to were invariably white European; from the appeal to the descendants of those arriving in New York Harbour at Ellis Island to the values enshrined in the Constitution and expressed by the founding fathers. The mainstream into which minorities were encouraged to assimilate, the Americanness prized and aspired to was unquestionably white European in origin. Latinos were not just criminalised because of their assumed illegal status, but also because of the numerous other crime-related activities in which they were assumed to be involved. It was not just Latinos inside California but Mexico itself which became the object of hostile media coverage invariably linked to crime, and especially to smuggling whether it be cars, drugs or tobacco.

Proposition 187 thus played a crucial role in securing and maintaining 'white-ness'. Its implied racialised discourse was about the defence of and support for white values, white populations, white privileges. It worked at a subjective cultural and material level. Its complexity, operating as it did at different levels even persuaded some black people to identify with a 'white' cause.

Conclusions

The two case studies examined, that is the UK's Immigration and Asylum Act, 1996, and California's Proposition 187, provide evidence of the continuing reso-nance of immigration as an object of political and media debate. Both countries shared historical and transnational conditions as well as discursive themes. The context which Cornel West described has formed the backdrop to the issues discussed throughout this book and is a conjuncture characterised by a crisis in both the US and England brought on by a loss of empire and a sense of declining global significance. It is also marked by the migration of peoples either fleeing persecution from regimes often directly and indirectly supported by western governments and transnational corporations, or seeking work in western economies as a result of domestic policies promoted by such agencies as the World Bank and International Monetary Fund.

The racialisation of immigration is nothing new in either the US or England. In the US, legislation to suspend Chinese immigration was passed in 1882 (Carter *et al.* 1996: 139). In 1939 such was the intensity of anti-Semitism that the Roosevelt administration turned a boat with Jewish refugees back to Nazi Germany against a backdrop of public opinion polls which confirmed opposition to the settlement of 10,000 Jewish children in the US (Duran *et al.* 1994: 6). Moreover, the themes around which immigration has been constructed in this, the latest phase of global-isation, have an all too familiar ring. They include the racialisation and criminalisation of particular groups; the simultaneous infusion of sexual/racial imagery through a vocabulary of contamination and defilement; and metaphors of drowning, swamping etc. Furthermore, the capacity to link macro-economic policy to private concerns, i.e. employment and taxes, as well as the fusing of the political and the personal, i.e. making ideas of national identity intelligible in terms of an individual sense of security, purpose and belonging have been signifi-cant in building a populist, anti-immigrant consensus.

Both the UK's Immigration and Asylum Act and Proposition 187 were concerned with procedures for dealing with illegal immigrants with a particular emphasis on rights to welfare and other social benefits. In fact both the focus and the timing (the UK bill was announced just four months after the 187 ballot and as other states in the US began to announce their own immigration initiatives) suggests that the 187's success might well have been another factor influencing the Conservative Government's decision to make it a key plank of its 1995–6 legisla-tive programme. Certainly there were some striking similarities in the way the Asylum Bill was publicly presented and debated in the media although, arguably, it never attained the same intensity and impact as California's Proposition 187. This could have been either because the battle for control was widely believed to have been won prior to the Asylum Bill, or because the immigration issue was suffering from battle/media fatigue, and that the re-assertion of national identity was finding other genres and pathways through which to find expression. In any event, exchanges in the public media domain, as well as private discussions between politicians, have cross-fertilised the issue on both sides of the Atlantic. In the most recent period, it could be said that whilst 187 might well have reminded the Conservative Government of the electoral possibilities of immigration control, immigration was an issue on which, for once, Britain pre-figured the US. Rather than Britain looking for inspiration or a barometer reading from across the Atlantic as it has on other issues, some US commentators were taking their lead from Enoch Powell in their arguments for immigration control.

As far as particular media were concerned there were some interesting and contrasting differences between the US and England. In the US radio proved particularly significant, especially local and syndicated talk radio shows. In England, once again, the tabloid press proved distinctive and decisive in its handling of the Asylum Bill. By way of contrast, radio and particularly local radio offered opposition groups the most effective outlet to make their case. The Campaign against 187 was particularly successful in using alternative media to mobilise grass roots support. According to Christine Soto, a student representative on the Los Angeles Committee to Defeat 187, 'get out the vote' efforts relied on community networks established via phone banks, mailings, precinct walkings etc. (interview, 12 January 1995). Both campaigns faced an uphill battle to counter the white imaginaries evoked in influential sections of the popular media. The slurs of 'political correctness', 'reverse racism', 'thought control' 'national betrayal' etc., were used to undermine grass roots initiatives[21] and simultaneously to promote a unitary, backward looking, defensive and, at the same time, populist version of whiteness.

5

POLICING WHITENESS

In 1888 the dismembered bodies of six prostitutes were found in London's East End. Jack the Ripper was never caught, but he entered annals of English villainy and became the object of numerous books, films and television programmes, not to mention waxwork sculptures. At the time, one unsubstantiated rumour spread as to Jack's identity. The 'Illustrated Police News' issued descriptions of Jack that resembled a caricature of an Eastern European Jew. It also reported that 'the criminal was a sexual maniac of a virulent type . . . and . . . that he and his people were low-class Jews' (cited in Gilman 1991: 115). Reports such as this provoked physical and verbal attacks on Jews in the East End of London (ibid.: 117). Not for the first time, Jews and prostitutes were linked: two icons of deviant sexuality akin to the image of the black and the monkey (ibid.: 121). Gilman traces the Jew–prostitute connection back to the image of Moll Hackabout, the 'Jew's mistress' in Hogarth's Harlot's Progress. It re-appears in Marcel Proust's 'Remembrance of Times Past' in the relationship between a Jew, Charles Swann and a courtesan. The significance of the linkage lies in their commonly forged status; deviant, promiscuous, diseased, 'fallen'. Both sets of images played on white fears, 'all the dangers felt to be inherent in human sexuality' (ibid.: 120). Each was defined in relationship to the other: she as 'out-of-control' white femininity, he as 'perverse' Jewish male sexuality. The 'Ripper' case thus played on anti-Semitic and gendered themes and in so doing helped to secure existing racial/sexual hierarchies.

In 1994, the football legend, film star, media celebrity, O.J. 'Juice' Simpson was arrested for the murder of his wife Nicole Brown Simpson and her friend, Ronald Goldman. The subsequent unfolding of events in court can be understood in part against the backdrop of the Rodney King verdict and the Los

Angeles uprisings in 1992 (see below). O.J. became a 'black criminal', an identity encapsulated in his mug shot which was used in *Time* and *Newsweek* as well as the *New York Times*. *Time* magazine even blackened the police photo-shot, as Fiske suggests, to 'Hortonise' (see below p. 147) the imagery, i.e. to tap into criminalised meanings of blackness (Fiske 1994: xvi). But O.J. also came to stand for the threat of black male sexuality, as the bloodied images of Nicole symbolised the vulnerability of the white femininity and her death worked as a metaphor for imminent threat to the social order (ibid.: xvii). Photographs of the Simpson family seemingly shot in happier times neverthe-less served to remind the spectator of its underlying dysfunctionality rooted in its interracial foundations (ibid.).

O.J.'s African-American status, which had hitherto been subordinate to that of his class and celebrity identity, was 're-discovered' only after it became known that he had physically abused his wife and allegedly murdered her. Whilst much of the media coverage was coded, racialised discourse surfaced once more with the release of the so-called 'Fuhrman tapes' in which detec-tive sergeant Mark Fuhrman talked about 'giving blacks a good beating', not unlike remarks made by LAPD officers as they radioed back to base after the Rodney King beating. One important reaction to the tapes, having witnessed the Rodney King beating and now Fuhrman's racist outpourings and admis-sion of the systematic racist beatings inflicted on African-American men, was to see the trial not so much about the murder of Nicole Brown but as an opportunity to make amends for Rodney King. O.J. Simpson was no longer in the dock; the LAPD were. For others, the tapes, incriminating as they were, could not detract from Nicole's brutal murder and the evidence against O.J. Simpson. Whilst opinion was not polarised entirely along racialised fault lines, polls suggested that such divisions played a decisive influence in shaping people's view of the trial and O.J.'s innocence or guilt. Television not only covered the verdict. It also covered the television coverage of the verdict! Audience reactions confirmed the above split. White audiences met the verdict with stunned silence, whilst African-Americans appeared relieved and vindicated. For the latter, the trial had become less about O.J. than a test of the endemic racism in the criminal justice system. On the other hand there were those millions of white viewers, made up of those who followed the trial live on Court TV in the US or who sat in the court's public gallery every day (because they had queued outside the court each morning from the early hours and won the entrance lottery), or those from around the world, who sent faxes, e-mails and phone messages to Sky TV legal experts. For this alterna-tive, global, white jury, there was only one verdict. O.J. was guilty.

The above cases, a century and an ocean apart, nevertheless share a number of themes of interest in this chapter. Historically, policing has played the role of last resort, when all appeals to morality, common sense, religion etc. fail. In the case of whiteness, policing has not been just about the defence of material privileges built around property laws, etc., but also about the defence of a more symbolic order, one to do with identities (both masculine and feminine), values and borders. The perceived threats to both material and symbolic orders have been simultaneously racialised and underpinned by sexual fears, as illustrated by the Ripper and O.J. cases. Hence the murdered prostitutes stood for a wayward white femininity in the Ripper story whilst Nicole Brown Simpson embodied the risks associated with interracial sexual relations.

The cases also illustrate how whiteness has been constructed in opposition to both 'black' and subaltern 'white' ethnicities. I will begin by illustrating these themes historically with reference to different ethnic groups. The Fuhrman revelations in the O.J. trial scratched the surface of what goes on behind the scenes in routine, institutional policing. I then examine some aspects of what has been dubbed 'canteen culture'. Rather than talk about the media's relationship to policing in general terms it is easier to examine it with reference to particular events or issues. In some instances, of which the history of mugging in Britain is one, the tabloid press undoubtedly put its ideological weight behind policing decisions and practices. Mugging will be the focus of the next section.

Elsewhere in the media (for example, television documentaries, community radio and an array of local, alternative media), initiatives have been taken to challenge police racism and, in the case of local media, to build new community alliances. I will then examine such strategies with reference to Newham Monitoring Project in London. The trial of the police officers accused of beating Rodney King, resting heavily on an amateur video, provides an opportunity to address the question posed in Chapter 1 with regard to the potential role of new media technologies in challenging and democratising dominant culture. The King video, as it turned out, arguably endorsed the cynic's viewpoint over the optimists in this debate. Above all, it illustrated the idea that what is 'seen' is constructed. In particular, whiteness induced a particular way of 'seeing' the video which fed on deep-seated fears and anxieties, the mobilisation of which was made easier by the make-up of the jury and the location of the trial. Again, as in Britain, the US media has not spoken with one voice on police brutality, and the role of community radio in challenging police racism and building new communities of resistance will be illustrated with reference to WBAI, a New York-based station.

Historical themes

It is no surprise that the modern police force, from its inception in the nineteenth century, played an instrumental role in supporting national identities structured around capitalist property relations. The role of the police was thus inextricably bound up with the legal and ideological framework necessary for the maintenance of the nation state. Against this backdrop the police sought to maintain both class-drawn and racialised boundaries. Thus white interests were constructed which both cut across class divisions and supported them. Police were charged with the role of defending 'racialised' boundaries both internally and externally, i.e. through policing immigration. In Simon Holdaway's view there is 'no better an English institution to separate British way of life and immigrant presence' (1996: 98). In Britain, different immigrant groups have, over time, become the object of racialised policing. The Chinese and Irish communities in the nineteenth century were particular targets and still are, although in media terms they have become somewhat eclipsed by the attention paid to black immigrants and their descendants.

Perhaps because of their physical as well as moral role, and/or perhaps because, like the military in times of war, they offer a last line of defence, the police have commonly elicited heightened white sexual and racialised anxieties. A recurrent theme in Fiske's analysis (1994) was the way in which the African-American male protagonists (i.e. O.J. Simpson, Rodney King and Willy Horton) were defined in terms of the threat they posed to white femininity. Such constructions were not without historical precedent, as Vron Ware has argued in her exploration of the role played by imperial law and its custodians (notably the army and the police) in defending white women. The unique role of white women was always bound up with the reproduction of the 'national stock' and the corresponding threat of moral and physical degeneration. Discourses surrounding the 'black monster' were suffused with invisible white values; values which claimed a moral monopoly when it came to family relations and respect for the law. According to Fiske, the Simpson, King and Horton cases all served to illustrate how the black male has been inextricably linked to the 'social body of black America', whilst the police and criminal justice system have been charged with defending whiteness and white femininity.

In the US policing had its origins in the slave patrols who were given absolute powers of arrest and punishment to enforce the slave codes which prohibited Africans from assembling in groups, possessing weapons or leaving plantations. Vigilance was increased after Nat Turner led a slave revolt in Virginia in 1831 and rural slave patrols had the direct responsibility of regulating the slave population (Dulaney 1996: 6). Punishments, which were harsh and arbitrarily applied, included castration, whippings, maimings and of course hangings/lynchings. Slave patrols 'thus set the pattern of policing that Americans of African descent would experience throughout their history in America' (ibid.: 2). In fact the history of white policing of 'black' urban areas has been summed up by Homer Hawkins and Richard Thomas as, 'another form of white social control which had evolved over the centuries in response to whites' racial phobias of black people' (1991: 65).

Writing in 1993, Ellis Cose illustrates the continuing impact of this legacy. In a conversation with a *Washington Post* Executive Post Editor, Cose remarked that he was writing a book 'about race' to which the journalist replied that he was worried about what 'race' was doing to him and illustrated this by saying that his home had been broken into more than once (1993: 93). What is interesting, from the point of view of this chapter, was not just that the journalist equated 'race' with crime, but that he and Cose used 'race' to mean African-Americans, as if whites were not implicated in the same racialised discourse. In any event, politicians, in conjunction with sections of the media, have succeeded in forging the 'race/crime' link through the selective construction and reporting of crime statistics. The latter have created the wholly erroneous impression that whites are law-abiding and African-Americans are not (Cose 1993: 94). In one set of figures, African-American males were allegedly responsible for 45 per cent of violent crimes, a figure which would mean that every African-American would need to be a violent criminal, even 'lawyers, teachers, salesmen . . . getting their jollies (during their lunch breaks, one supposes) by cracking hapless innocents over the head or 'wilding' in big-city parks' (ibid.).

In the development of urban police forces, US cities took their lead both from southern practices and, later, from the framework laid down in England. From the late seventeenth century many cities developed watches, city guards or constabulary forces to control the 'dangerous classes' that they attracted (ibid.: 3). The idea that African-Americans were habitual criminals had been built into the white psyche well before the Civil War and before city police forces like those in New York and Chicago became full-time units modelled on the Metropolitan Force in London. The creation and establishment of areas of 'black' urban settlement was dependent on systems of white policing (Hawkins and Thomas 1991: 66). Moreover, police forces, in responding to pressures of white popular opinion, 'often refused to allow red light districts to develop anywhere except in or near black neighbourhoods' (Kusmer, cited in Hawkins and Thomas 1991: 76). The politics of policing in northern US cities in the nineteenth century was a microcosm of wider developments in which the Irish were given jobs and enhanced status in exchange for votes, and were 'whitened' in the process. The outbreaks of violence in New York, Baltimore and Cincinnati enabled the Irish to assert their newly conferred (white) racial credentials.

The history of urban uprisings in the US during the nineteenth and twentieth centuries provided white police officers with a chance to engage in legalised terrorism against the African-American community. An uprising in St Louis in 1917 was initiated by white workers who felt threatened by an African-American workforce taking their jobs. In Chicago, two years later in 1919, whites attacked African-Americans who were swimming on a whites-only beach and in Detroit in the 1940s white tenants attacked African-Americans in an effort to stop them moving into a housing project. In each case the police were seen to be underprotecting and over-policing African-American communities. In St Louis in an incident where thirty-nine African-Americans were murdered, 'the few police-officers who remained on duty actually encouraged white mobs to lynch blacks' (Johnson cited in Hawkins and Thomas 1991: 77). The Report of the National Advisory Commission on Civil Disorders (1968) into the uprisings in the 1960s in Watts, Los Angeles in 1965 and, again, in Chicago in 1967, held white police forces responsible for triggering the violence. In 1980, in Miami, the catalyst for uprising was an incident in which Arthur McDuffie, an African-American insurance worker, was killed by two white police officers whilst being arrested. The officers were subsequently acquitted (Hawkins and Thomas 1991: 82). The term 'riots' in the US has become synonymous (as it has in Britain) with black urban uprisings, the initial spark for which has invariably been prompted by an incident of police brutality.[1]

Since the mid 1960s, British politicians have had one eye on racial conflicts in the US as a gauge to measure and/or anticipate future developments in Britain. Examples of the uprisings in the US in the 1960s formed part of the case put to Parliament for anti-discrimination in Britain in the 1960s and again in 1976 (Ben-Tovim *et al*. 1981). It has been commonplace for English tabloids to frame US inner-city disturbances with the question, 'could it happen here?'. Policing the alien threat has thus been a source of great anxiety to policy-makers, but it has also been a source of pleasure to movie-goers who, from the safety of a multiplex cinema in Britain, have thrived on a steady diet of Hollywood films fictionalising the urban nightmare experience of being white, and particularly white and male, in the US. 'D-Fens' (Michael Douglas) in Joel Schumacher's *Falling Down* (1993), is an obvious example of one such 'white victim', although similar characters are found in numerous other apocalyptic visions of both New York and Los Angeles (Gabriel 1996). The opening scene of Jerry Zucker's *Ghost* (1990), for example, shows a Latino appearing out of the shadows of a dimly-lit street corner to murder his white victim, Sam (played by Patrick Swayze). Likewise, Tom Wolfe's novel *Bonfire of the Vanities*, which was published in 1987 and very soon became a best seller, played on similar themes, as does Brian de Palma's screen version (1990). The story hinges on the events of one night when Sherman McCoy (played by Tom Hanks) and his lover, Maria (played by Melanie Griffith) took a wrong turn and ended up in the South Bronx. What happened there, the classic 'racialised/yuppie nightmare', eventually cost him his one million dollar-a-year job as a Wall Street 'master of the universe', his home, his marriage and his family; adding up to what might be described as the spiralling, downward flight of a WASP.[2]

The impact of such US films in Britain has been heightened at those times when the state has been at its most vulnerable; in other words, during times of economic restructuring and retrenchment and when the political ideologies accompanying such developments have attracted minimum consent. In exploring some of these connections, Tony Jefferson (1991) has argued that racialisation has been part of a wider process of winning popular consent for policing in response to the changing composition and location of the labour force. Divisions within the working class, between 'the roughs' and 'respectables', has been reflected in different patterns of policing; 'negotiated order' characterising relations with the latter and the brutal imposition of statutory order on the former. Immigrants thus became the new 'roughs' in the 1960s and 1970s and, hence, the object of repressive policing.

Similarly, Michael Keith has argued that waves of moral panic and phases of criminalisation, which punctuated the 1980s, lent legitimacy to measures of social control *and* were simultaneously 'consonant with restructuring of the British economy' (1993: 232). Police clashes with the miners, the print workers and poll-tax demonstrators, manifested Thatcherism's attempt to integrate Britain into the global circuits of capital: 'someone had to pay the price for postmodernisation' (ibid.: 235). Racialisation, both as a process of group formation and as a social construction, was thus part of an attempt to legitimate a wider national political project with global aspirations. Tony Jefferson has also argued that inner-city rioters were one of a number of groups, including striking miners and Irish Republicans,[3] who were scapegoated as deviant and dissenting in the crisis conditions of the 1980s (Jefferson 1991: 174). The role of the police in the 1980s was not just to impose order, but to sharpen the divisions between 'the enemy within' and Thatcherism's version of English national identity.

Canteen culture

My aim here is not to provide an exhaustive review of research evidence on police racism, but rather to select from this body of evidence to illustrate some of the processes associated with the construction of whiteness. For example, an insider study of the Police Academy in the US carried out in the early 1970s found evidence of racialised thinking amongst police recruits which was expressed as part of a wider 'ethic of masculinity' (Harris 1973: 89). Elsewhere, it has been reported that in the US, police officers have been prominent opponents of civil rights initiatives and active in racist political organisations of the extreme right (Reiner 1985: 100). In another study of the New York police, carried out in the 1970s and revealingly sub-titled 'a study of a beleaguered minority' (Alex 1976), white officers repeatedly asserted that minority officers were bringing down the standard of policing, gaining unfair advantages and 'were a breed apart'. One officer expressed some of these views in recalling a training course in which, 'the average IQ of this group went down to 70. And they were all minorities . . . (later) they found that 70 per cent of them were already in serious trouble . . . you can't motivate morons' (1976: 39). The references to inherited deficiencies of trainee officers were complemented by their views of 'black' crime, as the following extract illustrates: 'the majority of them, I don't want to sound like a racist or anything, are the minorities . . . look at Attica (New York State's prison), it's all Negroes' (ibid.: 129). According to another officer,

> blacks have more rights than they have ever had and they want more . . .
> blacks are a different breed of people, the way they think. They have no
> family life. They are screwing everybody here and there . . . they don't
> want to work . . . they love to commit crime . . . they love to stick the knife
> into you . . . they are a ruthless people.
>
> (ibid.: 130)

It might be argued that a researcher, returning to the NYPD in the 1990s, would find a different culture. On the contrary, evidence from Amnesty International's report on the NYPD (1996) has confirmed a pattern of cases in which African-Americans and Latinos have been the target of police brutality and that such routine practices were condoned, sanctioned or excused via the norms of policing culture. Equally compelling have been studies of policing culture which confirm similar patterns with respect to other social groups. For example, in a study of gay police in New York, Stephen Leinen observed over 150 homophobic incidents, including graffiti on lockers and bathrooms, verbal intimidations, denials of police services and outright assault violations committed by the police against fellow gay officers (1993: 37).

The prevalence of racialised and homophobic norms of white masculinity within US police forces have been echoed in research conducted in Britain. In 1966, Joseph Hunte produced a report for the West Indian Standing Conference entitled 'Nigger-Hunting in England?', so-called because 'nigger hunting' was a common expression overheard as police left their stations for patrol duty (Benyon 1986: 239). In general, gaining access to the British police for research purposes has never been straightforward. Occasionally evidence comes to light, as it did in 1982, when essays, written by police cadets and revealing extreme prejudice, were leaked to the press (Benyon 1986: 256). On another occasion, an officer, Peter Johnson, let slip a racist slur (a reference to 'coloured brethren or nig nogs') in the course of a speech to the 1984 Police Federation Conference (ibid.: 255). Apart from this more piecemeal evidence, more systematic research, collected in the 1960s and 1970s, confirmed widespread racism amongst rank and file officers (Reiner 1985: 100). For example, a study by Colman and Gorman found that the police attracted conservative and authoritarian personalities and, whilst basic training had a liberalising effect, the longer police stayed in the force, the more illiberal they became (cited in ibid.).

In another major study, this time of London's Metropolitan Police, in the 1980s, David Smith and Jeremy Gray found widespread evidence of the 'casual, automatic use of racialist language' amongst police officers, both in conversations amongst themselves and in their contacts with the public (1985: 390ff.). Such views clearly fed into policing practices, notably 'stopping' a disproportionate number of young African Caribbeans on the streets. The authors' observational study highlighted the importance of humour as a source of in-group identification amongst officers. Moreover, from the numerous recorded instances of racist and sexist jokes, including some scrawled on staff toilet walls (ibid.: 392), the in-group was 'white and male' both in outlook and appearance. Whilst there were cases of officers who objected to such language and behaviour (ibid.: 396), the authors' overall findings suggested that racism was the norm rather than the exception amongst junior ranks within the Metropolitan Police and not unheard of at a senior level, too.

Whilst such studies have always been subject to methodological criticisms (for example how far the police simply reflect the views of the wider society), there is more than a suggestion in research to date that 'police culture' has, indeed, promoted racism. Once again the methodological problem arises as to how we make hard and fast connections between views expressed 'in the canteen' and policing outcomes (e.g. arrest and conviction rates). However, it is not unreasonable to assume that if, by definition, ideologies and discourses provide explanations as well as motivations to act, then there is no reason to suppose that racialised ideologies and discourses will be any different. Nevertheless, what makes conceptual common sense by no means always satisfies the statistically-minded, especially those with particular political leanings. Any findings, to this extent, are open to criticism and re-interpretation and so, whilst there is evidence of racist views amongst the police and of the over-policing and under-protecting of black communities, proving the connection beyond doubt has always been fraught.

Simon Holdaway, a British sociologist, carried out research as an 'insider', working covertly as a police sergeant. His findings bore many similarities to Alex's study referred to above. For example, he found that terms like ' "coon" , "nig-nog", "spade", and "nigger" were common verbal currency among the lower ranking officers' (1996: 78). Moreover, exchanges with black suspects were thus invariably couched in racial terms, for example in one case a suspect was asked 'why don't you go home . . . to India or Pakistan, or wherever you fuckin' come from?' (ibid.: 73).

Such discourses are reproduced and reinforced in numerous cultural settings. I will take one such setting, a performance given by Bernard Manning, one of England's most popular comedians, to a gathering of Greater Manchester Police officers in March 1995, to illustrate the processes to which I refer. Humour, as indicated by Smith and Gray's study, has played an important role in forging group identities amongst white male police officers. The comedy show in question was subsequently the subject of a Granada television production of *World in Action*, an investigative documentary series. The overriding purpose of the programme was to challenge Manning's racism and to provide a space for 'alternative', anti-racist perspectives. The following extracts are taken from his show.

> Manning: They actually think they're English cause they're fucking born here that means if a dog's born in a stable it's a fucking horse. Them Los Angeles police kicking that fucking nigger on the floor. I thought fuck me that's not on. Not enough police there (laughter).

The following was addressed by Manning to the one black officer in the audience:

> How are you son? This is better than swinging through fucking trees . . . I was in Bradford last week. I felt like a spot on a fucking domino. What a fucking place that is. Dial 999 and you get the Bengal Lancers. They've got their own programmes, Asian magazines, Aap Kaa Hak. You've never heard such shit in your fucking life . . . social security free rent rebate. They actually think they're English because they're born here.

World in Action challenged this overt racism in a number of ways. It gave black officers an opportunity to describe their experiences 'on the beat'. One such officer,
who refused to disclose his identity for fear of reprisals, commented,

> the people I was working with were like a gang of bigots and racists.
> When we went to a black part of town they would often make comments
> like 'look at those black bastards', and they would refer to black people as
> 'niggers' and 'coons'.

World in Action also introduced 'expert' research opinion to confirm the prevalence
(i.e. beyond anecdotal evidence) of racism within the police, particularly at a junior
level. Simon Holdaway, interviewed for the programme, stated that, 'the world of
the lower ranks is a very highly enclosed world and it's a world where there's a lot of
banter and joking which easily slides over into racialised joking'.

The last word was given to a Rastafarian, who left the viewer in no doubt as to
the general sympathies of programme makers. He said,

> People who you are supposed to trust in the community, who you are
> supposed to look up to and who you are supposed to go to for help if you
> need it – I am angry that they can wear a uniform and when they wear
> that uniform they think they can do what they want to people.

Racism may have been highly visible in both Manning's jokes and in police banter,
but the white masculine norms forged by such exchanges, nevertheless, remain
well hidden. Racism was quick to specify its ('black') object but never its ('white')
subject. It has been suggested in previous chapters that the power of whiteness lies,
precisely, in its ability to deny its own dominance and to pass off its own white
norms as universal. Moreover, the presence of the odd black and/or woman police
officer has been used, strategically, to confirm its universalism.

However, it is not just white norms but white interests, too, which have been
constructed and derived from such racist practices. Patterns of normative inclusion and exclusion, of 'getting on', having your 'face fit', of being 'one of the lads'
hold the key to both job satisfaction and, more significantly, to promotion. The
World in Action documentary was important, given that it spotlighted the role of
racist humour in forging and sealing patterns of white racialised inclusion.
However, a one-off documentary programme will always struggle to compete with
everyday racism, circulating as it does within the routines of institutional cultures
and fed by the likes of Bernard Manning. Moreover, such media interventions
have also proved no match for the British tabloid press, as I shall now argue with
reference to a succession of 'mugging' scares.

Mugging: the media and the Met

In 1972, the *Daily Mirror* referred to a new crime which the reporter described as alien and unBritish and said to have originated in the US. It was not just considered 'alien' because of where it came from, but also because it was assumed, from the outset, that its perpetrators were black. This belief has been sustained by the 'moral panics' around mugging which have intermittently hit the headlines, firstly in 1972, again in 1975 and more recently in 1995. Stuart Hall *et al.*'s important study of mugging (1978) reveals the use made by the media of folk ideologies in the making of news. The authors cited the case of Paul Storey, a sixteen-year-old from Handsworth, who received a twenty-year sentence for 'mugging' an Irish labourer in 1972. The press made strategic use of the term 'mugging' to evoke a growing pattern of lawlessness amongst young blacks. Moreover such claims were supported by the comments of institutional authorities or 'primary definers' (police chiefs, politicians, etc.) who called for tough penalties (ibid.: 84). In this and subsequent cases, the racialisation of mugging was also achieved by the highly selective use and dissemination of crime data and its association with US 'ghettos', 'white victims' and 'black' perpetrators (Benyon 1986: 237).

'Mugging' fuelled the white imagination, not just because of a set of immediate circumstances, but because it tapped into ideas of black masculinity which had a much longer lineage. These representations, for example, have been reworked powerfully in cinema from D.W. Griffith's *Birth of a Nation* (1915) to the 'Blaxploitation' films of the 1970s and the urban nightmare films of the 1980s and 1990s referred to above. In their well-known study, *Policing the Crisis*, Stuart Hall and his associates analysed the phenomenon of black mugging as an attempt to criminalise a section of the working class and to racialise and divide it (1978: 395). Black crime, according to the authors, could thus only be understood with reference to the history of post-1945 black immigration, the deteriorating position of black labour and the imposition of an authoritarian consensus on a resistant young black working class.

'Mugging' panics have provided the police with yet a further excuse to impose statutory order on black communities in Britain, using whatever means at their disposal. For example, in the 1970s and early 1980s the British police used a clause of a nineteenth-century vagrancy act to pick up disproportionate numbers of young blacks on suspicion that they had committed, or were about to commit, a crime. The law was used in 1981 as a basis for an operation which became known as 'Swamp '81' in which London's Metropolitan police targeted young blacks in a series of raids for suspected drug offences and robbery. 'Swamp '81' was seen as pivotal in provoking the Brixton uprising of the same year. The Scarman Report into the 'disorders' as they were called, criticised the police for the heavy-handedness of their methods which had alienated many in Brixton's black community. In a cycle which has often been repeated, the police released statistical evidence allegedly to prove the participation rate of young blacks in street crime and hence the need to maintain existing policing practices. Community pressure, which was mobilised around the 'Scrap SUS' campaign, eventually succeeded in getting the Act repealed. However, its supporters had not anticipated the government's willingness to re-package 'SUS' under a new name, the Police and Criminal Evidence Act. This Act, which gave police increased powers to stop and search those under suspicion was passed in 1984.[4] The history of mugging can be picked up again just over a decade later.

In July 1995, the head of London's police force, Sir Paul Condon, wrote a letter to community representatives which stated that 'very many perpetrators of muggings are very young black people'. The letter was leaked to the media and widely covered by the national tabloid and broadsheet press alike. Whilst *The Times* covered the issue with an article under the headline CONDON TACKLES BLACK MUGGERS (7 July 1995), the *Sun* ran with the headline, MOST MUGGERS ARE BLACK SAYS TOP COP (7 July 1995). The following day, the *Sun*'s editorial began, 'a smoke screen of political correctness is in danger of blinding us to the truth' (8 July 1995) and went on 'how can it be wrong to say what he honestly knows to be true?' Once again, a 'taboo' had allegedly been unmasked and political correctness attacked for its curtailment of free speech and concealment of the 'truth'. The leader view was illustrated by a cartoon showing Sir Paul Condon in the dock with the caption reading 'Paul Condon, you are charged with telling the truth'. The cartoon was accompanied by a double-page feature article, entitled, VICIOUS MUGGERS WRECKED MY LIFE and a selection of letters from *Sun* readers on the topic. Summing up readers' views was the headline SUN READERS BACK TOP COP FOR SAYING MOST MUGGERS ARE BLACK. The correspondents, most of which did not reveal their whiteness, at least openly, referred to 'no-go areas' and 'fear of going out at night' as well as fear of speaking up and being accused of racism. One final, yet as I have suggested, hardly unique, feature of this reporting was the use of black spokespeople to support the chief constable's claims. Hence the *Daily Mail* ran an article by John (not uncoincidentally, now Lord) Taylor, former Conservative Party election candidate, under the headline THEY CALL HIM A RACIST BUT THE FACTS WON'T GO AWAY.[5] The choice of a black spokesperson served to strengthen the case against 'black muggers'. The fact that John Taylor held the same views as Condon suggested that the Police Chief's remarks had a universal appeal rooted in a common-sense truth which was as obvious to 'reasonable' blacks as it was to whites.

The above common-sense, racialised understanding of mugging prevailed but did not exhaust media reporting of Condon's remarks. For example, the *Independent* ran a full page article on the topic (4 August 1995), which, although taking Condon's remarks as its starting point, made a counter-argument based on research carried out by Jock Young and his colleagues. This enhanced the critical approach of the report in a number of ways. Firstly, the definition of mugging, so readily accepted in other press coverage of the debate, was called into question. Mugging was not a crime *per se*. Rather, it was an inclusive term which referred to different street crimes, e.g. theft, assault, robbery. The idea of lumping crimes together in categories is unusual to say the least, unless the point is to link them to a particular group. The selection of data from London and for these particular offences was also misleading, since research in other parts of Britain, e.g. Newcastle and Glasgow, had suggested that 'mugging' was a white offence. Moreover, in 1994 'muggings' (bearing in mind the term stood for a number of crimes) represented only 4 per cent of all crime in London. Fraud and forgery accounted for as many crimes and greater monetary loss. In addition there were five times as many reported car crimes and burglaries as there were 'muggings' (ibid.). Not only then were 'white muggings' concealed but more generally what could be described as 'white crime' was rendered invisible and insignificant along-side the racialised anxieties induced by Condon's remarks and the tabloid reporting of 'black mugging'. Once again, the odd piece of academic research and the odd broadsheet article and piece of research did little to dent either the associ-ation of whiteness with law-abiding behaviour or the view that whites were the 'victims', rather than the perpetrators, of such crimes.

White discourse not only succeeded in equating young black males with mugging but also managed to turn inner-city working-class uprisings involving white, African Caribbean and south Asian into acts of black criminality, i.e. 'race riots'. At the same time, popular 'global' uprisings, which were beamed live around the world on CNN and splashed across the pages of the world's press, were widely understood as legitimate political protests. For example, no commentator thought to describe events in Berlin in 1989, as protesters tore down (vandalised?) the Berlin Wall or student/workers' protests in Tiananmen Square in 1989 as acts of criminality or riots, let alone explain them in racial terms. In both cases, presum-ably, the protests, by and large, endorsed norms of western bourgeois democracy, or at least could be read as such. Irrespective of ethnic background, the protesters had 'white' on their side. In contrast, the use of the vocabulary of 'rioting' in the British context not only reinforced the 'criminal', as opposed to the 'political', dimension of the events but also pre-empted explanations which attributed what happened to disadvantage, unemployment, repressive policing and poor ameni-ties. On the contrary, as John Solomos has pointed out, explanations became increasingly racialised/criminalised to the point that, in 1985, Labour politicians, like their Conservative counterparts, were blaming 'riots', albeit in coded terms, on mindless ('black') criminality (Solomos 1989).

The shift towards a more racialised account can be attributed, in part, to Falklands jingoism, the defeat of the miners' strike and to the mounting attack on 'loony left authorities' discussed in Chapter 3. One of the lessons of Thatcherism's early years was that the violent suppression of trade unionists, foreign powers, Irish Republicans and left labour councils proved a sound political investment. Now it was the turn of inner-city blacks. The militarisation of the police during this period, from 1981–5, highlighted the limits put on 'negotiation' by the state and its willingness to apply overtly repressive measures and to use high-tech weapons and riot equipment to maintain order. Ironically, both the Brixton and Broadwater Farm Estate uprisings in 1985, which led to the death of one black woman,

Cynthia Jarrett, and the police shooting of another, Cherry Groce, were sparked by police actions (Benyon 1986: 264).[6]

In the 1990s, new discourses concerned with drugs, gangs and 'Yardies' have served to strengthen 'black crime' associations. The mugging scare, however, has continued to play an important political role and, along with the drug threat, served to justify the shift towards an increasingly militarised and repressive style of policing. Whilst negotiation and consultation measures have been implemented, the practice of picking up disproportionate numbers of young blacks under stop and search rules by London's police force continues to be sanctioned, giving new meaning to the idea of lip-service and tokenism. According to Amin, 'the number of black people stopped and searched by the Metropolitan Police in London is more than double and often treble their number as a proportion of the population' (1995: 6). The Police and Criminal Evidence Act 1984 empowered the police to 'stop and search', on occasions where they 'have reasonable suspicion of finding a stolen or prohibited item'. 'Reasonable suspicion' is of course partly informed by pre-judgements of the kind set in motion, reinforced and amplified in the press coverage of Sir Paul Condon's leaked letter. The success of the practice (or rather lack of it) bears witness to its dubious assumptions. 'In 1993, only 13 per cent of the 442,800 people stopped and searched were actually arrested' (ibid.: 7). Police harassment of young African Caribbeans was evident in the data, irrespective of class. The Irish, too, were stopped and searched in disproportionate numbers partly, according to research, because of their (working-) class background (ibid.: 7) but also presumably because of an analogous set of assumptions regarding the Irish and terrorism.[7] Whiteness has thus continued, in the post-1945 period, to define itself in opposition to subaltern, white ethnicities (in the case of the Irish) as well as in opposition to 'blackness'.

Community strategies and the media: the case of Newham Monitoring Project

The mobilisation of policing around dominant white interests has been witnessed, on the one hand, in zealous over-policing and, on the other, by the under-policing of cases of racial harassment, including those perpetrated by the police themselves. The disparities in both policing and protection accord with the historical role assigned to the police which, as I have suggested, was not just to defend bourgeois property rights through the imposition of order, but also to police marginal communities in ways which served to re-assert dominant norms. Whiteness here is defined, not by who or what it is, but by who or what it is not. The under-protection of black communities has been evident in both cases involving racial harassment [8] and deaths in police custody.[9]

Newham borough in East London was at one time a thriving industrial region. The docks, which were at one time the busiest in the world, attracted industries, including Tate and Lyle, Barking rubber company and Standard Telephone and Cables, to Canning Town in the south of the borough. Immigrant workers, predominantly from the Caribbean and the Gujurat in India, worked in these industries as well as in the service sector (e.g. the Post Office and London Transport) often doing the night shifts and sometimes in unsafe conditions. From the 1970s, a decline in investment and radical changes in telecommunications, transportation and containerisation, led to a dramatic decline in the local economy and loss of jobs. African Caribbean and south Asian workers struggled against both their employers and often their unions to improve their working conditions and protect and enhance their job opportunities.

Racist activity grew during this period. In 1968, local dockers marched in support of Enoch Powell and in 1973, Newham Ratepayers Association, encouraged by the council's discriminatory housing policies, marched to prevent Ugandan Asians from settling in the borough. And when racial attacks increased and black communities sought to defend themselves, it was their members who were criminalised. It is also worth noting that, according to evidence provided by local organisations, including Newham Monitoring Project (NMP), black women have been the most vulnerable to racist attacks. This pattern was also reflected elsewhere; in one Manchester-based survey, as many as one in three women had been attacked (Dunhill 1989: 69). What is more, this evidence confirmed that racial attackers were not only white men, but also white women, boys and girls (ibid.).

In April 1977, the day of a National Front march in Wood Green, three brothers, the Virks, were attacked by a gang of white youths. The Virks defended themselves and in the course of the fight, one of the white youths was stabbed. The police arrested the Virks, not the white youths, and the brothers were subsequently charged with grievous bodily harm. All three were found guilty and one brother, Joginder, was given a seven-year custodial sentence. In July 1980, against a background of growing racial tension, Akhtar Ali Baig was stabbed and murdered by a group of white skinheads. Despite overwhelming evidence to the contrary, the police maintained that it was a street crime and not racially motivated. Hence,

> an organisation was needed that was capable of speaking to new politically active constituencies, whilst also combining the organisational skills and wide community base of the elders with the vitality, militancy and black politics of the youth. In 1980, representatives from all these tendencies came together around the issue of racial harassment to form the Newham Monitoring Project.
>
> (Newham Monitoring Project 1991: 44)

In the mid 1990s there was still considerable racial harassment but the focus had changed. According to Piara Powar of the NMP,

> [we] have been in existence sixteen years. Every day people come through the door. We see people racially harassed or messed up by the police . . . nowadays refugee communities are often victims of racial

attacks and settled communities less so . . . and deaths in custody are an issue too. It's all linked to the way our communities are policed – someone who gets abused or slapped on the street – it's part of the same process as someone who dies in custody.

(interview, 24 October 1996)

The media pose a particular set of problems for NMP. The first relates to Piara Powar's point about deaths in custody. Routine police harassment, on its own, was rarely newsworthy enough to make the headlines. Incidents needed a 'hook' to generate media attention and NMP were mindful of this in planning their campaigns. For example, the case of Ibrahima Sey's death in police custody received considerable media attention because the police had sprayed him with CS gas.[10] Here, possible dangers of a new police technology gained national attention for Sey's case. Similarly, in the case of Brian Douglas, who died as a result of injuries inflicted by a (US style) long baton, the novelty of the police equipment helped to generate media interest. Otherwise, all that seemed newsworthy to journalists was the prospect of 'trouble' at the demonstrations against police brutality. Since 1969, there have been fifty-nine deaths of black people whilst in police custody, including eighteen since 1990 (NMP 1996).

Even when the mainstream media covered such cases, they rarely put them in a wider perspective of a history of routine police harassment, both verbal and physical, and the inadequacy of internal mechanisms within the police to bring perpetrators to justice. Moreover, the media have invariably qualified their concerns about racial harassment by 'counter-balancing' them with the 'authoritative' view of the police.[11] In the case of Ibrahima Sey, for example, the local *Newham Recorder* covered the case including the protest demonstration, but on the same page ran a story of a police officer who had been run over in a getaway incident and who was quoted as saying that he would not have been in hospital with a broken leg had he been able to use CS spray.

Outside of campaigning around specific cases, NMP staged events, partly to mobilise local support and, relatedly, to secure media interest. Local community radio had proved the most willing to publicise the activities and perspectives of the NMP, although the problem with this medium has been its vulnerability to closure. Stations like Dil FM, based above a kebab shop, survived about six months. Others, including Sunrise (a south Asian station), Choice FM and GLR all advertised the Ibrahima Sey demonstration (interview, 24 October 1996). The Internet also offered possibilities which were recognised but as then untapped by NMP, although the group did download an advert for CS gas from the World Wide Web which provided information subsequently used in campaign work. In addition, campaigns had been built around use of CCTV and audio cassette tapes, both illustrating the possible uses of new technologies for community groups. Newham's experience, however, bears out the difficulties encountered with the Rodney King video in the US. So, according to Piara Powar, in one case, someone who was getting a lot of racial harassment put a CCTV in his shop – he called the police on one occasion and they responded by accusing *him* and ended up arresting *him* . . . we took that case up focusing on the lack of police response to black people when they call them out for assistance . . . the footage on the CCTV tape showed these officers saying things to him . . . anyway (BBC's) *Panorama* used the footage and the officers concerned sued the BBC because they said they could be recognised, and the BBC ended up paying £2000 damages and £200,000 costs.

(interview, 24 October 1996)

The effectiveness of organisations like NMP cannot be understood without reference to wider economic and political developments within the borough; the collapse of the local economy, the rise of the far right, changes in policing practices and the role of the local media. The organisation has supported numerous complainants in cases of racial harassment, including those involving the police, since the early 1980s. Its recent concern with asylum seekers and refugees reflects not only the shift in migration patterns and public concern but the success of groups like NMP in empowering and supporting settled black communities. Its success otherwise is hard to measure. In individual terms, compensation, bringing perpetrators to justice is one kind of measure, but changes in wider policing practices and mechanisms of accountability is another, still-to-be-realised, objective. Community monitoring has undoubtedly played a preventative role. Who knows how many more cases of harassment might have been perpetrated but for the organisation and vigilance of groups like NMP? The forces of opposition – a collusion of white interests, made up of local politicians, the *Newham Recorder* and the police, have been formidable, so much so that the organisation was funding down in 1997. Sustained efforts to discredit it, ignore it and starve it of funds, finally paid off. In one sense its 'official' closure (it was continuing to operate, without funds, in 1997), therefore, was a testimony to NMP's success in challenging racism and dominant white interests whilst simultaneously helping to build a legitimate, alternative community base.

The racial production of the visible: the case of Rodney King

If the jurors came to see in Rodney King's body a danger *to* the law, then this 'seeing' requires to be read as that which was culled, cultivated, regulated – indeed, policed – in the course of the trial. This is not a simple seeing, an act of direct perception, but the racial production of the visible, the workings of racial constraints on what it means to 'see'.

(Butler 1993: 16)

The Los Angeles police beating of Rodney King in the early hours of 3 March 1992 has been the subject of considerable, detailed, critical discussion (see Gooding-Williams 1993; Fiske 1994; Feagin and Vera 1995). The media's role was paramount, both in the events surrounding the incident and in those, including the so-called 'LA riots', which followed in its wake. The transformation of George Holliday's local amateur video of members of the police beating Rodney King into a global media product was of particular significance. The fact that it was an amateur, 'undoctored' video served to enhance its authenticity and had initially, at least, conveyed unambiguous proof of the racist brutality of the Los Angeles police. The video's initial impact thus vindicated those who have argued that new technologies, like the camcorder, could serve the masses in their confrontations with corporate power.

Or could they? The last but by no means least significant factor about the event, was the naive belief that the video could indeed serve as unambiguous, incontrovertible and once-and-for-all proof of police guilt. In fact, as many excellent studies of the Simi Valley trial of the officers accused of the beating indicate, what we see is always mediated through chains of meaning or ideological narratives. We can be told the same story from different viewpoints until it becomes a different story. In the King case, this was made possible, in part, by turning Holliday's 'video low' into a 'video high' by computer enhancement, freeze framing and the addition of explanatory circles, etc. (Fiske 1994: 127). It was also made possible by what Kimberlé Crenshaw and Gary Peller have called 'disaggregation'. In King's case, this meant taking the video, frame by frame and re-telling the story as one of 'black lawlessness' and the need to contain it (1993: 61). According to this version, the police officers were merely doing their job, subduing a 'hulking, ferocious criminal suspect' (cited in Feagin and Vera 1995: 95).

The latter point of view was one subscribed to by Stacey Koon, the officer in charge of the beating, who used the video to tell a different story. In his view,

> It was the first time the jury – or anyone else, other than the defence – had had an opportunity to see it in such detail as to prove Rodney King was always in control of the situation, not the officers. When viewed in detail, not casually in its edited form on the evening news, the tape also proved that Rodney King had deliberately assaulted Officer Powell, even while on the ground he was constantly rising, constantly threatening officers engaged in the legal performance of their duties. It would be our strongest argument.
>
> (Koon 1992: 182)

What was ultimately seen was not just a black man out of control but black sexuality out of control (*Los Angeles Times* 16 May 1992). In his book, Stacey Koon described King's movements in the following way: 'then he grabbed his butt with both hands and began to gyrate them in a sexually suggestive fashion'. Koon's sexualised descriptions of King's movements suggest that King's body was both an object of fascination as well as fear. Koon's next comment suggests that, in his view, King was not the only one out of control. A white female highway patrol officer also needed to be 'contained'.

> Melanie's Jane Wayne and Dirty Harriet hormones kicked in. She drew her pistol and advanced within five feet of the suspect . . . . As far as I was concerned, LAPD was in charge, not the CHIPS (California Highway Patrol) . . . that's when I got involved. I had to . . . I quickly formed a tactical plan.
>
> (1992: 33–4)

Fiske refers to this focus on King's body and sexuality as a process of 'Hortonisation', i.e. the recoding of the racial/sexual threats to white supremacy into the discourse of law and order (1994). Willie Horton became a household name in the 1988 presidential election campaign when his face appeared in Republican-sponsored adverts. Horton, who had been convicted for murder, was then convicted of rape which had taken place whilst on a furlough (weekend release) programme. His case was used to symbolise both the Democratic Party's softness on law and order and the sexual proclivities of African-American men set loose on society. In fact one Republican campaign letter sent to Maryland voters stated that people could expect a visit from Willie Horton if Dukakis were elected President (Feagin and Vera 1995: 116).

In the King case, the transformation of a story of police brutality into one of law and order was an important feature of the process of disaggregation. It turned a police beating into a potential threat to the rule of law. It thus helped to 'obscure the everyday character of racial power' (Crenshaw and Peller 1993: 62). That 'everyday racial power' has been borne out in the number of cases of malpractice brought against the LAPD. Complaints by African-Americans represented 41 per cent of all claims between 1987–90 despite only constituting just over 12 per cent of the population. Moreover, although very few complaints were upheld, African-Americans were less likely to succeed than whites (Feagin and Vera 1995: 90–91).

There is another aspect of the wider context which adds perspective to the police officers' acquittal. The year 1992, according to Gilmore, in both Europe and the US, witnessed the 'rehabilitation of the white male' from Columbus (through the quincentennial 'celebrations') to *JFK* (courtesy of Oliver Stone) (1993: 30). However, this rehabilitation required what Gilmore calls the odd ideological zap, 'a function of the I'm proud to be American rah-rah' (ibid.). Successive forays into Nicaragua, Grenada, Panama, and Iraq were examples of such nationalist zaps as well as reminders as to who was 'boss'. The actions of the police officers thus ultimately came to mean something similar to the jury: a chance to assert the power of whiteness made possible by the police's strategic role in the US state.

Cedric Robinson has taken a somewhat different view of the idea of white rehabilitation. He has viewed it more as a temporary blip, masking the long-term crisis of white male civilisation. He associated the latter with the late 1980s slump and the politics of the Reagan/Bush era which brought unparalleled deregulation as well as massive disparities in wealth. Between 1977 and 1989, the wealthiest 1 per cent benefited from 60 per cent of the growth in net income whilst the poorest 40 per cent suffered a real decline (1993: 75). Robinson pointed out that, under such circumstances, it was only a matter of time until the vast majority of the electorate began to 'wake up'. This arguably happened in the 1988 presidential election when Bush only gained a mandate of 30 per cent of the electorate (ibid.: 76). Strikes against external enemies certainly brought temporary respite but cost money and lives. Battles against the 'enemy within' served the same purpose in national terms, i.e. promoting white national identity, but had the relative advantage of being cheap and less costly in human terms.

The narratives of white masculine re-assertion were less likely to work on an African-American jury, which is why the decision to try the case in Simi Valley was crucial. The Simi Valley jury was almost entirely white and drawn from a predominantly white county, Ventura, renowned for the high percentage of current and retired police officers. They were more likely to accept a version of the incident which cast police officers as upholders of law and order at a more superficial level, and more invested in defending white interests against the racial and sexual threat of a black male at another, perhaps less conscious, one.

The successful (neo-conservative) re-coding of the incident into one of law and order served to frame interpretations of the events which followed the not-guilty verdicts handed down by the Simi Valley jury. As it transpired, the law and order discourse turned what might have been seen otherwise as a more rational uprising/insurrection into a riot. Moreover, the filming and subsequent transmission of the beating of a white truck driver, Reginald Denny, served to justify the King beating; 'black men' were out of control after all (Fiske 1994:149).[12] Pat Buchanann's version of the events broadcast on CNN took up the racial/sexual threat by describing them as 'an orgy of rioting, arson, murder and lynching' (cited in Fiske 1994: 148). Republicans like Dan Quayle and George Bush also emphasised the importance of family values in resisting the amorality of the rioters. Even liberal responses to the events tended to talk in a language which redirected 'white power from its centrality among the causes of the problem and relocate it as the key to the solution' (ibid.: 150). Elsewhere the media did make the connection between the beating and the not guilty verdict and the uprising. According to Feagin and Vera, 'across the country newspaper editorials reflected the national shock at the injustice of the Simi Valley jury verdicts' (1995: 99).

The Los Angeles uprisings of 1993 also provided one further opportunity for white liberal and conservative discourses to join forces against the threat of black on white violence. Sister Souljah's remarks, which were quoted in the *Washington Post* were an example of this. She was reported to say, 'I mean if black people kill black people every day, why not have a week and kill white people' (cited in Feagin and Vera 1995: 124). This comment was met with a barrage of liberal condemnation, notably from President Clinton, who equated Sister Souljah's remarks with those of the extreme right. He said, 'if you took the words white and black and you reversed them, you might think David Duke was giving that speech' (ibid.: 125). The limits of such versions of white liberalism were not lost on Sister Souljah, who suggested on NBC's *Today* programme that,

> Bill Clinton is like a lot of white politicians. They eat soul food, they party with black women, they play the saxophone, but when it comes to domestic and foreign policy, they make the same decisions that are destructive to African people in this country and throughout the world.
>
> (cited in ibid.: 128)

Waves of resistance: WBAI, Amnesty International and the NYPD

There are two aims in this final case study. The first is to highlight the role of community radio in taking up issues of criminal justice in general and secondly to look at one particular intervention, prompted by the publication of Amnesty International's investigation into police brutality in New York (1996). The radio station, WBAI (99.5FM), is based in New York City and was, in 1996, one of four listener-sponsored community radio stations under the licensing authority of the Pacifica Foundation. It was, therefore, not reliant on advertising and corporate sponsorship, which gave it a certain latitude. Its staff were predominantly, but not exclusively, African-American. Brother Shine, a producer, had this to say about sponsorship: 'we don't have any allegiance to any companies . . . we're not beholden to anyone . . . we can talk bad about GM , the medical system because we know they won't be taking away their money' (Brother Shine, interview, 31 July 1996).

Success was partly measured in terms of survival and WBAI has managed to secure continued funding through 'marathon' appeals. In January 1996, the station received over $1 million and over $700,000 in March 1996. 'Marathon' programmes were geared to popular listener interests and in this respect, alternative health programmes and those with a historical slant were particularly good fund-raisers. Above all, the success of the marathons had ensured the station's independence and limited the need to compromise. In the words of one of WBAI's presenters 'you can't play by the other party's rules and still smell like a rose' (interview, Utrice Leid, 31 July 1996). According to Utrice, who discovered the potential of radio whilst listening to the BBC as a child in Trinidad, the success of community radio depends on its ability to,

> make airwaves a tool or instrument of learning, an exchange of information. Information is power. The reverse is also true – a lack of it is powerlessness. In the US there is little distinction between the role of mainstream media and government. Both are involved in a conditioning process – what Chomsky calls the manufacture of consent. However, through the creative use of media (with a little humour thrown in too!),

149

people can begin to make sense of their environment and the forces culti-
vating that state of oppression. Radio can change things . . . of all the
media it is the most portable, the most democratic, the most interactive.

(interview, 31 July 1996)

In 1996, WBAI was in 'negotiations' with its parent body, Pacifica. At root the issue
for Pacifica is one of finance and their attempts to secure grants from foundations
such as Ford and the Pew Trust. It is at this level that corporate influence has been
felt and undoubtedly influenced the decision to cut ties with forty unpaid program-
mers at KPFA in Berkeley with the (no doubt intended) result that numerous
public affairs programmes were cancelled, including those concerned with Native
American struggles, prisons, gay rights, civil liberties and central America (*Stop
Pacifica's Turn to the Right, Save WBAI 99.5*, unpublished campaign leaflet, 1996).
The programmes were replaced by music shows, a trend repeated at other Pacifica
stations. By 1996, WPFW-FM in Washington, DC had an 80 per cent music
format and the decision had been taken at KPFT-FM in Houston to make it a
Texan-based music station (ibid.).

In 1996, however, WBAI was able to run a schedule which was predominantly
devoted to listener call-ins around topical debates, and current affairs. So, for
example, WBAI has been at the forefront of defending the rights of black people at
the hands of the criminal justice system. According to Brother Shine,

About a month ago our Sunday night programme, 'Emanations' began a
campaign for Zion Israel, a black prisoner on death row in Indiana. We
took that up, listeners protested to the prison governor but we lost. In the
end he was given a lethal injection. After that we continued with the
death penalty issue . . . you know we were the spearhead behind the
Mumia issue.[13] Most of the information about his case came from this
station . . . we were the only station to run his commentaries when other
public radio stations refused.

(interview, 31 July 1996)

The community which WBAI serves extends beyond African-Americans. Those
involved in the station see their role in terms of the formation of a wider community. According to Shine, this includes, 'people of colour, poor people. We're
talking about poor people whether they're white, brown or whatever they happen
to be – the ones who seem expendable' (ibid.).

WBAI seeks to provide information to extend the scope of debate and choice
and provide the basis for reaching conclusions and viewpoints outside the spectrum of mainstream opinion. According to Utrice Leid, presenter of the afternoon
Talkback programme 'we should not make choices but define the parameters within
which people can make informed choices' (interview, 31 July 1996). The issues
which set the agenda for each programme often emerge from listeners' comments
and the station's links with grass-roots organisations.

150

One strength of WBAI lay in its mobilising potential, not just in terms of getting people to telephone prison governors or demonstrate about the welfare bill outside city hall but in developing a political awareness which cut across colour and ethnicity. The station prioritises 'the issues of the poor' but in ways which have not excluded others from participating in its struggles. Somewhat perversely, its threatened status is a measure of its success in disrupting and seeking to displace dominant, liberal and conservative versions of whiteness with its own distinct political and cultural agenda.

One issue of recurrent concern to WBAI was racism in the NYPD, hence its interest in Amnesty International's report of 1996 which likened the oppressive atmosphere surrounding policing in New York to that found in a police state. Evidence for the report was collected over an eighteen-month period from over ninety individual cases of alleged brutality. It concluded that 'police brutality and unnecessary force is nevertheless a widespread problem . . . with minorities most at risk of being victims of excessive force' (1996: 13). The report pointed out that in exercising such brutal force, the NYPD was in breach of the United Nations Declaration of Human Rights, the UN Convention against Torture etc. and the International Covenant on Civil and Political Rights, the second and third of which had been ratified by the US (ibid.: 9). The report also noted that its findings were nothing new. Cases included Michael Stewart who died in police custody in 1983 after being arrested for spraying graffiti in the subway[14] and Eleanor Bumpers, an elderly mentally disturbed woman shot by armed police who broke into her apartment to evict her after she had got behind with her rent (ibid.: 6).

Fifteen of the victims investigated by Amnesty had died. These included Chinese, Puerto Rican, Latino, and African-American men and women. In another case, an African-American, off-duty, police officer, Desmond Robinson, was shot four times in the back in 1994 by a white police officer. According to witnesses the latter continued shooting after Robinson had fallen to the ground (ibid.: 52).[15] In many of the cases investigated by Amnesty International, bystanders who tried to intervene or take photographs at the scene of an arrest were themselves objects of police brutality. Three other findings are also worth noting. The work of the so-called 'independent' Civilian Complaint's Review Board, the body designated to monitor the NYPD, was found to be subject to police and political influence through its appointments procedure. Furthermore, the body had also experienced a lack of co-operation from the police department. Amnesty International referred to a number of occasions in the course of its investigation when the police department were unwilling to provide information either on individual cases or aggregate data. Finally, research revealed a common pattern of police response to allegations of brutality which entailed charging victims with assault in order to justify brutality and deflect attention away from police officers themselves. This tactic appeared successful, since very few officers were subsequently convicted. Many, on the contrary, were promoted.

On 26 June 1966, Amnesty held a press conference in New York to coincide with the publication of their report. Pacifica's *Democracy Now*, which WBAI transmitted daily in 1996, devoted one of its programmes to Amnesty's report (27 June 1996). The researchers, who were part of a panel of guests, emphasised the long-standing and persistent problem of police brutality in New York and that the most serious complaints involved minorities, particularly African-Americans and Latinos. They also pointed out the discrepancy between police guidelines which state that force should only be used in life-threatening situations and the cases cited where alleged offences were trivial, the victims were unarmed and posing no threat.

The programme documented individual cases and gave voice to the families of victims of police brutality. For example, Anibal Carasquillo was shot in the back by police officers in January 1995. His mother, who attended Amnesty's press conference, said, 'this kind of killing is happening every month and they're getting away with it'. In another case, Anthony Biaz was kicking a football around in his neighbourhood when the ball accidentally hit two cars. Police officers intervened and set about beating him as a result of which he died shortly after arriving in the hospital. In all but two of the cases the victims were unarmed. Other victims were shot in the back with police claiming suspects were 'reaching for something' although in all cases the victims turned out to be unarmed. Finally, panellists referred to 'the blue wall of silence' in which police officers refused to testify against each other or to provide statistical evidence on arrests or deaths in custody etc. and pressed charges of resisting arrest against victims as a way of justifying police brutality, only to drop the charges later for lack of evidence.[16]

The presence of community activists on the panel enabled the discussion to relate research to community mobilisation and to legitimate such action. It helped to publicise organisations like Parents Against Police Brutality and the National Congress for Puerto Rican Rights and to add pressure for a genuinely independent community complaints board as well as for local congressional hearings. Finally, it pointed to trends of escalating numbers of cases and costs to the city taxpayer. There were fifty-four deaths in police custody in the period 1990–94 and the figure was rising in 1996. In 1994, $24 million was paid in settlements against police brutality, a figure which was also rising in 1996.

Aside from Amy Goodman's radio programme, *Democracy Now*, media and police reaction was deafeningly silent.[17] On the contrary, the NYPD tried to preempt publicity surrounding the report by publicising its own city code, ironically titled, 'Courtesy, Professionalism and Respect for Public'. WBAI, itself, gave detailed coverage to the report as well as publicising 'The Coalition for Community Empowerment', a local campaign which had organised a public hearing in Brooklyn, with the intention to probe recent cases involving the police killings of two young African-Americans. In one case the victim had eighteen bullet wounds and in the other the victim had a bullet removed from his back suggesting police interference with evidence. In addition to these cases it was hoped to question the Justice Department of the Civil Rights Department over its follow-up action in the case of Sergeant Mark Fuhrman, the white officer in the O.J. Simpson case. A black activist, interviewed on WBAI, hoped that an independent office would be set up to deal with complaints against the police and that police would be recruited from those who lived in the neighbourhood. He made the point that such killings did not happen in white areas. 'White communities', he stated, 'don't have a record of police brutality' (WBAI *Wake Up Call*, 30 July 1996).

Conclusions

This chapter has been concerned with the role of policing in the construction and consolidation of white identities. This has been evident at a number of levels. Firstly, research studies of the 'canteen culture' in the US and England, have confirmed the importance of racialised discourse in the socialisation of the ethic of white masculinity. This was found throughout the police, amongst trainees, junior officers and even at senior levels. Humour has proved a particularly effective sealant in the construction of whiteness, as revealed in Smith and Gray's observational study in London and Bernard Manning's performance to members of the Greater Manchester Police force. Secondly, whiteness has not only been expressed in jokes, banter and abusive comments, but also in policing practices as indicated in the 'stop and search' figures in England and the numbers of deaths in police custody in both the US and Britain.

The role of policing, I have argued has been inseparable from that of the media. The latter have responded in diverse ways to the policing patterns and practices discussed above; invariably, although not always, in ways which have sanctioned dominant white norms. In the case of 'mugging' the press played on 'folk ideologies' both to reinforce narratives of black lawlessness and to sanction heavy-handed policing and tough sentencing policies. The Rodney King incident illustrated the limitations of alternative media, an amateur video, when matched against those dominant ideologies circulating on both media and everyday culture. George Holliday's video, which was beamed around the world, appeared to provide undeniable proof of police racism. Yet when put into the context of folk ideologies of 'black beasts', 'rapists' etc., disaggregated into a succession of stills through freeze framing and narrated to an all-white jury in Simi Valley, the video became something else; the legitimate containment of an out-of-control black man. The folk ideology of the rapist also underpinned police officer Koon's anxieties and fantasies in his interpretation of the actions of the police at the scene of the beating. The 'LA riots' which followed in the wake of the verdict merely served to both confirm and feed white paranoias and sanction the upward spiral of authoritarian policing.

The emphasis on policing and media reactions with respect to particular groups, e.g. African-Americans, should not be to the exclusion of other ethnic groups which have also been the object of racialised policing. Nor should it be forgotten that the policing of the working classes has remained a priority throughout the history of policing, although increasingly eclipsed from the public domain with the rise of nationalism and the use of policing to construct a cross-class, white national identity. In nineteenth- and twentieth-century England, this latter strategy has also entailed the racialisation of subaltern white ethnicities, for example Irish, Chinese and Jewish immigrants. Whilst media, political and academic discourses have highlighted the policing of black communities since the 1950s, anti-Irish policing has continued in Britain with the strategic use of the Prevention of Terrorism and Police and Criminal Evidence laws. Overall, history has witnessed a succession of racialised out-groups which have been targeted in defence of an in-group whose ethnicity and racialised status has remained hidden.

The history of policing has provided a fascinating example of the intertwined histories of both England and the US. On the one hand, England was implicated in both the establishment of informal policing methods under slavery as well as providing the model for police forces established across US cities in the nineteenth century. On the other hand, in the contemporary era, England, in turn, has 'borrowed' a racialised language (e.g. mugging), equipment (e.g. long batons, CS gas), models of community policing and more generally, folk ideologies (e.g. the threat of 'race riots') to frame many of its inner-city, social and penal policies. Increasingly both countries are subject to global pressure, as witnessed in Amnesty International reports on human rights violations perpetrated by the police in both the US and England, which in turn have been taken up by local media and pressure groups in their campaign activities.

At a local level, numerous initiatives have been formed to counter the worst excesses of police racism and to promote new community alliances which have cut across ethnic ties and have sought to dismantle a powerful bloc of white interests which spans much of the mainstream media, political and police establishments. In the case of both Newham Monitoring Project and WBAI radio in New York, pressure was exerted using a variety of media, including local radio, the Internet, leafleting and pamphleteering. The strategic use of the media has been developed in conjunction with more traditional forms of protests, including pickets, marches and public hearings, which built support from sections of the community hitherto on the margins of local politics.

6

THE FRINGE AND THE FABRIC: THE POLITICS OF WHITE PRIDE

Studies of 'far right' organisations have inevitably focused on their political successes and failures and yet the prior task of establishing what it means to be 'on the far right' is not as easy as it might appear. Academics, in particular, have struggled to establish universal, clear-cut criteria for using 'extreme' and 'far' right, for the simple reason that what may be considered 'extreme' in one historical and spatial setting may not be in another. The need for definitions which are contingent and provisional notwithstanding, I have used the terms 'far' or 'extreme' right below to refer to those groups and ideologies which have made the defence of whiteness an integral *and explicit* part of their political agendas. Even this is difficult to sustain, since the relationship between what I refer to as 'white pride' and mainstream political discourse has already shown signs of disruption.

This last point touches on an important theme running through this chapter: the relationship between 'white pride' and more coded expressions of whiteness and the continuities between the fringes and the fabric of political culture. I begin with the specific aim of exploring the peculiarities of whiteness in both the US and England and the role of history in shaping particular expressions and formations of 'white pride' identities. Such histories have been complex and uneven, with some distinctive marks and moments in each of the two countries: Christianity, Vietnam, and gun culture in the US; immigration and skinhead culture in England.

In this chapter, mainstream media representations of 'white pride' culture and politics form the basis of two case studies. The first takes English press coverage of a Dublin 'football riot' instigated by British neo-fascists, as its focus. Images and reports of the violence and the 'official' response to the events, worked at a number of levels: satisfying a detached curiosity with the lifestyles of 'the violent', exploiting national myths and stereotypes about the Irish and distinguishing acceptable from illegitimate versions of white English masculinity. An interesting feature of the coverage of the riot was its adeptness in concealing the ideological links between the rioters' rationale for violence and widespread assumptions regarding political conflict in Ireland. The second case study examines the role of the media in the politics of David Duke and the National Association for the Advancement of White People in the US. An important aspect of the local

Louisiana media was its attempts to 'normalise' Duke's politics and to suppress his extremist background in favour of his cultivated celebrity status. Oppositional campaigns against David Duke used the media strategically in an effort to isolate 'white pride' from mainstream politics and culture. Such tactics eventually paid off in the sense of stalling, if not ending, Duke's own political career. What the campaign was less able to prevent was the re-appearance of many of Duke's ideas in more respectable political contexts. 'White pride' may have been marginalised, but normative whiteness was able to adopt many of its assumptions without being tainted by its Nazi associations. The activities of the Southern Poverty Law Centre in countering both explicit and implicit white pride discourse will be the basis of a third case study.

'National' or 'local' specificities such as those explored in the histories and case studies in this chapter have increasingly been re-configured by new, global conditions, typified by the rapid expansion of telecommunications and information technology. In the case of 'white pride' identities, the Internet and music have provided opportunities for the formation of new global alignments around whiteness which have encouraged interchange and convergence between the US, England and the rest of Europe. Such developments suggest that the very global processes which might have undermined racialised identities within a national context, have served to re-configure them on a global scale. A discussion of these developments will form the basis of the concluding section of this chapter.

Continuities and 'local' peculiarities in far right-wing politics in England and the US

Immigration politics and the far right in England

Analyses of the 'far right' in the period since 1945 have drawn heavily on Marxist theories of fascism.[1] In broad terms and internal differences aside, Marxist writers have identified a number of conditions, seen as 'ripe' for fascism. These are: economic restructuring, e.g. the growth of monopoly capital; the failure of dominant political forces to represent expanding economic sectors; the capacity of fascist ideology to incorporate elements which cut across class divisions, and the blinkeredness of socialist discourses, including their inability to go beyond a narrow economistic agenda (see e.g. Poulantzas 1974; Laclau 1977). Correspondingly, the analysis of post-war Europe has linked the revival of fascism to a down-turn in the economy, insecurity of employment and/or economic restructuring, including the growth of multinationals and international agencies like the World Bank and the IMF, and the resultant social dislocation which has provided the backdrop to the mobilisation of political forces. Politically, fascism has been seen to fill an ideological vacuum on the right created when mainstream parties inhabit a middle-ground consensus. It has also thrived on anti-progressive backlashes, crises of national identity prompted by political upheaval (e.g. the collapse of the Soviet threat), migration and the emergence of transnational political blocs of which the European Union and the North American Free Trade Association have been two good examples.

A second set of theoretical accounts of the far right have been rooted in psychological factors, drawing on both the psychoanalytic ideas of Eric Fromm and the Frankfurt School, particularly Adorno's empirical study of the 'authoritarian personality'. Psychology, like Marxian political economy, is a diverse field, but running through its accounts of fascism and the far right has been the key concept of alienation, a condition brought about by the conditions described above, i.e. modernisation and the consequent loss of security and communal ties. Such changes have prompted the simultaneous need for a higher authority (masochism) and the need to direct aggression at marginal groups (sadism). Many of these theories and those that have followed have worked, both implicitly and explicitly, with the idea of a scapegoat, a construct which has allegedly enabled people to compensate for their own weakness or powerlessness by attributing weakness and inferiority to others.

This last point highlights the first of a number of objections which could be raised with respect to these psychological theories. The traditional scapegoat at the heart of their theories of authoritarianism, i.e. the Jew, far from weak and powerless was perceived as all-powerful in fascist accounts. Moreover, the theories have invariably been applied equally to both leaders and masses, when in fact authoritarian leadership and mass compliancy arguably merit distinct psychological explanations and processes. Thirdly, a number of these theories also focus on individual psyches at the expense of wider political, economic and cultural factors, although psychological theories do not themselves necessarily preclude the latter. For instance, Adorno, whilst acknowledging the significance of the parent–child focus in his account of the formation of an authoritarian personality, also admitted that those family relationships were themselves determined by social and economic processes (1950: 972).

One final, yet politically apposite, critique of this tradition emerged in the US in the anti-left witch-hunt era of McCarthyism. Adorno and others were criticised for concentrating on right-wing extremism and not linking it to extremism on the left (cited in Billig 1978: 50). The real distinction according to authors like Roekeach was between rational, open-minded liberalism and closed-minded dogmatism, whether the latter was from the left or right (ibid.: 50–51). This attempt to collapse left- and right-wing extremism has proved a very powerful discursive tool in critiques of political correctness, antiracism, and left-wing politics generally. It has served to hide the dogmatism of its liberalism, the particularism of its notion of universalism and the monoculturalism implicit in its 'open-mindedness'. As I argued in Chapter 3, an integral part of the discourse of whiteness has been its capacity to render extreme those attempts to dismantle it.

The far right in Britain, unlike a number of its European counterparts, has achieved only limited success, some would say failure, if measured by membership numbers and/or votes cast in support and elections won. Its success has been more in terms of shaping values than winning seats. The three most successful far right parties in the twentieth century have been Oswold Mosley's British Union of Fascists in the 1930s, the National Front in the late 1960s and 1970s and the British National Party in the 1990s. The National Front's best local result was in 1976 when it polled 27.5 per cent of the vote in Sandwell, in the West Midlands (Taylor 1982: 46).

According to research carried out by Chris Husbands, NF voters are typically white, unqualified, males often in marginal self-employment, but by no means predominantly young or necessarily from authoritarian working-class backgrounds as previous research had found (Eatwell 1992: 182–3).[2] Locally, far right-wing political parties have done best where post-1945 economic expansion was subsequently followed by industrial collapse in the 1970s (ibid.: 183). This evidence notwithstanding, there have always been deviant areas of far right support that do not conform to these characteristics, e.g. Blackpool (ibid.: 183). Moreover, there has been some dispute as to whether the far right has done better in areas with a high immigrant or black presence or whether it is more the threat of such a presence that inspires allegiance. Voting patterns have tended to confirm the former point of view. On the other hand, the media's role in mobilising fears of an invasion are evident in the peaks of National Front support which coincided with intensive tabloid coverage of the immigration of expelled Ugandan Asians (1972–3) and Malawian Asians (1976–7). In the case of the latter, President Banda's policy of Africanisation led to the immigration of less than a hundred south Asians, mainly from Goa, India (Taylor 1982: 45). Despite the numbers involved, the tabloid press greeted their arrival with the headlines, NEW FLOOD OF ASIANS INTO BRITAIN (*Daily Mirror*, 6 May 1976) and SCANDAL OF £600 A WEEK ASIANS (*Sun*, 4 May 1976). The following May the National Front gained some of its best election results in the local elections, including the Sandwell result referred to above.

The British National Party was formed by John Tyndall in 1981 two years after he left the National Front. In the 1983 General Election, the BNP support peaked in Walsall south in the West Midlands with a vote of 1.3 per cent. In 1992 they gained over 3 per cent in two east London constituencies and won their first victory in a by-election in Millwall, in east London in September 1993. In May 1994, the BNP took 33 per cent of the vote in the local council elections in the Beckton ward of Canning Town in Newham, East London, a predominantly white district. In line with the above explanations, the district was a once thriving area which has suffered from industrial decline since the late 1960s and, at the same time, it bordered on wards where there was a much higher black population. But what is also important to note is the longer-term history of racialised politics in the area and the role of the media and liberal establishment in legitimating whiteness (see Chapter 5).

'White pride' has a long history in east London. The BNP inherited a legacy bequeathed by Mosley's brownshirts and the National Front, both of whom were active in the East End. The BNP's national organiser, Richard Edmonds has said of his Party, 'we are 100 per cent racist, yes' (cited in Newham Monitoring Project

1995: 6). The Party has thus campaigned on a 'rights for whites' platform and mobilised support around individual 'cause célèbres'. One such case was that of John Stoner who was stabbed by Bengali pupils at a school in the Newham borough of London in 1990 after weeks of tension between rival gangs of white and Asian youths. The BNP leafleted in support of John Stoner and a march was organised by local whites who were ostensibly concerned about their children's safety. The racialised fears of local white parents were endorsed by the local bishop and by the views expressed in the local press. The march was dominated by slogans like 'Rights for Whites' and 'Pakis Out' and John Stoner's foster grandfather was quoted as saying that Asians 'take our businesses. They take the heart out of this place' (ibid.: 11). The speed and intensity of the media response and the legitimisation of the white community's response to the assault of a young white man stood in marked contrast to the silence which greet the vast majority of racial attacks, both in Newham and nationally.[3]

The significance of the National Front in the 1970s has been summed up by Stan Taylor in a way which could apply to the BNP in the 1990s. The NF provided an outlet for white hostility to blacks and black immigration 'during a period in which the established parties, particularly the Conservatives, were seen by some voters as having abandoned the "interests" of whites' (1982: 173). Immigration control has thus been cited as one, if not the, common thread running through far right ideology in both England and, not unexpectedly given continental-wide political developments, in Europe since 1945 (Hainsworth 1992: 7). According to Geoffrey Harris, political and economic factors apart, what has made success possible has been the chance to become respectable (1990). Immigration provided one such opportunity in Britain (see Chapter 4) as it did elsewhere in Europe, for example Le Pen's FN party in France which also campaigned under the slogan '2 million unemployed means 2 million immigrants too many' (ibid.: 21). Immigration was not a new issue, as I have argued, but in the 1980s and 1990s the political climate across Europe was particularly receptive, thanks to demographic trends, population changes and the economic trends cited above (ibid.: 26). These conditions, widespread across Europe, have in turn provided the basis for European-wide alliances and the idea of a European brotherhood 'against both communism and decadent democracy' (ibid.: 29). In 1986, the far right organ, *Scorpion*, urged its readers to think European which would be 'based on the notion of identity and opposition to what is non-European' (ibid.: 18–19). The symbol of the Celtic cross, which was found on walls, banners and in publications of the far right across Europe in the mid-1990s, provided further evidence of such an alliance (ibid.: 28).

However, since most mainstream parties from centre left to right have advocated immigration control and passed legislation limiting immigration, the tactic of the 'far right' has been to connect it to other issues, for example anti-Semitism, anti-communism and national-populism (ibid.). Its anti-abortion stance too, was not so much rooted in pro-life but in the call to whites to reproduce and maintain their dominance (Taylor 1982: 161). The significance attached to different issues has varied over time and from place to place. In the case of national populism, the target constituency has been a disaffected working class, lacking support structures like churches, community networks and trade unions who would be responsive to political appeals which have gone over the heads of governments to the people. Of course, the tactic has not always worked and this begins to explain the limited success of the far right in England, at least in electoral terms. Its failure has had to do with the relationship between the far right and mainstream politics in both England and, I shall argue, the US. What is particularly notable here is the incorporation of what were, at one time, thought fringe, if not lunatic, values, into the fabric of mainstream society's culture.[4] In the case of the UK, David Edgar has argued that the demise and break-up of the National Front was in large part due to the rise of Thatcherism, which used the same populist rhetoric about immigration but without the taint of Nazism (1977). Conversely, it can be argued that many of today's lunatic ideas were once yesterday's common sense. In cyclical terms therefore, the lineages of present-day mainstream political culture may be traced to what were once extremist outpourings, which in turn can be traced historically to the highly legitimated institutional foundations of modernity.

Aside from the appropriation of far right ideas by the mainstream, the limited success of the British far right has also been attributed to the success of anti-fascist politics. The latter were able to forge connections, personal, ideological and political, between the far right and Nazism and fascism. In making these links and highlighting the far right's themes of intolerance and self-congratulatory racism, anti-fascist politics have put forward a construction of the far right which is sharply at odds with the outward displays of civility/decency and political democracy associated with Britishness/Englishness. The success of 'Rock against Racism' in the 1970s and the Anti-Nazi League in the 1970s (Gilroy 1987) and again in the late 1980s and 1990s, as well as the mobilisations against fascism in areas like the West Midlands and East London have all played a part in limiting the electoral impact of the far right. The innovative campaigns of organisations like Newham Monitoring Project are also illustrative of this strategy. In the 1990s popular anti-fascist campaigns have included the 'Kick Fascism out of West Ham Campaign' in 1995–6 (NMP 1995, 1996) and the 'Vote for Equality not Hatred Campaign' in 1995 in which celebrities (including some from the television soap EastEnders, former boxing champion Terry Marsh and the Bishop of Barking) were invited to public events (NMP 1995). However, the fact that the far right's articulations of whiteness have been coded, re-packaged and sold under a different party's banner have secured its continuing impact on mainstream culture.[5] Regrettably, as the individuals and parties of the far right have been marginalised, many of their ideas have found a niche within the platforms of respectable political parties.

Guns and God in the USA

In his account of the rise of the 'warrior cult' in the US, James Gibson has assessed the impact of the military defeat in Vietnam in the following terms:

whether they fought in the war or not, these men drew the same conclusion from the defeat of the United States in Vietnam as did a certain part
of the mass media: the white man's world was gone; dark forces of chaos
had been unleashed and dangerous times made it not only permissible
but morally imperative for them to take their personal battles far beyond
the law. Paramilitary mythology offered men the fantastic possibility of
escaping their present lives, being reborn as warriors, and then re-making
the world.

(Gibson 1994: 196)

The racist right attracted the 'cult warrior' for a number of substantive, ideological
reasons. Both racists and warriors, were, for example, fervently anti-communist.
The murder of five members of the Communist Workers Party at an anti-KKK
demonstration in Greensboro, North Carolina in 1979 helped cement the bond,
although anti-communism had always been integral to the far right's penchant for
conspiracy theories. Furthermore, both were disaffected with federal government,
an antipathy brought home to many veterans in the conviction of William Calley
for the murder of 400 Vietnamese civilians at My Lai. Lastly, and by no means
least, was the degree of convergence between religion and the far right around a
vision of a millennial, apocalyptic battleground. This is best illustrated in William
Pierce's novel *The Turner Diaries* and its take-up by the Christian Identity
Movement. In the novel, the white underground, called the Organization, many of
whom are Vietnam veterans, fight back against the forces of ZOG (Zionist
Occupation Government) who are intent on mass 'miscegenation'. White liberals
are hung from street lamps bearing signs that say, 'I betrayed my race', whilst white
women known to have slept with black men are likewise hung with signs that say, 'I
defiled my race'. Jews are shot and African-Americans, Latinos and Asians are
exiled. The novel is set a hundred years in the future, when the Turner diaries are
found. The diaries record events in the 1990s and to readers in 1980 they seemed
to prophesy an imminent 'race' war. The 'cult warrior' thus had his battleground
marked out and pre-figured by the religious right.

With some notable exceptions, the media has received scant attention in what is
a growing and fascinating literature on the far right in the US. One such exception
has been Sara Diamond's account of the Christian Right in the US (1989). She
traced the media's role in promoting the religious right, beginning with the media
ministries of Father Charles Coughlin in the 1930s and 1940s, renowned for their
anti-Semitic and pro-Nazi sympathies (1989: 3). In the six years after Jerry Falwell
began the Moral Majority in 1979 the percentage of all local radio stations affiliated to evangelical or fundamentalist Christianity had risen to over 10 per cent
(Singular 1987: 89). In addition, in the 1980s, over 20 per cent (i.e. 16.3 million) of
all households with televisions in the US tuned into TV evangelist Pat Robertson
every month, 9.3 million to Jimmy Swaggart, 7.6 million to Robert Schuller and
5.6 million to Jim Bakker/Oral Roberts. In 1985 Pat Robertson's CBN collected
$230 million and was broadcast on nearly 200 stations and syndicated to about

sixty countries (ibid.: 13). It provided the 'most valuable and consistent forum for new right figures' (ibid.: 13) during the 1980s. Techniques used by Robertson to encourage the 'right' audience response included presenting 'debates' between two almost identical sides and using loaded terminology, outrageous statements attributed to unknown sources and shocking background footage over which ran a commentary about the enemy (e.g. the Sandinistas in Nicaragua who were a popular target of anti-communist propaganda) (ibid.: 15). According to the admittedly 'predisposed' Christian Broadcasting network, 50 per cent of all households with televisions watched at least one such programme very month (ibid.).

In his fascinating account of the Christian Patriots in Idaho, the 'Mecca' for evangelical groups in the 1980s,[6] James Aho explained the make-up and emergence of 'Christian patriotism'. Amongst the 'Patriots', there were 'Constitutionalists' and 'Identity Christians'. The former were so-called because of their preoccupation with the 'organic constitution', made up of the Constitution, the Bill of Rights and the Pentateuch, that is the first five books of the Bible. Their selective readings of all three enabled them to appeal, on occasions, to a higher law than the Constitution and to a morality which did not necessarily coincide with the law. The Constitution, in their view, did not confer rights. Its role was to protect those rights acquired at birth (Aho 1990: 48). Such arguments have provided a rationale for attacks on the federal government and its institutions (for example, the Bureau of Alcohol, Tobacco and Firearms) and has led some 'Constitutionalists' to bring charges against those agencies, notably the police, when they have tried to infringe their right to protection from self-incrimination! (ibid.: 45). The ideas of the Constitutionalists have been taken up by a number of far right factions, including the Posse Comitatus. If these ideas sound familiar it could be because they echo those of Philip Howard and a seemingly more respectable group of thinkers discussed in Chapter 3.

Identity Christians, aptly named in an age of identity politics, trace their ideology back to its allegedly Anglo-Saxon origins. Barkun viewed them as a millennial cult who vacillated between revolutionary confrontation and withdrawal (1994). Of particular historical significance for this 'Christian cult' was the supposed migration of the tribe of Joseph over the Caucus mountains. Their supposed 'British' origins, known as British Israelism, not surprisingly, have been downplayed in the US since the demise of the British Empire.[7] Consequently, the idea was promulgated that Joseph's sceptre had been transferred to the US, thus enabling Identity Christians to re-iterate the biblical references to global colonisation by God's chosen seed without reference to a fallen (British) empire (Aho 1990: 53).

The beliefs of 'Identity Christians' have informed numerous sects and factions, including the Aryan Nation's Church. In the 1970s, the Aryan Nation's Church began a series of annual congresses in Idaho at which they ran survivalist workshops and organised target practice using cut-out silhouettes wearing the Star of David (ibid.: 59). They attracted disaffected war veterans, some of those responsible for the attempt to bomb a rally at the Hollywood Palladium to which Martin Luther King, Jr had been invited to speak. They also drew in members of Posse

Comitatus in Norman crusader battledress and ex-convicts, whose presence was the direct result of an active prison recruitment drive by the Church. An important theme underpinning these congresses was a version of Pierce's impending racial war, the outcome of which was to have been the realisation of America's covenant with the Lord, the repulsion of Satan and the creation of an Aryan homeland. The church had already earmarked five states for this purpose: Oregon, Montana, Wyoming, Washington and, of course, Idaho (ibid.).

Frustrated members of the Aryan Nation left the organisation to join numerous rival groups, off-shoots and splinter groups, including White American Resistance (WAR), The Order, Odinists[8] and finally 'The Group' or 'The Company' formed at the Aryan Nation's headquarters, which sought to re-enact Pierce's Diaries. Its attempts to do so culminated in the murder of radio personality Alan Berg and the conviction and imprisonment of a number of its members for this crime. Alan Berg, a talk radio host for KOA in Denver provoked his Christian audiences with mention of the joys of oral sex, the white man's fears/white woman's fantasies of black men and, to top it all, contradictions in the Christian message (Singular 1987: 15). Berg was shot dead in his drive as he was about to get out of his car after work. The significance of white consciousness in the politics of those responsible for Berg's murder was illustrated in a description of one of those convicted. David Lane was described by a friend in the following way: '(David believed) white people need to love themselves more. They're lost. They need to learn they have a soul . . . to have a spiritual pride in themselves, to see what a beautiful thing it is to be white' (cited in ibid.: 107).

It is interesting to reflect on the waning popularity of the Christian right since its heyday in the 1980s. According to one gallup poll, people put fundamentalist Christians high on their list of least desirable neighbours. According to one report, groups like the Christian Coalition formed in 1989, were having to articulate their demands in ways which would appeal to non-fundamentalists in order to maintain their political and electoral influence in the mid 1990s. One consequence of this shift, and one by no means limited to this particular extremist coalition, was the loss of some of its hard core members, who were not prepared to make the necessary compromises or to speak in more coded terms.

Some of those hard core members have formed part of the now infamous religious and militia cults of the 1990s which have been shaped ideologically by a complex synthesis of their militaristic and Christian fundamentalist backgrounds. In 1995, groups of this type were reported to exist in forty states across the US (*Observer*, 23 April 1995). They shared, in common with their Idaho 'compatriots', a preoccupation with survivalist training, opposition to gun control bordering on the fanatical and an intense dislike of federal government. Conspiracy explanations have thrived on efforts to connect such events as the deaths of Branch Davidians, including their leader David Koresh, at Waco in April 1993, and a murderous federal government. The extent of the ire that the Federal Bureau of Alcohol, Tobacco and Firearms' raid on the Waco complex had provoked was manifest in the April 1995 bombing of the federal building in Oklahoma. The bombing had coincided with the anniversary of the raid on Waco and it targeted a building housing offices of the Bureau of Alcohol, Tobacco and Firearms. In 1997, Gulf War veteran and militia member, Timothy McVeigh was convicted of the bombing and sentenced to death. At the time of writing his co-conspirators were still awaiting a trial.

Both David Koresh and the militia movement also clearly shared survivalist strategies in common and a commitment to the creation of a community outside of the jurisdiction of federal law. The bombing of April 1995 spotlighted the extent of right-wing militia groups and the zealotry of their members.[9] It also confirmed the ideological continuities between more respectable versions of Christian fundamentalism and the far right. The successful inroads of the far right into the political mainstream have, in no small part, been due to the right's effective exploitation of the media and the propagandising of its religious message. I will examine the role of the media more specifically now with reference to two case studies, the Dublin football riot of 1995 and the campaigns surrounding David Duke's efforts to win political office in the US in the late 1980s and early 1990s.

English football hooligans, fascists, and the media

On 15 February 1995, the National Socialist Alliance, an umbrella organisation for neo-Nazi groups, including Combat 18 and Blood and Honour, planned and instigated a riot at an international football match between Ireland and England, held in Dublin. Combat 18 was formed in 1993 as a result of a split with the British National Party. They dismissed the latter's electoral strategy and preferred instead to return to the streets and football terraces from which the BNP and NF attracted young recruits in the 1970s and 1980s. Combat 18 took the number '18' from Adolph Hitler's initials which were the first and eighth letters of the alphabet. In 1995 its membership numbered about one hundred and fifty, according to the *Sunday Telegraph* (19 February 1995). Moreover, all its leaders were, at one time, known members of northern Ireland's Protestant terror organisation, the Ulster Defence Association ('The Terror Squad', *World In Action*, Granada Television, 19 April 1993). Since the organisation includes members first recruited in the 1970s, it has an 'older' membership than its 'teenage skinhead' image suggests. The activities of C18 have been well documented in *Searchlight*, a journal which documents the activities of the far right[10], including evidence of numerous racial attacks, its sectarian clashes with the BNP, its support for the Loyalist movement in northern Ireland and its links with the three young Britons who killed themselves in a triple suicide pact in the US.[11]

According to the Finlay enquiry into the events in Dublin, fifty to eighty English 'hooligans' were directly responsible for the riots, with a total of 200 taking part. Forty people were arrested and twenty injured (*Daily Telegraph*, 5 April 1995). The riots were not just 'media events' *per se* but were important cultural sites for the expression of 'far right' politics. As regards the latter, the match was both an 'away match' (i.e. away from England) and a 'home' match for members of Combat 18 in the sense that, given its history, any football ground was 'home territory'. The idea of 'home' and 'away' thus prompts us to think about 'locality' in terms of culturally and not just geographically, defined spaces. But there is a further dimension to the idea of 'locality', which in this case has to do with the far right's alliances with Protestant para-militarism in Ireland. In a wider political context, the fixture enabled Combat 18 to express both its English nationalism and its antipathy to the Irish Republican (anti-colonial) movement against a back-drop of the then cease-fire in northern Ireland and the Conservative Government's willingness to negotiate with Sinn Fein, the political wing of the IRA. In predictably opportunistic terms, the far right thus aimed to fill the vacuum created by the Government's, admittedly gestural, attempts at consensus politics.

In media terms what was interesting about the Dublin riots was how interpretation of the events drew on three racialised themes. Firstly, in ways which resonated with coverage of the 'riots' in English cities in the 1980s, the media could not decide whether what took place in the football ground in Landsdowne Road, Dublin, were the spontaneous acts of mindless hooligans or the result of a deliberate and planned act of right-wing political extremism. Whilst the mainstream press acknowledged the role of right-wing groups in the riot, ultimately most columnists were reluctant to attribute too much rationality to the rioters for fear of contradicting the 'mindless criminality' explanation which predominated or to probe the rioters' motivations too far for fear of making uncomfortable connections with more widely held views and understandings. Initially, therefore, *The Sunday Times* ran a full-length feature in which it told the story of a sophisticated operation carried out by the Football Intelligence Unit, Special Branch and the International Crime Branch of Scotland Yard which, together, had collected data on Combat 18. The Unit had gathered information from the Internet and had raided the homes of the group's members finding bomb-making handbooks and racist magazines calling for the deaths of gays and Jews and a thousand CDs of Nazi propaganda (*Searchlight*, 247, January 1996: 3). Security forces also uncovered plans of other 'firms' (a term used by football gangs to describe themselves) to meet up in Dublin.

The tabloids, too, were generally quick to attribute the violence to right-wing extremism. The *Daily Mail*, for example, the day after the match, reported 'National Front thugs and Hitler movement behind violence' (16 February 1995) and went on to talk about 'Charter (sic) 18's' connections with disturbances at the Chelsea and Millwall football grounds. Similarly, the *Daily Mirror* referred to 'right-wing thugs' and reported that the Dublin 'match was abandoned after a mob of fifty skinheads giving Nazi salutes, screaming anti-IRA slogans and carrying union jacks daubed with "NF" hurled missiles down on fans and their children sitting below them' (16 February 1995).

However, sections of the media presented the rioters as mindless as well as mindful; wantonly violent as well as cunningly conspiratorial. Television documentaries and liberal Sunday supplements had a particular penchant for such stories. For example the *Independent on Sunday* ran a piece on Millwall supporters at the Dublin riot who were identified by their Union Jack/Millwall FC banner. In one incident during the match a piece of concrete was thrown at the Millwall fans. The rioter who was hit described what happened, 'The next thing . . . I was waking up on the ground with my hand on my head and blood pissing through my fingers. Later on my mate said I'd been hit by a piece of concrete about a foot square' (*Independent on Sunday*, 19 February 1995).

Such articles allow their predominantly professional readers to get a taste of a lifestyle far removed from the outward civility and containment of their own. Their attraction undoubtedly lay partly in the ambivalent feelings of pleasure and repulsion they elicited or, to put it another way, a chance to taste the thrills without the spills.

Overall, however, the politics of those responsible for the riot was downplayed in order to emphasise their mindless violence. The passing references to Nazi symbolism and anti-IRA slogans glossed over the ability of the rioters to plan and execute the violence despite the best efforts of the Football Intelligence Unit, Scotland Yard and the local Irish police. Neither did the press probe too deeply into the motivations of the protesters, again because to do so would detract from the alleged irrationality of their actions and because such motives might just coincide with the views of many of their readers. The difficulties here can be illustrated with reference to a reported quote from one of the rioters, who asserted that 'the Irish need to be taught a lesson for all the IRA bombings. The buzz of giving them a kicking they'll never forget was all I wanted' (*Sun*, 17 February 1996). The potential problem with this quote is that for a lot of *Sun* readers the idea of giving the Irish a good kicking might not have been such a bad one, but it was one at odds with the punishments advocated by *Sun* readers for the Dublin rioters, which included castration and horsewhipping in front of a full crowd at Wembley. The more generous, less imaginative, amongst them suggested locking the rioters up for a very long time. The hesitancy of the press to delve too deeply into the politics of the far right, I would argue, is a reflection of the contiguity of views, if not behaviour, between the rioters at Dublin and mainstream values.

Secondly, the English media did not miss the opportunity to contrast the expertise of the English intelligence service with the incompetence of the Irish police. Both tabloid and broadsheet press played on war and cold war themes of English fiction writing and popular cinema whilst re-iterating widely disseminated stereotypes of the Irish. In a curious mixture of twentieth-century spy thriller fiction and nineteenth-century cartoon humour, *The Times* praised the role of the English intelligence, whilst at the same time ridiculing the role of the Irish Garda. It contrasted the performance of both sides in the following terms:

> all this intelligence information, painstakingly gathered was passed on to the Garda in the weeks and days leading up to the game. The Garda's failure (to respond) was most graphically illustrated by the early withdrawal of its riot units from Landsdowne Road. When the violence erupted the riot squad were recalled only to find themselves unable to get

in. After hammering on its steel gates for five minutes and radioing inside for assistance, they finally smashed their way through one of the locked entrances. That is why the English hooligans were allowed to run amok for more than 20 minutes.

(ibid.)

The riot was thus (indirectly) blamed on the Irish Garda who were depicted as both incompetent and comic, i.e. stereotypically Irish. The article did admittedly go on to acknowledge that English security forces, armed with all this intelligence information, still allowed known suspects to travel to Dublin, a fact not dwelt on too long for fear of undermining the *Boys Own* version of English intelligence and the *Punch* version of Irish intelligence.

Thirdly, the press seized the opportunity provided by the riots to promote an alternative version of Englishness. The riots prompted a sense of national humiliation in the tabloids which was only tempered by their strenuous efforts to isolate this 'thuggery' from mainstream English values. Two story lines, shared by all the tabloids, serve to illustrate these efforts. The first began with a photograph of a spectacled man with blood streaming down his face. Published in the *Sun* the following day, the paper reported that 'The blood soaked victim pictured in yesterday's *Sun* was a kindly bank clerk who never hurt anyone in his life, who, according to one of his colleagues "was one of the kindest, gentlest guys I know"' (*Sun*, 17 February 1995). The reporter also interviewed neighbours at his family home who said how he had been taken to matches as a boy by his father who had recently retired from East Midlands Electricity. The story served to remind readers of another version of Englishness, one harking back to an era when it was safe for boys to be taken by their fathers to watch football and when the only male values on display were decency and gentility. Likewise, the figure of the diminutive James Eager, another innocent bystander, inevitably stirred memories of times past when football grounds were safe for dads and lads and there were such things as family values. James' innocence was juxtaposed alongside other, less innocent, versions of masculinity . 'Disgusting scum', 'vermin' with faces 'contorted with hate' were some of the ways used to describe the rioters. Exposed as cowards ('louts turn to little cry babies') and named individually in some reports, they were deliberately cast as the antithesis of supposedly twin English virtues of innocence and courage.

A second storyline, which complemented that of isolating the perpetrators, was to shift the blame on to an 'outsider'. *The Times'* attempts to blame the Garda is one example of this. Elsewhere the origins of what happened in Dublin were traced back to the actions of a French footballer, Eric Cantona, who had been convicted of assault following an incident with a fan from an opposing team who had been chanting anti-French slurs at a match between Manchester United and Crystal Palace. In addition to Cantona, Richard Littlejohn, writing in the *Daily Mail*, also managed to blame the only black English player at the time, Paul Ince, for his conspiring role in the Cantona incident (17 February 1996). Like their broadsheet counterparts, the tabloids attributed the violence to the Irish, but in this case confirming the links between the far right and the Ulster Volunteer Force which, it was claimed, had orchestrated the violence by selling tickets in Belfast pubs (*Daily Mirror*, 17 February 1995).

David Duke, campaign politics and the media

'Whiteness' in the politics of the National Association for the Advancement of White People

In this section, my aim is to examine a central theme of this chapter; the continuities between 'extreme' and 'mainstream' political discourses. I will do so with reference to the politics of David Duke, ex-member of the Ku Klux Klan and the White Student Alliance (the youth arm of the National Socialist Liberation Front). After breaking with these organisations, Duke became the leader of the National Association for the Advancement of White People (NAAWP). Duke has not just remained on the political fringes, however. His career has encompassed his election to the Louisiana State Legislature in 1990, his Presidential candidacy and his electoral bids for seats on both the US and Louisiana Senates in the late 1980s and early 1990s.[12] Despite his apparent courting of the political mainstream, Duke managed to retain some key elements of his white supremacist position, as the following quotation suggests:

> We need to prepare the white race to preserve America. If we lose the heritage of America's founding race . . . there will be no turning back from the United States becoming just another third world country. America is facing a dangerous crossroad.
>
> (cited in Zatarain 1990: 298)

On the contrary, far from Duke leaving the wilderness to join his colleagues on the floor of the Louisiana House, it could be argued that his fellow Republicans and even Democrats went some way, possibly more than half-way, to meet him in the wilderness. The early to mid 1990s witnessed a shift to the right in Republican politics and many of the ideas Duke promoted became increasingly part of the mainstream. His comment on Newt Gingrich's 'Contract with America' was to scoff and state 'that's mine. That's the exact platform I ran on in 1990 and 1991' (cited in Boulard 1995: 31). A closer look at *NAAWP News*, the mouthpiece of the NAAWP, confirms this. It also illustrates what coded whiteness looks like in its raw, uncooked state. NAAWP discourse has been proudly unapologetic in its defence of white interests. I shall illustrate such expressions of 'deciphered whiteness' with reference to six themes: law and order; family values; welfare moms; white victims; big government; and censorship.

The NAAWP's stance on 'law and order' has proved an enduring and politically profitable theme. In 1995, in ways prefigurative of California's Proposition 209 (see Chapter 3), the NAAWP turned civil rights discourse on its head by demanding, 'we have a civil right to know *who* is killing us with crime. We demand the race of criminals once again be made public' (*NAAWP News*, no. 80, 1995). Instead of using Willie Horton as a code for 'black crime', the NAAWP openly attributed crime rates to race: CRIME WEARS A BLACK FACE (*NAAWP News*, no. 81, 1995). The NAAWP have made much of their willingness to break taboo silences on this and other issues. In one edition of *NAAWP News* the organisation defended KETC talk radio host, Bruce Bradley, who had been sacked for stating that most crime was committed by blacks who were destroying the city of St Louis (*NAAWP News*, no. 81 1995). An NAAWP rally in 1995 thus had as its main topics that 'behind the scenes, invisible, never-to-be-mentioned "thing" killing America, Negro crime and welfare fraud' (*NAAWP News*, no. 80, 1995).

'Family values' have proved a second, recurrent source of white anxiety and their defence has allowed the NAAWP to simultaneously promote a particular set of norms for femininity, sexuality and ethnicity. Once again, a striking feature of this writing has been its capacity, and the willingness on the part of its authors, to unscramble coded, conservative discourse. For example, in an article under the headline NEGROES CONDEMN VIRGINS FOR NOT GETTING PREGNANT AND CLIMBING ON WELFARE WAGON, an editorial rider states that 'this disgusting reversal of family values is what 30 years of bribing negroes for their vote with the sweet, sweet narcotic of welfare has done' (*NAAWP News*, no. 80, 1995). The article went on to condemn the media for masterminding 'the whole welfare bribery scheme to further their hidden agenda to destroy Christian White America' (ibid.). Duke's defence of genetic determinism sought to underpin this argument. Furthermore, in his view, whilst blacks were criminogenic and black women promiscuous, the homosexual psyche drove lesbians and gays 'to seduce powerfully' (Boulard 1995: 32). Another of Duke's targets was the liberal establishment for its 'godlessness and commitment to socialism'. In his view, 'we have a government establishment dedicated to the complete elimination of God . . . overwhelmed by heathen hordes subverting religion, undermining the traditional family, redistributing wealth and fostering anti-American multiculturalism' (*NAAWP News*, no. 80, 1995). His apocalyptic vision was one of a liberal take-over and the promotion of non-traditional families and lifestyles. Duke's one and only interest in feminism was its stance on birth control and only then because he was able to link contraception to eugenics and the protection of the white gene pool. His solution to AIDS was an indelible tattoo 'placed in the private area . . . with glow-in-the-dark ink' (Boulard 1995: 32).

The 'welfare mom' has been a third object of NAAWP concern. In fact, advocates of the 1996 Welfare Bill, signed by President Clinton could have looked no further than the columns of NAAWP News to find much of the legislation's underlying rationale. Those provisions of the bill aimed at curtailing rights for legal and undocumented immigrants could not hide their racial basis. However, the broad attack on the unemployed, fatherless families and 'welfare mothers' had kept its racialised message thinly concealed, at least, that is, until the NAAWP put the case for the bill in the following terms:

Negroes are seven times more likely to be on welfare than whites . . . if the new Republican controlled congress make radical cuts in welfare be prepared for the liberal media to fill the air with pitiful pictures of welfare mothers holding starving babies in their arms. If you think Negroes won't let their children starve so they look right on TV, you do not know negroes. This dis-proportionate, disgusting, and unacceptable ratio is the dirty little national secret the liberal media has been hiding.

(*NAAWP News*, no. 80, 1995)

This was a simultaneous attack on the black underclass *and* the white liberal establishment. In another piece, the NAAWP wrote in similar terms, 'Thanks to Welfare State Liberalism giving cash rewards for illegitimacy, (black) underclass women not only have more children, they also give birth at an early age' (*NAAWP News*, no. 68, 1993). Arguably, these comments became the unspoken rationale behind the 1996 Welfare Bill.

Fourthly and predictably, 'white victims' also preoccupied the NAAWP in its efforts to invert conventional understandings of civil rights and racism. According to an argument already rehearsed in Chapter 3, whites were the new minority. It was *their* civil rights which were now being threatened by reverse discrimination and racism. In one instance, the NAAWP expressed its solidarity by giving financial help to a white farmer who, it alleged, had suffered reverse discrimination (*NAAWP News*, no. 79, 1995). Under the headline NAAWP DEFENDS WHITE FARMER IN REVERSE DISCRIMINATION CASE, readers were told how federal courts denied Larry Moore a federal loan programme designated for minority applicants. They were also informed that Mr Moore was a white, working, male, who was not on welfare and who had always respected the laws only to be treated like a second class citizen (ibid.). In another case, a policeman, who was accused of beating up an African-American, received financial support from the NAAWP. The officer subsequently wrote to the organisation expressing his gratitude, 'I wish your organisation could afford to provide legal assistance to many whites that are being abused by our corrupt political system' (*NAAWP News*, no. 73, 1994).

At these moments, the NAAWP, as its name would suggest, has promoted whiteness through a defence of those perceived as white skinned. At other times it has been less concerned with skin and more concerned with values. For example, in several issues of *NAAWP News*, the organisation advertised for 'Jewish and Negro patriots. Regular Negroes are good patriotic Americans. Regular Jews are good patriotic Americans. Be a leader. Help the budding Jewish and conservative movements grow' (*NAAWP News*, no. 79, 1995). Of course, the organisation's main motive could well have been to boost its membership and its funds.[13] A more likely explanation is that 'white' has been a reference to values as much as to people. The tension between ontological and normative whiteness has also facilitated the organisation's vitriolic attacks on the white, liberal establishment *and* its use of black conservatives like Thomas Sowell to endorse its editorial line. At the same time, such overtures to African-Americans like Sowell could always be withheld or at least overshadowed, simply by reminding readers of the organisation's stance on genetic determinism and innate racial and sexual pathologies (see e.g. *NAAWP News*, no. 71, 1994).

Fifthly, the evils of 'big government' in the context of immigration and affirmative action preoccupied the NAAWP. David Duke was quick to point out that whilst *he* had been participating in the 'Klan Border Watch' along the US/Mexican border, California's Governor, Pete Wilson, was busy defending illegal immigration. Fifteen years later, in 1994, Wilson, who by now had been converted to Duke's point of view, was spearheading Proposition 187 (see Chapter 4). Duke's own proposals to end affirmative action have become the focus of respectable debate on Capitol Hill and another Wilson-backed initiative, California's Proposition 187 (see Chapter 3). Attacks on 'big government' have become commonplace in the mid 1990s and by no means restricted to the political fringes of the militia movement and the far right.[14] According to Duke, it was 'angry white men' who fuelled the Republican electoral gains in 1994 when they took over both houses of Congress for the first time. The attacks may not go as far as 'the theory', i.e. the Jewish/communist conspiracy, but they have converged on key issues like welfare and affirmative action. The attack on big government and the call to give power back to the states and the people has proved yet another effective veil for the defence of whiteness. The fact that Duke and his Louisiana allies were, in the mid 1990s, at the forefront of a secessionist campaign, could likewise prefigure political trends in the US.

Finally, the NAAWP attacked the mainstream media's role in restricting freedom of thought. In fact Duke's only kind word for the media was reserved for talk radio which he claimed was 'the only media outlet not controlled by the liberal thought Gestapo'. (Although the reference to Gestapo in this instance was intended to underline the absence of freedom in the media, elsewhere, Duke expressed sympathy for what, in his view, was National Socialism's defence of 'family values'.) The problem with the establishment media, according to Duke, was its connections with the federal government and the finance sector. The conspiracy theory, which underpinned this argument, ascribed pivotal roles to Jews and communists. If we cut momentarily to the liberal, progressive end of the political spectrum, e.g. as expressed by FAIR (see Chapter 3), we also find a critique of the media bias based on the power of corporate interests and the marginalisation of alternative, oppositional media. How, we might ask, can mainstream media be perceived in overwhelmingly negative terms from both sides of the political spectrum? The answer must in part be down to different interpretations or 'readings' (e.g. one of NAAWP's white victims would be one of FAIR's white racists) and in part down to the preoccupation of both sides with questions of bias and the implied notion of some objective yardstick, i.e. truth.

The media and the anti-Duke campaign

The Louisiana Coalition Against Racism and Nazism (LCARN) was founded in 1989. Its more immediate aim was to destroy David Duke's political ambitions, both in Louisiana and his bid for the US presidency. This was set against a longer-term goal 'to provide research and accurate information in order to combat the influence of those who advocate Nazism, racism, and religious and ethnic intoler-ance' (LCARN articles of incorporation, December 1989). LCARN was disbanded in May 1992 at the end of Duke's presidential bid and after he was defeated in the elections for State Governor. LCARN's success was built around its media strategy which remained at the forefront of its campaign priorities. According to a founding Coalition member, Lance Hill,

> we knew from the outset that the war against Duke would take place in the public sphere by and large governed by media . . . (so) we did two things – became experts on Duke to the extent that media came to rely on us for up-to-date information on Duke and his movement and, secondly, our aim was to define the terms of debate about Duke.
>
> (interview, 26 August 1996)

Underlying both strategies was the view that Duke had to be isolated politically. LCARN's goal was to 'identify him as an extremist, hater and a fraud' (ibid.). To accomplish this, the organisation worked as closely as they could with journalists, providing them with information and using their contact as a chance to win them over to LCARN's position.

The media varied in their receptivity to Duke and hence to LCARN. According to Jason Berry, the local press treated Duke as a personality rather than probe his neo-Nazi links (Berry n.d.). In doing so, it facilitated the emergence of Duke's new role as underdog spokesman for disgruntled whites. Likewise Julie Sternberg's study of the local TV station, *WWL* and the *Times Picayune*, concluded that both withheld critical information about Duke's past which allowed him to develop a moderate facade which was 'a veneer of sophistication and sweet reason' (cited in Sternberg 1991: 71). Duke himself had worked on his image. In 1988, when he stood as Democratic presidential candidate, he appeared on a thirty-minute commercial, having literally reinvented himself. Not only had he eschewed white sheets for a coat and tie and button down collar but there was much evidence to suggest a plastic surgeon had been kept busy; lips, chin, eyes, smile, skin, all helped to make him telegenic (Sternberg 1991: 41). The failure to remind viewers about his Klan connections and his continuing neo-Nazi links enabled Duke to establish himself as a credible candidate. Journalistic conventions took over. Hence the electorate was invited to judge Duke by his successful campaigning, his skill in attracting outside coverage and his stance on clear cut issues (ibid.: 72). Those issues included the abolition of affirmative action and set asides (or fixed employ-ment quotas) and the reform of the welfare system (ibid.: 32). His opponent's platform, in contrast, was less clear cut and less amenable to sound bytes that resonated in popular discourse. Moreover, the common practice of turning elections into contests (television studios full of pundits, computer graphics and swingometers) helped detract viewers and readers from the political contexts of election issues, let alone the longer-term background of the candidates.

Both Berry and Sternberg concentrated on *local* media. According to Hill, national media covered the Duke campaign differently. He maintains,

> the national media were always more prepared to treat Duke as an object of investigation . . . the local media didn't want to touch the story – they feared if they singled out Duke for critical coverage there would be a backlash against them by their viewers/readers – they told us that . . . . So, you had journalists trying to diminish the Duke threat, making out he wasn't really appealing to racism and that his followers weren't motivated by racism . . . that he was just another conservative candidate . . . they were also more cynical – they did not think their readers could be appealed to in terms of moral reason.
>
> (Hill interview, 26 August 1996)[15]

The result of this reluctance to touch Duke led to what some have termed a 'media quarantine' or 'embargo' during the 1989–90 period. For Hill, it was no coincidence that Duke's popularity gained most in the first half of 1990. LCARN, in response to this 'blackout', went on the offensive – a kind of guerrilla information war. In the summer of 1990 the organisation began a direct mail campaign, sending out 100,000 brochures to voters. LCARN also wrote letters to newspapers (some under the 'ghost' name of the Rev. James Stovall).

During his period as elected member of Louisiana's House of Representatives, David Duke put forward a proposal to pay 'welfare mothers' to go on a sterilisation programme. The controversy it aroused prompted LCARN to produce a sixteen-page report on the issue and to get some air time on a local radio station, WYLD. Lance Hill, LCARN's spokesperson on this occasion, refuted Duke's claims and assumptions:

> we think that poverty is not caused by excessive family size. The average welfare family in Louisiana has two children. The problem is not excessive population. It is that there isn't economic opportunity, there aren't jobs for people and there's not adequate training. The state legislature should treat this as a social and economic problem by providing training and jobs rather than trying to solve this problem on the operating table by sterilising black people.
>
> (cited in interview, 26 August 1996)

The above proposal to sterilise and implant contraceptives in women in receipt of government assistance, thus provided LCARN with an opportunity to highlight the continuities between Duke's ideas and Nazi sterilisation programmes. In the call-in programme referred to above LCARN reported that

> In 1986 Duke advocated genetic engineering . . . in 1988 he (Duke) stated that the ultimate issue is Darwinian – who will propagate and who will not . . . (in addition to blacks) he also targets . . . criminals (and) he has advocating sterilising mentally defectives since the early 1980s . . . . Remember that in the . . . 1930s ideas of sterilisation were all based on voluntary programmes to begin with.
>
> (WYLD, audio archive, Amistad Center, Tulane University)

The second tactic of LCARN was to debunk the specific myths surrounding Duke's proposal, namely that: welfare does not provide an incentive to have children since figures suggest birth rates are highest where welfare rates are lowest; illegitimacy rates for white women have increased more than for African-American women; women had been entitled to free contraception from the AFDC since the 1970s; and the amount offered as an incentive to participate in the proposed sterilisation scheme was derisory and hardly likely to encourage women to suffer the physical and mental side effects of the proposed treatment. The last point was picked up by a number of callers to the above phone-in programme. A number of women, for example, mentioned internal bleeding as one of several side effects of Duke's sterilisation plan. One woman telephoned saying 'I'm a 27 year old woman. I won't subject myself to what David Duke is proposing' (ibid.). Another suggested that if there had to be guinea pigs then perhaps Duke should ask his own wife to test the implant procedures.

The third tactic was to use the campaign to promote employment and training initiatives. Although the Coalition did not regard itself as a policy-making organisation, when pressed on policy alternatives to Duke's proposed programmes, it emphasised economic regeneration. LCARN talked about capital flight from the inner cities to the third world and/or white suburbs and the collapse of employment opportunities which was Louisiana's experience, as it had been for other parts of the US . One caller to the WYLD programme from the African-American business community endorsed this view and argued for policies which brought jobs to the region rather than exacerbating racial tensions.

Aside from such opportunities to participate in local radio, LCARN's relationship with national media was altogether stronger. In Hill's words,

> we did a lot of work with national media based on our assessment that they would change the local media and get them to do the job they should have been doing all along – CBS, national network TV, talk shows, *Newsweek*, all ran pieces with information we provided and questions we crafted for them.
>
> (interview, 26 August 1996)

The only drawback to this strategy was that it exacerbated local Louisiana resistance to 'the north' or, more specifically, a collusion of the 'pinky', liberal establishment, federal government and Jewish interests. In fact, Duke attacked the local *Times Picayune* because of its Jewish proprietorship: 'The New York-owned *Times Picayune* and other powerful voices outside our community don't want you to hear my side of the story. And why? because I am speaking for you' (Sternberg 1991: 36). In Sternberg's view, a vote for Duke became a vote for freedom from outsiders, so that every time another political boss endorsed his opponent it gave an added incentive to vote against the party machine and for Duke (ibid.: 37). Duke continued, 'we don't need anyone from the north coming down to dictate our politics for us. We've got enough Jews down here to take care of that' (ibid.: 38).

The turning point came in the summer of 1990 when, as a result of LCARN's direct mailing strategy, Duke was forced on to the defensive and to explain his Nazi past for the first time. LCARN pressed home their advantage. They circulated a cassette tape in which Duke talks openly in anti-Semitic terms and the need to remove the parasites along Hitler's lines. The Coalition also organised workshops at which they discussed their perspective on the resurgence of racism and the radical right. Increasingly, the tide was turning in their favour. Anti-Duke lyrics were put to country and western ('David Duke, he makes me puke'), rap, punk and twelve bar blues. Musicians sent them tapes of anti-Duke music:

> the great white hope washed his sheets
> and changes his names
> but in his eyes you can still see flames
> he is the monster you thought was fifty years ago in Germany
> (Amistad Center, Tulane University, David Duke archive)

and,

> he speaks in code
> crime means black work means white
> they clap they're hands that's right that's right!
> (ibid.)

The anti-Duke movement built up a momentum of its own. One dentist sent anti-Duke material out to all his patients. One man went door to door with a cassette recorder playing the recording of Duke's interview with Evelyn Rich in which he elaborates his sympathy for Nazi values (17 February 1986, Duke archive, Amistad Center, Tulane University). Film producers threatened to boycott New Orleans if he got elected. One taxi driver reported that Duke would be bad for business and, on top of that, he was a racist bigot! (interview, Hill, 26 August 1996). The question as to why people stopped supporting Duke was a vexed one for LCARN because it touched the core of the anti-Duke campaign. Did people vote for his opponent in 1992 because they were morally outraged by his extremism or because in the words of the taxi driver he would be bad for business? The local press supported the view that people voted because of their pockets, not their conscience. But Lance Hill and others thought differently. According to Hill,

> In a *New York Times* exit poll, they found that people voted against Duke because of his racial beliefs. This confirmed our strategy that the way you defeat a right wing political insurgency like Duke is to build the broadest possible visible, vocal coalition and transform it from a political to a moral contest – [the] business community initially couched their opposition in terms of boycotts etc. but began to drop economic for moral arguments, thus helping to shatter the white consensus built around Duke's movement. Don't forget he went from 55 per cent of the white vote in 1989 to 2 per cent in last year's [1995] vote.
>
> (interview, 26 August 1996)

LCARN helped forge a popular anti-Duke movement which was built on a tactic of letting people know 'the truth' about Duke's past. In the end Duke's failure is in part testimony to the Coalition's success in building a broad-based movement of people who did not want to be identified with Duke or his racist ideas. They wanted to identify themselves as opposed to racism and anti-Semitism. In doing so, the Coalition even forced a wedge between Duke and the right of the Republican Party, so that in its strategy paper, the Coalition distinguished Reagan's nostalgia and regret about affirmative action and levels of welfare spending with Duke's vision of an America in which 'Race is the source of all maladies' (LCARN Strategy Summary: 2). The success of LCARN, measured in terms of Duke's failure to realise his personal political ambitions was beyond dispute. However, the fact remained that many of his ideas were reborn in more respectable guises and settings and without the taint of a Nazi background to help defeat them.

Anti-'white pride' politics: the case of the Southern Poverty Law Center

The SPLC was founded in Montgomery, Alabama, in 1971 by two civil rights lawyers, Maurice Dees and Joe Levin. According to Joe Levin, 'we began it in order to continue on a broader basis the civil rights litigation cases primarily in the south . . . that we [had] begun as private lawyers' (interview, 16 August 1996). In the early 1970s the Center brought a number of landmark cases to the Supreme Court, including one involving the Alabama State Troopers. The state court agreed that discrimination had occurred (there were no African-American state troopers at that time) and as a consequence the troopers were required to hire one African-American for every white hired until the latter reached 25 per cent of the total. The Center then took up the issue of promotion within the troopers and won a similar quota requirement. The State and President Reagan's Justice department objected and the case went to the Supreme Court in 1987, which found in favour of the Center (SPLC 1996: 5).

In 1996 the Center was still involved in litigation cases (I shall return to some below) but its strategy had shifted since the late 1970s as members began to focus on 'novel' cases which '[were] sufficiently different [and] controversial that some other lawyer [wasn't] going to [accept them]' (ibid.). This decision was also due, in part, to financial constraints which made it impossible for the Center to take on every case. It was also due to changes in attorneys' fees which meant that there were more lawyers available to handle discrimination suits. As a result, the SPLC became more selective in the number and type of cases it pursued and coincided with the organisation's growing interest in the far right and, initially, in the KKK. Out of this interest grew Klanwatch, an organisation set up to monitor Klan activities. According to Levin,

> its original intent was to monitor what was at that time a rising tide of Klan activity around the country but principally in the south, and to litigate against Klan groups and try to injure them – where we could demonstrate that the Klan organisation itself had some legal liability for violence and injury.
>
> (ibid.)

One of its best known cases was that of nineteen-year-old Michael Donald who was abducted in 1979 after which he was beaten, his throat was cut and his body was hung from a tree. The SPLC took up the case as a civil suit on behalf of Michael's mother and won $7 million in damages against the United Klansmen who had also been responsible for the Birmingham Church bombing of 1963, when four young African-American girls were killed, the murder of a civil rights activist during the Selma to Montgomery march to demand the vote for African-Americans and the attacks on the freedom riders who rode integrated buses as a way of testing the anti-segregation laws (SPLC 1996: 7).

High profile, widely publicised cases like the above served to heighten awareness, as did the SPLC's *Klanwatch Intelligence Report*, which is published quarterly and circulated to individual subscribers as well as 7000–8000 law enforcement agencies 'from the FBI to local, county and state police' (Levin interview, 16 August 1996). According to Levin,

> we probably have the largest data base in the country on extremist groups and extremist individuals – maybe bigger than the FBI – so we're a good resource. We do a lot of investigation and we have a lot of confidential sources employed around the country who help us keep tabs on what's going on in the extremist movement and we disseminate this.
>
> (ibid.)

One of the main features of *Klanwatch*, a magazine not dissimilar in format and type of coverage to the British *Searchlight*, has been to demonstrate connections between individuals and organisations of the far right and to piece together the flawed logic which has inspired acts of racist violence and terror. For example, the group Phineas Priesthood found its licence to violence in the Book of Numbers in the Old Testament, where an Israelite man was described as having a relationship with a woman from another tribe. Phineas slayed the couple and thereby appeased the wrath of Yahweh (*Klanwatch Intelligence Report*, no. 83, August 1996). Numerous acts of violence have since been committed in the name of the Priesthood. What is more such crimes have not only been motivated by racism. Robert Jackson, reportedly a Phineas Priest, was charged with the murder of three men in a gay bookstore (as well as subsequently convicted of plotting to bomb the SPLC). Paul Hill, an anti-abortion extremist, who was convicted of the murder of a Florida doctor and his bodyguard in 1994 had promoted Phineas actions a year prior to these murders. The particular significance of the biblical tale of an inter-tribal relationship was not lost on John Paul Franklin who murdered at least eleven partners of interracial couples and declared his commitment to Phineas in his prison letters. The Sect's transparent use of Christian discourse to attack gays, African-Americans and those defending women's rights, reveal, all too clearly, the inter-articulation of homophobic, racist and patriarchal discourses.

The growth in militias, Christian identity groups and other right-wing sects like Phineas led the SPLC again to broaden its focus beyond the Klan. According to Levin,

> as the Klan began to subside somewhat in the '80s, we began to find a lot of the extremists who had formally been associated with the Klan or who we had seen crop up in some of these other neo-nazi organisations, . . . militia groups and some . . . patriot groups that have developed in the US and we've been heavily involved in monitoring and litigating against those groups now for several years.
>
> (interview, 16 August 1996)

One such case was that involving a skinhead gang from Portland, Oregon who killed an Ethiopian student, Mulugeta Seraw. The SPLC sued Tom and John Metzger and the White Aryan Resistance for sending a recruiter to train the gang who praised the skinheads for carrying out their 'civic duty' (SPLC 1996: 7). The jury awarded $12.5 million to Mulugeta's family. The Supreme Court refused to review Metzger's appeal. A final area of concern for the SPLC was the spate of church burnings across the south in 1995 and 1996. The SPLC took out an action against the Christian Knights (of the KKK) for the burning of two black churches in 1995 on the grounds that they incited two of their members to carry out the arsons 'in order to promote their organizational goals' (*Klanwatch*, August 1996: 6).

Twenty-five years on, the SPLC remains a white-led liberal organisation with its roots firmly in the legal profession and a commitment to using the law to seek redress for racial injustices. It has pursued this strategy in conjunction with a clear understanding of the media's potential role in mobilising liberal, anti-extremist sentiment. The SPLC's legal interventions have contributed to a general climate of antipathy towards the far right as well as securing redress for the individuals concerned. Its legal triumphs have financially weakened its adversaries in the process and its 'teaching tolerance' programme has sought to challenge curriculum bias and promote cultural diversity. Yet the overall shift in the SPLC's emphasis towards white pride organisations such as the KKK and militia groups, has left normative, not to mention liberal and progressive whiteness, largely intact and, arguably, less visible.

Globalisation, music and the Internet

Ehud Sprinzak (1995: 27ff) has identified a series of stages in the development of the far right: a crisis of confidence in which ideologies are challenged; a conflict of legitimacy which is characterised by sporadic acts of violence; and a crisis of legitimacy which is characterised by systematic terrorism. With regard to terrorist groups, Sprinzak distinguished five types: 'reactive' terrorist groups which aimed to restore the *status quo ante*, e.g. the Croats in the former Yugoslavia; 'vigilante' organisations which emerged out of the alleged failure of governments to enforce law and order; 'racist' terrorists; 'millenarian' groups which cannot seclude themselves from the rest of society (e.g. Christian identity groups); and finally, 'youth counter-culture' terrorist groups, which expressed alienation and isolation and were best illustrated, according to Sprinzak, by skinhead gang culture. It is on this last type of terrorist group that I will now focus.

Skinhead culture had its origins in British youth culture of the late 1960s and early 1970s. Doc Marten boots, tattoos, shaved heads had loose connotations at first but increasingly came to symbolise an aggressive, working-class masculinity which was both racist and homophobic. 'Paki' and 'fag' bashing, desecration of synagogues and Jewish cemeteries were thus part and parcel of its everyday culture. Skinhead attachment to a number of English football teams in concert with more organised groups like Combat 18 turned football grounds into sites for the distribution of neo-Nazi propaganda as well as ritual bashings. Whilst music has always played an important cementing role in skinhead culture, the latter's particularly strong links with a neo-Nazi music scene has been attributed to Combat 18 member, Ian Stuart Donaldson,[16] a former musician with the band *Screwdriver*, who formed the organisation 'Blood and Honour' in 1987 (the latter derives from a translation of an SS slogan). *Screwdriver* recorded such albums as 'White Rider' and singles as 'Fetch the Rope', releasing their albums in the US under the name of *The Klansman*. Donaldson died in a car crash in 1993 but 'Blood and Honour' lived on in the mid 1990s as an umbrella organisation for skin rock groups and a mail order service for 'white pride' paraphernalia. The service ran from West Bromwich in the West Midlands where *Razors Edge*, another skinhead band was also based. In 1996 other neo-Nazi bands included *English Rose* (from Leicester), *Celtic Warrior* (Cardiff) and *The Order* and *Warlord* (London). The last of these was named after a *Screwdriver* album track and included a number of ex-*Screwdriver* members, including 'whitey' on vocals. Magazines like *Resistance* and *Blood and Honour* were also distributed from its Midlands base. The profits from this enterprise were an important source of funding for Combat 18 which controlled ISD (Ian Stuart Donaldson) records. A rival organisation, The British Hammerskins, formed in 1995, was an independently operating section of the Hammerskin Nation Movement which was founded in the US in 1986 (*Searchlight*, no. 256: 11). Nazi skin music lyrics, whoever performed them, or whatever their record label, invariably returned to a familiar theme: the apocalyptic vision encapsulated in *The Turner Diaries* and a battle cry to whites. In the words of one such band, *White Warrior*,

> Fighting in the city
> It's a matter of life and death
> . . . When the battle's over
> and the victory is won
> The White man's lands are owned by the White people

In the mid 1990s, the Nazi music scene in the US was centred around Resistance Records, based in Detroit, and its magazine *Resistance*.[17] *Blood and Honour* and *British Oi* published interviews with George Eric Hawthorne, the editor of *Resistance* and lead singer with *Rahowa*. Moreover, Resistance Records used the Internet to advertise its merchandise and disseminate its ideas. In one article, George Hawthorne described the crisis of the white race, a phenomenon which he attributed to 'race-mixing' in the following terms: 'without the wombs of our women, we cannot reproduce our dwindling numbers. Race-mixing spells death', since 'WHITE PEOPLE [are becoming] the true "new" Minority. Non-Whites make up 92 per cent of the people on this planet. We DO have a reason to be concerned and to want to close our borders to non-European People' (web site Resistance Records, emphasis in original). And who was to blame? According to Hawthorne, the media and education were, for inducing a white guilt complex which had censored expressions of white pride. This situation thus called on Resistance Records to forge 'a new destiny for White Power Music' (ibid.).

Given the possibilities of global communication, it is not surprising that both music and the Internet have proved, not only an important expression of skinhead fascism, but also a means of forging connections across Europe and the US. For example, bands like *Razor's Edge*, *English Rose*, *Skullhead* and *Screwdriver* have formed links with groups such as C18 and the National Socialist Alliance, connections which have been well demonstrated by *Searchlight* (no. 251, May 1996: 6–7). C18's *Blood and Honour* developed extensive links with other European and north American fascist bands. These links provided the basis for promoting and distributing records and other merchandise. C18 produced *Viking*, a 'skinzine' for French Nazis (ibid.: 7) and a Belgian Nazi mail-order service was promoted and distributed in England through *Blood and Honour*. European publications have been translated into English whilst British bands have appeared on European labels, e.g. Botta in France and DI-AL in Germany (ibid.).

More generally, the Internet has become an increasingly important source of exchange between, and information about, far right-wing organisations. With a couple of clicks of the mouse, it has become possible, in the mid 1990s, to 'surf' numerous home pages belonging to organisations and Internet newsgroups of the far right. Some, like Stormfront (White Pride World Wide), provided a resource page linking readers up with other white nationalist organisations and Internet groups, for example the Aryan Corps and Vikings. The British National Party's homepage (updated monthly) gave access to its monthly organ, *British Nationalist*. Recurrent themes of BNP ideology formed the basis of new stories on: illegal immigration and asylum fraud; health risks to whites; cash hand-outs for black projects; black prostitution; anti-gay jokes, and anti-Semitism. Such stories bore remarkable similarities, at least in terms of themes chosen, to their mainstream tabloid counterparts (see Chapter 4).

Similarly, in the US, groups and organisations used the Internet to rehearse their ideas, provide information regarding related sites, membership details, frequencies for World Wide Christian Radio, conference applications and mail-order subscriptions for video and audio tapes and relevant publications. Different groups have become associated with particular themes, including: the biblical origins of the white race (e.g. Aryan Nations); anti-immigrant (e.g. American Nationalist Union); the imminent collapse of western civilisation (e.g. American Renaissance); the need to revive authentic southern culture and the causes for which the Confederate States fought in the Civil War (e.g. The Southern League of Florida);[18] rejection of 'alternative lifestyles and pro-traditional family' (The American Nationalist Union); a commitment to white living space (The National Alliance); anti-gun control laws, anti-government regulation (Christian Patriots); and anti-GATT, NAFTA, UN, foreign aid and NATO (American Nationalist Union).

The Internet has not just proved a space for the far right to promulgate their views but also served as a battleground on which anti-fascists and sectarian fascists have waged war with their adversaries. For example, an article condemning C18 written by BNP leader John Tyndall, which had originally appeared in the BNP's *Spearhead* magazine (September 1995), was reproduced on the Internet. In it, he condemned C18 for its stance on violence including physical attacks on BNP officials. He also challenged some of its allegations, including one which claimed the BNP welcomed transvestites as members.[19]

The information flow is not all one way, although the far right have exceeded their political opponents both in terms of sheer output and 'technical' quality (use of graphics, colour, etc.). Nevertheless, anti-fascist groups and individuals have been making growing use of this technology. For example, the Nizkor Project has published articles concerned with fascism, racism and Holocaust denial, including one on skinheads in the UK which gave details of their racist and anti-Semitic activities and connections with football hooligans and racist rock music. In another it ran an exposé of the Church of the Creator and its leader, namely the 'Rev. Eric Hawthorne' of Resistance Records, which, needless to say, highlighted their neo-Nazi skinhead base and connections with Canada's 'Heritage Front'. Organisations like 'People Against Racist Terror' have also published articles electronically, both to inform readers as to the state and scale of racist activities and expose the racist face of organisations like the Populist Party, its leaders and candidates (Novick 1994, Nizkor Project at webmaster@nizkor.almanac.bcca). In 1996 there was also an official UK Anti-Fascist Web Site as well as the Anti Racism Resource Web Site and Anti-Racist Action Toronto.

The Internet often serves to conceal the identity and/or perspective of the author, which can make for a more open and lively debate. It also lacks many of the conventional understandings commonly forged between different newspapers, television programmes and presenters and publishers on the one hand, and their audiences on the other. The possibilities of anonymity on the Internet and its relative 'openness' has thus increased the chances that its contents will be used for quite different purposes. An article which exposes racism for one reader might provide useful racist contacts for another and research data for another. The rapid expansion of personal computers, their user-friendliness and declining prices will undoubtedly increase their use. According to *Searchlight* by 1998 the Internet will have a user base of over five million (*Searchlight*, no. 249, March 1996: 13). Put into a global context, however, these figures only confirm the continuing exclusion of the vast majority from the Internet. Added to this the predominant use of the English language as the '*lingua franca*' of the net continues to act as an exclusionary mechanism and a barrier to more equal and equitable exchanges of information.

Conclusions

Michael Barkun has described the Christian Identity Movement as a *cultic milieu*, that is, existing within the realm of rejected or forbidden knowledge.[20] The idea of a 'cultic milieu' and 'forbidden knowledge' relates to the organic ties between fringe and fabric ideologies and, hence, to an important, recurring theme in this chapter. David Duke attempted, in vain, to cross the Rubicon from a cultic to a mainstream milieux. In the cultic context of the NAAWP, whiteness was a source of celebration and assertiveness, underpinning views on welfare, law and order, immigration and civil rights. As I have argued in previous chapters, mainstream politicians have taken up these themes in their campaigns and legislative programmes, yet invariably hidden their whiteness beneath a gloss of universalism and the strategic use of African-Americans, African Caribbeans, etc. to buttress their claims. In making these links, I am not suggesting that racist murders or the bombing of the Oklahoma federal building were equivalent to attempts to abolish affirmative action or legislate against asylum seekers. What is being argued here is that distinct political practices have been underpinned by a common defence of, and allegiance to, normative whiteness and the construction of white interests.

The particularities of 'white pride' politics in England and the US have been influenced by such factors as demography, religion, military involvement, domestic politics and cultural tradition. In the US the 'locality' has proved significant in different ways; Vietnam, gun culture and a strong anti-'big government' tradition have all proved decisive. In England, the polarisation between electoral and street politics within the far right and the use of both music and football as key sites for political socialisation and formation of far right identities have been central to the form far right activities have taken. Furthermore, England's particular historical relationship with Ireland, migration patterns and the histories of different localities like the east end of London, with their own peculiar traditions of both fascist and anti-fascist activity, have likewise helped to lend a distinctive edge to right-wing extremism. Such variations have prompted different forms of political mobilisation and, relatedly, the distinctive roles played by the national media.

Anti-white pride political strategies have correspondingly varied, too. *Klanwatch* and *Searchlight* have played a public education role, highlighting the Nazi connections, as well as debunking the myths, of the 'far right'. The Southern Poverty Law Center has developed what might be seen as a selective, legalistic approach, involving high profile court cases which have attracted maximum publicity in order to expose as well as bankrupt groups such as the KKK. Important as these interventions have proved, however, there is always the danger, to some extent reflected in the Louisiana Coalition Against Racism and Nazism's anti-Duke campaign, of isolating the far right from the mainstream and leaving the latter intact, perhaps even bolstering its legitimacy. Attempts to highlight the extremism of mainstream politics is a high-risk strategy, as Newham Monitoring Project found, in its confrontations with the local 'establishment', to its ultimate cost. Collectively, these counter-mobilisations have all had a direct impact on such organisations as the NF, the BNP, the KKK as well as the careers of white men like David Duke and John Tyndall. They have also helped to build alternative organisations (many white-led) and identities around liberal, progressive and anti-racist political agendas.

Far from eroding whiteness, new global conditions, including the rapid expansion of telecommunications, economic restructuring, class and political fragmentation and what has been described as a crisis of national identity, have all assisted in the re-configuration of global white identities. Globalisation has also provided opportunities, in the shape of the Internet, for organisations and parties of the 'far right' to collaborate across north America and Europe and to merchandise their products world-wide. Likewise, skinhead organisations have harnessed their own brand of music to disseminate white supremacist messages and identities. In forging such links, again across the US, Britain and mainland Europe, they have been assisted by the rapid increase in use of Internet technology. The latter, however, has not only supported the 'far right' and a particularly aggressive, racist version of white masculinity, but increasingly has provided a space for resisting such politics and promoting alternative political and cultural agendas.

CONCLUSIONS

The imminence of a new millennium has encouraged the emergence and revival of cults, all anticipating the inevitability of some form of apocalyptic change. The most recent period in the history of whiteness has been shaped by its location at this temporal cusp and hence bears some similarities to what Barkun has termed 'cultic milieux', both in its expression of heightened anxieties and its breaking of taboos. More generally, whiteness has been understood throughout as an *essentialising strategy*, one which has attempted to: purge itself of extraneous impurities; construct itself as a unitary category without class and gender differences; and historicise its origins and development in highly selective terms. The intentions of such attempts have varied but the effects have been to build identities and interests around an allegiance to 'whiteness'. The latter have included 'white pride' politics, which has boasted this allegiance; 'normative whiteness' , which has built whiteness into a series of coded discourses; 'progressive whiteness', which has challenged dominant versions yet within political contexts which are 'white-led'; and finally, to 'subaltern whiteness', a status which, in the case of the Irish, has shifted over time and space, but which has always remained prey to dominant, white, racialised discourse.

Whiteness, therefore, with the exception of its subaltern forms, exists along a continuum. The politics of racist murders, church burnings and bombings is clearly not the same as one which advocates immigration controls, a monocultural curriculum or the abolition of welfare benefits for lone parents, let alone one which promotes anti-racism in the context of white-led and/or dominated organisations. In all its political guises, whiteness shares a point of privilege, a position of power from which it has been possible to define, regulate, judge as well as accrue material and symbolic rewards. I have suggested that 'normative whiteness' has hidden itself behind a claim to speak for everyone (universalism) or all its citizens (national identity). Normative whiteness has thus been rendered opaque and, simultaneously, re-worked around different universal themes, for example, family values, law and order, individual responsibility, as well as numerous sources of national allegiance, from wars to royal jubilees to sporting events. In these instances whiteness in an explicit sense has been written out of the script or 'exnominated'. Whiteness thus hails its subjects through a moral and

184

affective filter within which choices are made, actions sanctioned and loyalties secured.

The idea of 'coded' versus 'uncoded' whiteness has been used to underpin the distinction between discourses of universalism, etc. and those of the 'far right'. However, the more nervously 'whites' have reacted to global change, including migration, new forms of cultural representation and difference, antiracist politics, etc., the more likely coded whiteness will increasingly decode itself. There is a price to pay here, however, since the more whiteness appeals explicitly to its own ethnic particularity, the less 'universal' its appeal. This would inevitably undermine a key source of its legitimacy, as explicit associations of whiteness and the far right have also done. Hitherto, an open defence and celebration of whiteness, *per se*, has been restricted to the not-so-nether reaches of the 'far right'; 'not-so-nether' in so far as many of the motivations and assumptions underpinning 'white pride' political discourse have been found to resonate, rather than clash with, the values of main-stream culture. The discussion of backlash culture in Chapter 3, together with the discussion in Chapter 6, reflect these echoes and sublimations. The *historical* relationship between the fringe and the fabric, which is both relative and cyclical, also serves to dislodge any hard and fast distinctions. In some instances what was fringe today was fabric yesterday, and vice versa.

Since whiteness does not refer to some fixed, ethnic or physical characteristics, it should come as no surprise to find that its boundaries of inclusion and exclusion have shifted over time. This is particularly so in the case of 'subaltern whiteness', where relationships between white ethnicities have been characterised by domi-nance and subordination. The processes by which whiteness has been denied and conferred over time have not been once and for all, nor have they applied unilater-ally or universally. The subaltern status of white ethnicities has, at times, been eclipsed from the public (e.g. media) domain as attention has been focused on other racialised groups. The ontological status of 'being white' has also served to obscure processes of racialisation and the strategic use of one version of whiteness against another. But subaltern whiteness in common with other ethnicities should not be conceived exclusively in terms of its subordinate status but also in terms of its fissures around gender, class and sexuality. Moreover, its 'ethnic' boundaries, too, have shifted, merged and fused with other ethnicities and at times hidden behind dominant representations of whiteness. Indeed, an important feature of white-ness, I have argued throughout, has been the deployment of 'outsider' spokespeople in the reporting of 'riots', attacks on affirmative action or immigra-tion, etc. Their interventions have sought to neutralise the terms of debate by speaking from a position, allegedly, outside of ethnicity.

With the exception of subaltern whiteness, the continuities referred to above have been forged through particular versions of white masculinity depicted in popular culture, notably Hollywood film and music, as Fred Pfeil's study, *White Guys* (1995) has confirmed. Moreover, the characteristics and qualities on display arguably underpin a range of masculinities along the continuum of whiteness. Both Richard Donner's *Lethal Weapon* films (1987, 1989, 1992) and the *Die Hard* films (Dir. John McTiernan, 1988, 1995 and Renny Harlin's *Die Hard 2*) worked around narratives themes of lost innocence, devalued and discarded skills, and political and institutional corruption and/or incompetence. According to Donna Harroway, films like *Rambo II* and *Top Gun*, assert male violence but, in doing so, they undermine men's claims to male authority, what she has called the 'paradoxical intensification and erosion of gender itself' (cited in 1995: 27–8).

In Gibson's terms (1994), this paradox was integrally tied up with the military defeat in Vietnam but it was prompted also by those economic factors cited above, i.e. restructuring, the collapse of the manual labour sector and the feminisation of labour at the professional-managerial and sub-proletariat levels (ibid.: 28). Another cinematic expression of white masculinity in the 1980s was the iconic figure of Arnold ('I'll be back') Schwarzenegger, whose 'new'/'old' white working man invited audiences to respond, both to his Aryan, super-human physical presence and to his 'ridiculous implacability, obscene violence, and hulking insensitivity with a sneer that then permits the qualities sneered at to be embraced and enjoyed' (ibid.: 31). The fantasy, surreal-like quality of the sci-fi genre, moreover, made Schwarzenegger's masculinity open to multiple readings from 'neo-conservative' to 'far right'.

Rock music, too, has expressed some of these themes in a succession of white male icons from Elvis Presley, Mick Jagger, Bruce Springsteen to Axl Rose, all admittedly displaying differing manifestations of masculinity. Springsteen has been particularly interesting because his popularity has been partly rooted in his expression of white working-class culture, both lyrically, in tracks like 'The River' and 'Born to Run', and in his physically 'buffed' appearance. According to Pfeil, Springsteen's success has been achieved through his ability to bottle his aggression (but not so as to hide it completely), his attachment to national symbols (e.g. the American flag) and his reliance on 'white' musical influences (notably rockabilly and country-western). Overall, his image, as Pfeil argues, has transcended its class origins and appeals 'to (white) male dominance in the upper reaches of the economy and the state' (ibid.: 87). Whiteness, here, is not attributable to individuals but manufactured in this instance through politicised media discourses and the creation of a star or 'cult' following. Sometimes the 'stars' themselves do their best to resist appropriations of their image by the right. Bruce Springsteen, for example, objected to Ronald Reagan's use of *Born in the USA* and later urged his fans not to vote for George Bush in the 1988 Presidential elections.

The idea of a continuum of whiteness in the context of a discussion of Hollywood film and music is not meant to imply that *Born in the USA* and *Barbecue in Rostock* are equivalent or that John McClane in the *Die Hard* films or Riggs in the *Lethal Weapon* trilogy are mere fictional incarnations of Timothy McVeigh or David Lane.[1] Rather, the point is to emphasise the way in which elements of popular and fringe culture can often complement each other. Differences in both the degree to which white masculine norms are expressed and what behaviour accompanies them, or the capacity to invest contradictory meanings in films, music etc., should not detract from the point that some films and some kinds of music have an enhanced synergy with practices of the far right. This is not to suggest, either, that whiteness is necessarily associated with something intentionally malign. On the contrary, whiteness has been reinforced much more by routine than the conspiracies of the militias or Combat 18. It has been about maintaining traditions, representing culture and anchoring identities. The problem with such forms of whiteness, 'innocent' as they appear, has been their exclusivity and the inevitable hierarchies of representation and access which result. Such are the unspoken, unconscious, yet privileging effects of whiteness in both spheres of cultural production and consumption.

I have suggested that the eruption of whiteness, both coded and overt, has been facilitated by a set of conditions described by Stuart Hall as the 'global postmodern' or by Cornel West as the 'new politics of difference'. These conditions have called whiteness into question both as an epistemology (i.e. as a knowledge) and an ontology (i.e. state of being). The media has played a pivotal role in challenging age-old orderings of time and space and the corresponding identity-anchorings associated with these world views. Radio, film, and television have brought global messages and images into our front rooms, whilst the age of the Internet has initiated new forms of global dialogue as well as a breath-taking array of new sources of data. The expansion of such media forms has led to the transmission of ideas and information on an unprecedented scale, both in intensity and speed.

Meanwhile, global corporations and production lines, trading agreements and political alliances across north America or Europe and international banks and aid agencies are increasingly taking the national out of what were once unmistakably symbols of national identity, be it a Ford motor car or the sovereignty of Parliament. Even British Airways decided to take the overt national symbolism out of its designs in 1997 and opt, instead, for ones which allegedly had a more 'global', 'multi-ethnic' appeal. (Meanwhile, its multi-ethnic workforce were protesting at the deterioration of their pay and conditions.) Capital has been searching for new markets overseas with the inevitable economic fall-out, whilst slavery, indentured labour immigration, migrant labour and refugees have in turn shaped both labour markets and cultural patterns in their new localities. Whiteness has traditionally responded to these changes with renewed claims and assertions of national and ethnic identity. It has sought to essentialise its ethnicity around alleged characteristics of Englishness and Americanness.

The purpose of drawing on material from both the US and England has not been to undertake a direct comparison *per se*, but to explore the cross-fertilising processes of Anglicisation and Americanisation which have helped to configure whiteness on both sides of the Atlantic. Moreover, beyond its global impact, the crisis referred to above retains a 'local' flavour in both countries, according to the particularities of history, culture and global position, which in turn, for example, in the case of Hollywood film, has found its way back into the global spheres of distribution and consumption. The pilgrim, frontiersman and slave-owner were to the US what the overseas missionary, adventurer and absentee landlord have been to

England. These corresponding versions of white masculinity thus reflected the respective patterns of historical development in the two countries. The defence of whiteness was much more of a pressing domestic concern in the US. Settlers defined themselves and were defined as 'white'. White supremacy was enshrined in the law. In the US, therefore, white ethnic claims of 'belonging' and 'authenticity' always had to negotiate their status *vis-à-vis* the presence of Native Americans and forced settlement of African slaves. In its English version, whiteness was defined, initially at least, in terms of a distant empire. It was more mediated than immediate. Whilst colonial practices were often brutal and harsh, a collective self-image could always be cloaked in the language of diplomacy for those back home. Philomena Essed's comparative study of the US and Holland (1991) suggests that there is a greater rhetoric of tolerance and civility in the Netherlands, characteristics less apparent but none the less present in popular representation of Englishness, and arguably made possible by those differing antecedents of expansion and empire.

From their respective histories, it might come as little surprise to find that whilst Hollywood have been making action adventure films of the kind referred to above, the English have been preoccupied with films about weddings, funerals, mountains and matchmaking frivolity in the English countryside.

Other cultural sites have been important for the promotion of such values. National sporting events, for example, have served to evoke and reinforce a sense of national pride and the values associated with a militarily-conquered empire or the realisation of an American dream. Representations of 'Britpop', too, can be understood as an attempt to trace a lineage of popular music from the Kinks to Blur and Oasis, purged of its diverse cultural influences and typifying, or sometimes parodying, a somewhat awkward, deviant, self-deprecating version of English masculinity. It is no co-incidence that such efforts to 'whitewash' English music are being made in the mid 1990s just as they were in the 1960s, when more diverse music traditions were on the ascendant. In the 1960s it was blues, soul and Motown. Today it is bhangra, jungle and rap. This is not meant as a criticism of any forms of music *per se*, but rather, to argue that: Britpop was never unadulterated in terms of ethnic influence; there has always been a lot more to Brit(ish)-pop(ular music) than 'Britpop'; and finally that Waterloo sunsets were always enjoyed by an ethnically more diverse mix of young people than just white boys from Croydon.

Elsewhere in the media, I have noted particularly interesting parallels between talk radio in the US and the tabloid press in England. What distinguishes these two media from others has been their willingness to break taboo silences and decode the discourses of normative whiteness, as well as confirm and forge the continuities and connections between mainstream political common sense and the excesses of the fringe. These media in particular have served to resonate and make intelligible some aspect of their listeners' and readers' lives to whom they have appealed directly via phone-ins and readership polls. In so doing, they have helped to build a respectable, coherent, common-sense whiteness. The 'unfairness' of affirmative action and immigration, the plight of the white male victim, the 'mindlessness' of black criminality and the case for tougher policing and the 'reasonableness' of ending welfare payments for lone parents whilst leaving Ivy league and Oxbridge networks intact, have all been legitimated by this discourse.

An important aspect of Avtar Brah's notion of a 'diasporic space' (1996: 208ff.) is the idea that multiple social identities are simultaneously forged. Although the focus of the discussion here has been on whiteness, the latter has not been 'made' in isolation from other social constructions. So, for example, the 'making' of white Irishness in the nineteenth century was tied to class divisions and political alliances in the development of US capitalism. Likewise, the celebrated cases of Jack the Ripper and O.J. Simpson were both used by the media and other sections of the establishment to define and regulate, once again implicitly, norms of white femininity. Since whiteness has defined itself according to norms of sexuality, gender as well as ethnicity, it has invariably exploited its own contrived links between 'deviant groups' as a way of heightening anxieties and of creating some apocalyptic vision of whiteness. So, despite its electoral failures, the Oregon Citizen's Association helped to build and mobilise an angry, disaffected, white, working-class constituency, one whose members' homophobia and racism worked in tandem to the enhancement of both.

I have distinguished three forms of intervention the aim and/or the effect of which has been to challenge the hegemony of whiteness. These are: the politics of representation; hybridising whiteness; and anti-racism. Plausible and persuasive as Chomsky's 'propaganda model' and Schiller's concept of cultural imperialism have proved to be, the politics of whiteness has nevertheless found room for various forms and strategies of resistance. In general these have resulted from a process whereby dominant versions of whiteness have been embedded in culturally disparate and discordant contexts which then resist, re-work and/or appropriate their preferred meanings. This has been achieved, in part, by taking dominant 'white' readings of 'white texts', e.g. the Pocahontas legend, the harem or minstrelsy, inscribing them with different meanings and re-inventing them for different audiences. However, the politics of representation has worked best when it has provided spaces for diverse forms of cultural production. Cinematically, this has been most obviously expressed in England in the work of film-makers such as Isaac Julien, Hanif Kureishi and Gurinder Chadha and the photography of Edith Pollard. Likewise, in the US, films like Mario Van Peeble's *Posse* (1991) served to remind or acquaint its audiences with the fact that one in three cowboys were black. This collective assault on the cultural hegemony of whiteness contrasts with strategies to counter negative with positive stereotypes. Instead, this generation of diasporic cultural producers have celebrated both the diversity and complexity of identity and the need to express it in culturally syncretic ways.

The second strategy has been directly to challenge and undermine the idea of an 'authentic' white culture. Martin Bernal's thesis regarding the black African origins of white western civilisation is one example (1987). So, too, is Paul Gilroy's analysis of the black contribution to modernity (1993a). Homi Bhabha's idea that we all exist in a 'third space' rather than in some hermetically sealed ethnic vacuum, also lends itself to the idea of a 'diasporic whiteness' (1994). Overall, the conclusions of these writers confirm that both English and US whiteness, from the 'outset' (which, like 'origin', is itself a problematic term) have been steeped in, and beholden to, cultural traditions which transcend the alleged purity and authenticity of whiteness. Such intellectual interventions as these have exposed 'white essentialism' for what it is; an attempt to 'bleach' historical processes against a reality of cultural fusion, exchange and interpenetration.

In *Whitewash*, I have been less concerned with these first two strategies and more with organisational attempts the aims of which have been to resist various forms of exclusion and racism and to promote diversity and difference. Such interventions have sought to dismantle white monopolies which have been expressed both in terms of a visible 'white' presence and less visible 'white' values. Organisations like Southern Poverty Law Center, Fairness and Accuracy in Reporting, Newham Monitoring Project and community radio station, WBAI, have been anti-racist whilst simultaneously seeking to promote new communities which cut across traditional ethnic lines. In some instances, these new communities have been actively mobilising across ethnic divisions, e.g. WBAI. In some instances they have remained white-led, e.g. in the case of SPLC. This version of whiteness has been portrayed cinematically in *Betrayed* (1988), *Mississippi Burning* (1988) and *A Time to Kill* (1996). Elsewhere, in the everyday cultural sphere the limits of liberal whiteness have been manifest in a cultural or class lifestyle which embraces ethnic difference when it comes to consuming Mexican tortillas, Chinese noodles, Irish beer or Alice Walker novels. Once again whiteness is defined by its capacity to control patterns of consumption, albeit on a class basis.

I have also discussed forms of political intervention and campaigning, the object of which has been to highlight the irrationality of whiteness and the possibility of correcting bias and injustice through legal campaigns. The role of FAIR and the SPLC are examples of this kind of politics as were elements of the campaigns against California's Proposition 187 on immigration, Proposition 209 on affirmative action and the UK's 1996 Immigration and Asylum Act. Despite their successes in mobilising opposition and, in the cases brought against the KKK by the SPLC, of financially damaging the extreme right, the limits of this kind of politics are manifest in the assumption that whiteness can be dismantled through an appeal to reason, when 'reason' itself, alongside racism, constitute defining characteristics of modernity (Goldberg 1993).

Finally, I have examined forms of community mobilisation built around campaigns and alternative media interventions which have transcended narrow ethnic allegiances and appealed to interests defined in terms of class, gender and sexuality. For example, the campaigns against Oregon's Citizen's Alliance acknowledged the latter's strategic use of race to marginalise homosexuals and vice versa. Newham Monitoring Project, too, has simultaneously sought to build links across different ethnic groups (e.g. established and refugee communities) whilst at the same time building innovative alliances around particular issues, e.g.

football violence. The embryonic use of the Internet, less advanced than in environmental politics, has begun to forge links across localities in and between the US, England and the rest of Europe. Again these initiatives have begun to establish an alternative politics to that of 'white pride' which has itself made extensive use of the Internet for information, contacts and merchandising its products. Whether or not new media technologies with their interactive focus will serve to weaken or to strengthen traditional identity allegiances, to democratise or render knowledge more exclusive, remains to be seen. There is nothing intrinsic in the technology which gives us a clue, yet there remain differences in access to and use of the Internet, as well as in representations in cyber culture, which may yet serve to reinforce in more subtle ways new forms of global whiteness.

NOTES

1 Globalisation, ethnic identities and the media

1 Jordan concedes that white supremacy does not have to be driven by a sense of divinity, although in the US it often is couched in religious terms.
2 There has been a more widespread revival of interest in the work of Fanon, Dubois and others, not just because of their comments on whiteness, but the importance of their work as part of a wider critique of the western canon and/or attempts to map a broader, pluralistic genealogy in the formation of mainstream intellectual debate. See also Chapter 2.
3 Fanon cites the example of Bigger Thomas in Richard Wright's *Native Son* to illustrate this point (Fanon 1986: 139).
4 Frye begins to do this in her discussion of class and gender in relationship to whiteness. A certain version of whiteness, gendered and classed in particular ways, has achieved hegemonic status in ways which have encouraged subordinate groups, white women and white working classes to buy into its assumptions and themes. This does not mean that such groups benefit. On the contrary, Frye argues, that white women's subordination is facilitated as a result of the support they lend to whiteliness.
5 Although even physical attributes have been contested through ideas of intersexuality, transexuality and hermaphroditism.
6 For a discussion of the events surrounding the publication of Salman Rushdie's *Satanic Verses* in these terms, see Gabriel 1994: 22–9.
7 The Labour Party's victory in the general election of 1966 had been widely attributed to England's world cup success of that year. Hence, the British media speculated as to whether John Major would hold a snap general election if England won 'Euro '96'.
8 In one front page article in *The Times*, a photograph of cheering English fans draped in Union Jacks ran alongside an article under the headline MAJOR CLAIMS VICTORY IN BEEF WAR.
9 Media portrayals of the centennial Olympics in Atlanta, Georgia, 1996, reflected a pre-occupation with these values (courage, dedication in the face of adversity) which are commonly associated with the early white settlers. Whilst these values were projected as international/universal, they came to encapsulate the characteristics of US athletes in particular (Keri Strug, Amy van Dyken) and were confirmed in the overall superiority of the US team.
10 One such story involved a two-month-old baby girl, Anna, whose mother was German and whose father was English and who had to choose their daughter's citizenship status. They decided that Anna would either become a German or an English citizen depending on the outcome of the game (BBC1 *Midlands Today* 26 June 1996).

11 A reference to Sir Francis Drake's preparations before the defeat of the Spanish Armada.

12 US originated popular culture was always used to work around themes of English national identity. For example one banner headline, LION KINGS, worked both as a reference to the Disney film and as a link to recurring association of lions, lionhearts, English flags and the Crusades.

13 Although women were present at the games themselves and were amongst the television audiences, their participation remained marginal, particularly when account is taken of the players, officials and near monopoly of male media commentators. On GMTV, the morning following England's defeat, counselling was offered for bereaved fans and their families by Anthea Turner and her guests. There was some dispute amongst participants as to the degree of female involvement in the games, but at least as far as one of the guests was concerned, women needed to take their husbands or partners' devastation seriously, encourage them to write a letter to the English team, cook their favourite meal and give them lots of cuddles! (*GMTV*, 27 June 1996).

14 The term 'indentured' was used to describe the labour at El Monte on *Donnahue*, a US talk show (12 July 1996). The women working at El Monte, it was argued, had to borrow money from a labour recruiter and subsequently used their wages to pay back the loan.

15 The show's format is similar to 'Richard and Judy' and 'Ann and Nick' in the UK.

2 Genealogies of whiteness

1 One of the strength's of Essed's research is her discussion of the marginalisation of black women and how this is maintained through everyday acts of harassment, threat, ridicule, insult and discouragement. Her account also illustrates the ways in which racism is gendered. Representations of black women have thus played a pivotal role in these discourses, offering both descriptive epithets and explanations of black behaviour.

2 W.E.B. Dubois encouraged blacks to boycott *Birth of A Nation* (Rhodes 1995: 38).

3 In saying this it is worth recalling Peter Fryer's point that Africans were probably in England with the Romans, i.e. before the English! (Fryer 1984).

4 Ann McClintock (1995) describes the map of the mines which appears at the beginning of Haggard's book. She writes, '(the map) written by a trader . . . while he was dying of hunger on the "nipple" of a mountain named Shebas's Breasts . . . inscribed with a cleft bone in his own blood . . . it carries with it the obligatory charge of first killing the black "witch mother", Gagool'. McClintock goes on, 'In this way the map assembles in miniature three of the governing themes of Western imperialism: the transmission of white, male power through control of colonised women; the emergence of a new global order of cultural knowledge; and the imperial command of commodity capital' (1995: 1–3).

5 The figure became an object of a campaign in Britain in the 1980s to have the labels removed from jam jars.

6 Motherlessness is a common state in Disney animated films, which might explain the corporation's decision to make a film based on the Pocahontas story (1995).

7 In 1850 there were 100,000 Native Americans and 15,000 others. In 1900 the Native American population was 17,500 out of a total population of 1.5 million! (Almaguer 1994: 29).

8 The 'mass' democracy which replaced the old aristocratic pro-slavery leadership was notable for its exclusion of Native and African-Americans. As Theodore Allen points

out, 'Regrettably, critics and defenders alike generally seem to ignore the most significant factor about the spoils system (e.g. at Tammany Hall), namely that it was first of all
a "white-race" spoils system' (1994: 186).

9 In 1791, Irish workers formed the basis of the first working-class organisation, the
London Corresponding Society, inspired by the ideals of the French Revolution and
committed to the overthrow of the English monarchy and the establishment of a
republic (Ignatiev 1995: 63).

10 The case involved a French Jewish soldier who was wrongly convicted of spying for the
Germans. Popular antipathy towards him was whipped up by the publication of the
(forged) Protocols of the Elders of Zion which advocated world Jewish/socialist domination.

11 The article provoked an angry response from Ernestine Rose, a Jewish abolitionist and
women's rights campaigner whose letters were published in the newspaper over the
period 1863–4 (Dinnerstein 1994: 31).

12 Arguably, the holocaust, as Bauman argues, was both a product of, as well as marking
the end of, modernity. Reason, rationality and bureaucracy, all stripped of emotion and
taken to their logical, yet terrifying, conclusion, combined with the nation state's last
ditch attempt to promote cultural unity (1989).

13 The example given by Dirlik identified 507 micro-consumption units per macro-
consumption unit , as part of a strategy referred to as guerrilla marketing (Dirlik 1996).

3 Backlash culture and the defence of whiteness

1 The commercial success of some books in the US is something of a surprise to an
English outsider. They look more like books for college reading lists than top ten sellers.
What distinguishes them is a well oiled propaganda machine which markets their work
for a much wider audience than is suggested by their content. In some cases this is
undoubtedly related to the fact that many of the authors have strong journalistic
connections either through their political background or because they are journalists
themselves. But the machine also relies on foundation backing. Authors thus receive
grants from wealthy foundations with the corporate connections and resources necessary to promote mass interest in such books. Dinesh D'Souza's *Illiberal Education* (1991)
and *The End of Racism* (1995) are two such examples. D'Souza received grants from such
bodies as the Bradley, Richardson and Olin foundations, all of whom aim to promote
the Republican Party as a way of securing lucrative business sponsorship. Both these
books and Allan Bloom's *The Closing of the American Mind* (the latter was backed by the
Earhart and John M. Olin foundations) have received widespread acclaim in newspapers and weekly journals which have themselves been closely aligned to Republican
politics as well as funded by media conglomerates with Republican leanings. It seems
ironic that, given this highly politicised management of knowledge, its producers have
been at the forefront of defending objectivity against their relativist critics.

2 For a critical discussion of 'race-evasive' socialist politics in England in the 1980s, see
Ben-Tovim *et al.* (1981; 1986).

3 According to cultural relativists and historicists, truths and judgements are never absolute but always relative to historically and culturally specific contexts.
Deconstructionism is premised on the idea that any text is inscribed with a multiplicity
of meanings.

4 Bloom has claimed that humanities and social sciences have admitted students under
affirmative action programmes who would have failed in natural science disciplines
where 'absolute' standards still apply. The result, according to Bloom has been that 'the

humanities and social sciences were debauched and grade inflation took off, while the natural sciences remain the preserve of white males' (1987: 351).

5 Ironically, there is plenty of independent evidence, i.e. the discovery of mass graves and confirmation of US financial and military support of the military regime which perpetrated these acts of genocide, including the execution and torture of members of Rigoberta's family.

6 This comment was part of an answer to a question about Susan Faludi's book *Backlash*, which, Sykes claimed, clung to the idea of women as victims.

7 According to D'Souza, Herrnstein and Murray's *The Bell Curve* (1994) which revived the idea that intelligence was racially determined was proof, not of biological differences but cultural pathologies within the black community. *The Bell Curve*, it should be added, received considerable media attention when it was published including full extracts in an issue of *New Republic* which was given over to debates surrounding the book.

8 1995 OCA campaign material was headed 'Stop Minority Status' and in 1992 the Campaign included a 'No Special Rights Committee'.

9 In one case, a gay man and lesbian woman, were killed when their house was firebombed in Salem, Marion County, Oregon. The background to the incident was a racial attack on the black nephew of one of the victims, Hattie Mae Cohens (*Oregonian*, 3 October 1996).

10 Yeo (pronounced Yo) subsequently resigned from office after allegations of an extramarital affair and 'love child' were reported in the press, suggesting that the minister had himself imbibed rather too much of the 1960s counter-culture.

11 This decision did not, as it turned out, silence the local press. On the contrary, the salary of the new Equalities Officer made headline news in the *Birmingham Mail* in January 1997.

12 Elsewhere, anti-racism has been accused of diverting attention from the real struggle, i.e. the class struggle and the real evil, i.e. capitalism (see, for example, Tom Hastie's contribution to Palmer 1986).

13 Even 'news coverage' of the O.J. Simpson trial brought together a number of entertainment genres – courtroom drama, characters, expert opinion and phone-in slots – in its nightly coverage on Rupert Murdoch's satellite channel, Sky.

14 The aim of a proposition or ballot initiative is to bring about changes in state law. Initiatives can only be put on the election ballot if they obtain a minimum number of signatories and hence have been the object of popular campaigning.

15 Wilson's growth in popularity which doubled between June–July 1995, was attributed to his stance on affirmative action (*Mail Tribune* 11 August 1995).

16 One of the men behind Proposition 209, Tom Wood, was a white teacher who had, according to his own account, been passed over for a teaching post. In an edition of NBC *Dateline*, it was suggested that his lack of publications had been decisive in the decision to reject his application (Teri Stein interview, 6 September 1996).

17 This reflected the involvement of 'civil rights bureaucracies' in the campaign (Kim Deterline interview, 6 September 1996).

4 Border guards, bodyguards, lifeguards

1 It is interesting to note the way in which the term alien was used rather than Jew. The term alien pauper worked more at a class level and included gypsies, although for many, including the leadership of the BBL, the term alien was merely a code for Jew (Holmes 1979: 94).

2 In a major BBC debate, *A Question of Immigration*, in 1978, Powell played a pivotal role in the discussion, with the chairperson Sir Robin Day constantly returning to Powell

himself or referring to Powell's views on numbers of immigrants, the consequences of immigration and repatriation. This was highlighted by Maggie Steed and Stuart Hall in the Campaign against Racism in the Media's (CARM) programme, *It Ain't 'alf Racist Mum* (for a fuller discussion of the CARM programme and the furore it caused see Hall 1990).

3 Rodney and Gail Pereira who did not live in the inner city but in an English village in Hampshire were successful in their campaign to avoid deportation after their white neighbours sent what the press described interestingly as a 'blizzard' of petitions on their behalf. *The Times* noted the following in justifying the Home Office's decision not to deport: 'they played an active part in village life . . . they showed a positive commitment to Britain and to the English way of life' (cited in Gilroy 1987: 63).

4 In this radio interview, Thatcher spoke of the need to 'end immigration in the foreseeable future to avoid the effects of being "swamped" by an 'alien culture' (cited in Barker 1981: 15).

5 This was revealed in an interview in BBC's *Panorama*, a documentary news programme. Whilst there had been prior allegations of an affair, this was the first time Diana herself had admitted to it.

6 These murders were committed in Gloucester, England, during the 1970s and 1980s by a married couple, Frederick and Rosemary West. Amongst their victims, whom they also raped and tortured, was their daughter, Heather. Frederick West hanged himself in prison before the case went to trial.

7 Much can be learnt from authors' acknowledgements, particularly in the US, where as I have suggested books written by journalist academics invariably receive grants from foundations with strong links to business and/or the Republican Party. Hence Brimelow's book begins with an expression of gratitude to John Tanton, founder of the right-wing population control group Federation for American Immigration Reform, and to English Language Advocates.

8 He goes on to describe Powell as 'the prophetic critic of Britain's disastrous post-imperial immigration policy' (Brimelow 1995).

9 The choice of acronym (SOS) conveyed a desired sense of urgency and fear as well as the more literal suggestion that immigration was the key to the state's survival. It is also the call used by ships in trouble, i.e. the use of yet another water metaphor.

10 The commercial was for Pete Wilson, the Republican candidate who stood and subsequently won the election for State Governor in California on a pro 187 ticket, despite the fact, it should be added, that Wilson himself had commercially benefited from the use of illegal immigrant labour over many years.

11 Ironically, 187 has subsequently been challenged by the Supreme Court precisely on the grounds of its constitutionality.

12 The arguments around 187 thus drew on both female and male imagery. The language associated with the former (Liberty), is associated with stereotypically soft, 'female' characteristics (e.g. vulnerability and compassion), whilst the Constitution is associated with physical and intellectual prowess, i.e. stereotypically 'male' characteristics. In their overt use of the Liberty symbol, proponents of 187 were thus seen to be defending those values embodied in white femininity and which the latter safeguards for white culture as a whole.

13 It is worth noting the way 'America' is used here to refer to the US whilst other parts of the continent require qualification, i.e. Latin America.

14 It is interesting to note how official spokespeople of the SOS Campaign were at pains to restrict the issue to that of illegal immigration. In the white popular imagination, however, inspired by talk radio hosts like Ray Briem and Joe Crummey, 187 was undoubtedly part of a wider agenda.

15 No attempt was made (predictably, given the wider assumptions of the campaign) to reconstruct American identity in terms of Native American culture.

16 In the 1996 presidential election campaign, the Democratic Party ran an advertisement defending President Clinton's attempts to secure the borders and at the same time linking immigration to crime. The advertisement, a direct response to Republican allegations, thus confirmed the impact of 187 on subsequent political debate (*San Francisco Chronicle*, 7 July 1996).

17 The term 'Heterodoxy' and the magazine's sub-title, 'Articles and Animadversions on Political Correctness and other Follies' are indicative of a wider agenda into which Proposition 187 was conveniently slotted and which talk radio hosts like Joe Crummey and Ray Briem and, above all, Rush Limbaugh, exploited.

18 The new Disney-financed Celebration, in Florida, is an interesting example of a new phenomenon of gated cities, which have sought to re-create small town values complete with white picket fences, porches facing the street, security guards and strict by-laws. These developments, which house four million people across California, Arizona and Florida, have been described as the logical extension of 'white flight', a reference to the exodus of whites from the inner cities to the suburbs in the 1960s and 1970s (*Guardian*, 27 July 1996).

19 The Federation for American Immigration Reform was formed in 1979. Its plush offices in downtown Los Angeles and glossy publications suggest lucrative sponsorship rather than the shoe-string budgets associated with many campaigning organisations.

20 Of the Asian and Black vote 47 per cent supported 187 and 23 per cent of the Latino population voted for the Proposition (*Los Angeles Times*, 10 November 1994).

21 For example, the decision to use lottery money to fund the West Midlands' Anti-Deportation Campaign was attacked in the national tabloid press as another example of 'political correctness gone mad'. What was also interesting about this reaction was the way the tabloid press managed to lump the Anti-Deportation Campaign together with organisations involved with other 'PC demons', i.e. women's and lesbian and gay rights.

5 Policing whiteness

1 For a full discussion of urban revolts in the 1960s see Feagin and Hahn. In their analysis the authors write that 'one category of taboo transgression [an act of insult or injustice to the community] is of overriding importance: the killing of, arrest of, or interference with black men and women by policemen' (1973: 144).

2 Other films have used animation and sci-fi genres to explore the same themes, albeit more obliquely. Ridley Scott's *Blade Runner* (1982) has been widely discussed in terms of its coded racial messages (Harvey 1989). The spectre of a city under threat or siege was also the dominant message of Steve Barron's *Teenage Mutant Ninja Turtles* (1990) with its criminal underworld masterminded by a demonic, despotic, oriental character. Even when films take on a more surreal, or stylised form, e.g. the *Batman* movies, the connection with New York, the prototypical urban space, remains strong, even with their futuristic settings. Moreover, the seeming timelessness and only half-connection with New York's urban landscape make them easier to translate into a British context. What these films have in common is a powerful and recurring theme of a criminal underworld, invariably 'marked' by ethnicity and/or physical disfigurement, eating away at the core of America's big apple.

3 For a discussion of the specific impact of policing on Irish women see O'Shea 1989.

4 For evidence of the racialised use of stop and search by the Metropolitan Police, see Human Rights Watch 1997: 77.

5 Taylor's own failure to become a Conservative MP resulted from a campaign full of racist slurs by his own fellow Conservative Party members. Despite this, he maintained his 'race evasion' brand of conservatism which endeared him even more to the media. In 1995 he presented his own nightly radio show on BBC Radio 2 and was one of the presenters on BBC1's *Talkabout*, a daily debate series.

6 The specific impact of the uprisings on black women has been explored by the Women of Broadwater Farm (1989).

7 See Paddy Hillyard (1993) for an analysis of the implementation of the Prevention of Terrorism Act and how it has been used to discriminate and harass the Irish community on the British mainland.

8 In their excellent study of racial harassment in London, Barnor Hesse *et al.* (1992) have illustrated the ways in which policy statements which appear to take racial harassment seriously have been undermined by a series of factors, including: the vagueness of the policy; the failure to communicate it down to patrol level; the failure to develop adequate mechanisms for evaluating the policy; the inappropriateness of categories to measure policy effectiveness, e.g. clear-up rates which give an inflated sense of success since they do not indicate what actions were actually taken against perpetrators; and, finally, disputes with victims over definitions of harassment. (ibid.: 48ff.). Both the macro- and micro-cultures of policing have created a climate conducive to the maintenance of these institutional conditions, where policing culture, aided and abetted by a sympathetic tabloid press, has acted as a major disincentive to win the approval of both victims of racial harassment and black community organisations. Another issue is that of domestic violence against black women. Here, police have been criticised for using racial stereotypes of black women as a basis for shaping policing responses to domestic violence (Southall Black Sisters 1989; Mama 1989: 183).

9 For a fuller summary of deaths in police custody in the United Kingdom, see Human Rights Watch 1997: 35ff.

10 Ibrahima Sey voluntarily gave himself up for arrest with a friend on 16 March 1996. At the police station he was assaulted, handcuffed and sprayed with CS gas spray. Within minutes he was dead.

11 In another well publicised case, Joy Gardner was killed by three police officers on 28 July 1993 in her flat in Hornsey, north London. The officers put chains on her legs, lay on top of her, put quick cuffs on her hands and wrapped 13 feet of sticking tape around her face in an attempt to enforce a deportation order. In addition to the three officers there was an immigration official and two local police officers present. The police officers were subsequently cleared of manslaughter. Press coverage of the incident concentrated on: the views of the police officers, who alleged they were being scapegoated (*Evening Standard*, 10 August 1993); Joy Gardner's violent disposition (ibid.); the use of the gag to avoid being bitten and possible contraction of HIV or hepatitis (*Evening Standard*, 5 August 1993); and renal failure or natural causes as the likely cause of death (*Daily Mail*, 3 August 1993 and *Evening Standard*, 2 August 1993). Only the *Guardian* and *Independent* conceded the excessive use of force, notably the use of a body belt and a four-inch-wide tape across Joy Gardner's mouth (e.g. *Independent*, 5 August 1993).

12 As Cose points out, Denny's beating exacerbated white fears, but what is forgotten here was the historic fear of black men – of beatings, lynchings and hate crimes. Just months after the Denny beating, 'a black Brooklyn man on a visit to Florida was kidnapped, drenched in gasoline and set aflame on the outskirts of Tampa by three white men packing handguns and slinging racial epithets' (1993: 108).

13 Mumia Abu-Jamal, a member of the Black Panthers in the 1960s, was convicted of murder and sentenced to death. In 1997 he was imprisoned on death row. The death penalty was abolished in 1972 on the grounds that it was being applied in arbitrary and discriminatory ways, i.e. overwhelming evidence suggested that African-Americans disproportionately received the death penalty for the same offence as whites. Death sentencing for rape was particularly marked in patterns of differential treatment. A federal court decision in 1972 had argued that the death penalty was unconstitutional because of the arbitrary and discriminatory manner in which it was administered and hence that it was an infringement of the 8th amendment of the US Constitution which prohibited cruel and unusual punishment (Haines 1996: 14). Within two years states had adopted new death penalty statutes which claimed to make the sentence less arbitrary. In 1976, the Supreme Court accepted that states could devise more rational sentencing procedures. It was ironic that the first person to be executed after the death sentence was reintroduced was a white male, Gary Gilmore who was executed by a Utah firing squad in 1977: ironic in the sense that the death sentence has since been used disproportionately against African-American men in the US. Capital punishment has been described as symbolic of 'rich white men – making their political careers from killing black people' (cited in ibid.: 185) and the backlash in defence of whiteness, against the gains of the civil rights era and against federal government, is perhaps no better illustrated than in the return of legally sanctioned racialised killings.

14 The case of Michael Stewart, who was killed by eight police officers, provided Spike Lee with the backdrop to Radio Raheem's death in *Do The Right Thing* (1989). Spike Lee's films brought cases like Stewart's to a much wider audience. Another was that of Yusif Hawkins, who was shot and killed in the Italian quarter of Brooklyn in August 1989. Thanks to well organised protest marches and demonstrations, the case received much media attention and the background to his death was subsequently taken up in Spike Lee's film *Jungle Fever* (1991). The film was actually dedicated to Hawkins and takes ethnic tensions and conflicts between the Italian and African-American communities and interracial heterosexual relationships as its focus. More often, however, such cases receive much less media attention and, even when they are reported, they often sink without trace and/or remain unresolved as agencies (police, health professionals and courts) have colluded, closed ranks and sometimes covered up in order to protect their interests.

15 Ellis Cose also refers to other cases of off-duty police officers shot or beaten by fellow officers, including one incident involving an attack on an African-American police sergeant, Don Jackson, which was filmed by an NBC camera crew (1993: 102–3).

16 The case of Henry Hughes is a further striking example of the 'thin blue line of silence'. In September 1989, Henry Hughes, a young African-American, died in police custody. According to the police, the medical services and the Coroner, Hughes had no outward or inward signs of injury. According to eye-witness accounts he was beaten for over twenty minutes by several police officers, thrown against a shop window so hard that it smashed and then pinned to the floor by some officers whilst others kicked him. In any event, he was dead on arrival at the hospital. The police denied accusations of physical assault (there was no amateur video recording of this particular incident) and although early official statements indicated an inconsistency between police and medical services' estimated time of death (a crucial difference of twenty minutes), subsequent statements by both agencies suggested the 'mix up' had been resolved (*New York Times*, 15 September 1989).

17 Both Mayor Guilliani and Police Commissioner Howard Schafer did describe the Report as 'statistically inaccurate, outdated and irrelevant' (cited in *Democracy Now*, 27 June 1996).

6 The fringe and the fabric: the politics of white pride

1 The significance of the impact of immigration on class politics has been the focus of Paul Spoonley's account of the extreme right in New Zealand politics (1987: 13–14), an examination which underlines the global nature of such processes and the possibility of exploring similar developments in England and the US. According to Spoonley, landowners and shopkeepers in New Zealand had become economically threatened by the growth of large corporations and companies, agribusinesses and food chains. This class had also lost out politically and ideologically too as the parties of the centre and left (social democratic and labour) appealed increasingly to the 'new' petty bourgeoisie, i.e. public sector employees, professionals and salaried managers (ibid.: 15). Social dislocation and isolation thus encouraged the old petty bourgeoisie to be backward looking, nostalgic and/or fundamentalist (see also Bourdieu 1984: 349). Against this background, a single issue, immigration, provided the petty bourgeoisie/extreme right with an opportunity for a 'public re-affirmation of values in the context of feeling powerless' (Spoonley 1987: 29).

   Spoonley also looked at the impact of those changes on working-class extremism which, like its petty bourgeois counterpart, was also linked to social dislocation resulting from the collapse of once relatively secure sectors of employment and the break up of old community ties. However, whilst working-class extremism was rooted in a spontaneous common sense, the petty bourgeoisie aimed at coherence and views suitable for public consumption (ibid.: 33). For example, the latter has drawn on eugenics to provide a rationale for consigning women to caring and nurturing roles, and to preserve racial exclusivity has used socio-biological theories of innate racial differences in intelligence (e.g. to be found in the work of Arthur Jensen and more recently Richard Herrnstein in the US and Hans Eysenck in England) to give racial theories of the far right their spurious scientific gloss.

2 In 1983, the National Front gained 35 per cent in a mock general election held at a school in Birmingham with a predominantly middle-class catchment area (cited in Cashmore 1987: 95).

3 Another such case in 1994 was that of Richard Everitt who was stabbed to death by a gang of Asian youths in the St Pancras district of London in 1994. Such was the outraged reaction to this case that Princess Diana was reported to have visited the scene to see the floral tributes (*The Times*, 8 September 1994). Two young Bengali men were subsequently arrested and convicted despite widespread protests and proof to the contrary. A campaign was launched in support of 'the Kings Cross two' to secure their release.

4 The distinction between fringe and fabric was used by Ridgeway (1990).

5 Newham Monitoring Project have sought to counter this process through a strategy of exposing the mainstream as extreme, for example through the use of sound-byte slogans, e.g. 'ethnic cleansing' in relationship to local Labour housing policies.

6 Such has been the colonisation of the state by the religious right that in Kootenai County all students were required to wear red, white and blue, pop music was banned and girls were not allowed to wear make-up, pants or to have their hair cut (Aho 1990: 24).

7 Barkun describes the early Anglo-Israelists as quintessentially English. They were middle-class Anglicans, with a smattering of aristocrats and military officers, curious but harmless, devoted monarchists who believed the Empire to be the fulfilment of divine promises, hence their inevitable adherence to the *status quo* (Barkun 1994: 243–4).

8 Odinism is loosely based on the Nordic myth of Valhalla, the place where Aryan martyrs are brought by the winged Valkyries and thence to immortality.

9 It was the leader of the Idaho militia who likened the scene at the bombing to a Rembrandt painting (*Observer*, 23 April 1995).

10 *Searchlight* has been the monthly magazine of an organisation which was formed in 1962 to combat racism, neo-Nazism and fascism. It has relentlessly pursued fascists and their organisations ever since. Its public campaigning, educational and investigative role was well illustrated in its October 1996 issue which was devoted to Nazi music. Articles exposed the European- and US-wide scale of the scene; the record companies, magazines and bands, mail order distribution networks exist throughout western Europe and in the Czech Republic, Slovakia, Poland, Slovenia, Serbia and Hungary (October 1996: 12–15). As part of its campaigning role *Searchlight* also took the lyrics of the album, *Barbecue in Rostock* performed by the band No Remorse to a barrister, who agreed that their incitement to murder Jews, Blacks, Asians, homosexuals and communists in such songs as *Exterminate Ya*, *The Niggers Came Over*, *We've Got the Guns* and *Zyclon B* contravened several sections of the 1986 Public Order Act (ibid.: 9).

11 The three were mourned in the columns of *Putch* which wrote of the 'loss of three comrades who took their leave for Valhalla' (*Searchlight*, April 1996: 3).

12 Duke had sought office in 1975 and 1979 as a Democrat when, it was claimed, 'his race-baiting, quasi-populism was not a particularly new phenomenon in the Louisiana Democratic Party' (Kuzenski 1995: 11). The Party shifted with the growth in power of the black electorate and the convergence with the values of mainstream political parties (ibid.).

13 Its fund-raising has included the sale of NAAWP T-Shirts, baseball caps and pins (badges), direct appeals for its legal defence fund and invitations to readers to bequeath money to the organisation in their wills.

14 The anti-government thrust is evident in the selection and slant given to numerous story lines from articles which claimed that mini Wacos were happening all over America (*NAAWP News*, no. 85, 1995), to those describing David Dukes' own clashes with the 'Federal beast' over unpaid taxes (no. 79) as well as demands to re-segregate schools (no. 74).

15 This point was captured in a cartoon in the *Ouachita Citizen*. A woman points a finger accusingly at her male neighbour. 'David Duke has 20 years of links to various Nazi groups! When he ran for president, his campaign manager was the western commander of the American Nazi Party. Until a few months ago he sold pro-Nazi books and tapes from his Metairie office', to which her neighbour replies 'Yeah, but I like what he says about affirmative action' (25 April 1990).

16 Donaldson, known as the Godfather of racist rock, always preferred to be known as a Nazi rather than a neo-Nazi.

17 In his three-year-long study of the Death's-Head Strike, a neo-Nazi group in Detroit, Raphael Ezekiel found that one of their overriding beliefs was in God-given and absolute racial divisions (1995: 311). Yet, this was integrally bound up with the idea of black male sexuality as both an object of terror and fantasy, a fear that both white women and men too, might be violated by a more powerful sexual force. The self-doubts regarding sexuality inevitably prompted an equally powerful homophobia. In Ezekial's view the young white males 'bristle with hatred and aversion toward the male homosexual community; gays are right at the top of their list of people to be hated and feared' (ibid.: 312).

18 The Southern League produced a half-page spread on its web site on the Hollywood film *Braveheart* which it informed its readers, 'is powerful and violent . . . unreconstructed Southerners will find it difficult to miss the parallels between the Scots and our Confederate forebears'.

19 Tyndall explained that when the person in question had been found to be a hermaphrodite Tyndall himself had instructed 'his/her' membership to be terminated.

20 It is interesting to note that Barkun sees very little difference between many of the ideas of the Identity Christians and the New Age movement, apart, that is, from their not inconsequential views on race and religion (1994: 248).

Conclusions

1 Although the Rambo character was said to be based on Bo Gritz, the former Green Beret Populist candidate in the 1992 Presidential election who had former ties to the Identity Movement and David Duke (Barkun 1994: 211).

BIBLIOGRAPHY

Adorno, T.S., Frenkel-Brunswick, E., Levinson, D. and Sanford, R.N. (1950) *The Authoritarian Personality*, New York: Harper.

Aho, J. (1990) *The Politics of Righteousness: Idaho Christian Patriotism*, London: University of Washington.

Alba, R. (1990) *Ethnic Identity: the transformation of white America*, New Haven, CT: Yale University Press.

Alex, N. (1976) *New York Cops Talk Back: a study of a beleaguered minority*, New York: Wiley.

Allen, T. (1994) *The Invention of the White Race: racial oppression and social control*, vol. 1, London: Verso.

Almaguer, T. (1994) *Racial Fault Lines: the historical origins of white supremacy in California*, Berkeley, CA: University of California.

Amin, K. (1995) 'Police Stop and Searches: Who, Where and Why', *Runnymede Bulletin*, London: Runnymede Trust, 283, March: 6–7.

Amnesty International (1996) *United States of America: police brutality and excessive force in the New York City Police Department*, New York: Amnesty International, USA.

Anderson, B. (1983) *Imagined Communities*, London: Verso.

Ang, I. (1991) *Desperately Seeking the Audience*, London: Routledge.

Anthias, F. and Yuval-Davis, N. (1992) *Racialized Boundaries: race, nation, gender, colour and class and the anti racist struggle*, London: Routledge.

Auster, L. (1990) *The Path to National Suicide: an essay on immigration and multiculturalism*, Monterey, VA: American Immigration Control Foundation.

Axford, B. (1995) *The Global System: economics, politics and culture*, Cambridge: Polity Press.

Balibar, E. (1991) 'Racism and Nationalism', in E. Balibar and I. Wallerstein, *Race, Nation, Class: ambiguous ethnicities*, London: Verso, pp. 37–67.

Barker, M. (1981) *The New Racism: Conservatives and the ideology of the tribe*, London: Junction Books.

Barkun, M. (1994) *Religion and the Racist Right: the origins of the Christian Identity Movement*, Chapel Hill, NC: University of North Carolina.

Barnet, R. and Cavanagh, J. (1994) *Global Dreams: imperial corporations and the new world order*, London: Touchstone.

Baudrillard, J. (1983) *Simulations*, New York: Semiotext.

—— (1988) *America*, London: Verso.

Bauman, Z. (1989) *Modernity and the Holocaust*, Cambridge: Polity Press.

—— (1992) *Intimations of Postmodernity*, London: Routledge.

Bendersky, J. (1995) 'The Disappearance of Blonds: immigration, race and the reemergence of "thinking white"', *Telos*, 104, Summer: 135–57.

Ben-Tovim, G. and Gabriel, J. (1979) 'The Politics of Race in Britain 1962–1979: a review of the major trends and of the recent literature', *Race Relations Abstracts* November, 4 (4): 1–56.

Ben-Tovim, G., Gabriel, J., Law, I. and Stredder, K. (1981) 'Race, Left Strategies and the State', *Politics and Power* 3: 153–81.

—— (1986) *The Local Politics of Race*, Basingstoke: Macmillan.

Benyon, J. (1986) 'Spiral of Decline: race and policing', in Z. Layton-Henry and P. Rich (eds.) *Race, Government and Politics in Britain*, Basingstoke: Macmillan, pp. 227–77.

Bernal, M. (1987) *Black Athena: the Afroasiatic roots of classical civilisation*, London: Free Association Books.

Berry, J. (n/d.) 'White Lies: David Duke in the Media Mind', unpublished monograph, Amistad Research Center, Tulane University.

Bhabha, H. (1994) *The Location of Culture*, London: Routledge.

Bhattacharyya, G. and Gabriel, J. (1994) 'Gurinder Chadha and the Apna Generation: black British film in the 1990s', *Third Text*, 27, Summer: 55–65.

Billig, M. (1978) *Fascists: a social psychological view of the National Front*, London: Harcourt Brace.

Birch, E. (1994) *Black American Women's Writing: a quilt of many colors*, Brighton: Harvester.

Bloom, L. (1987) *The Closing of the American Mind: how higher education has failed democracy and impoverished the souls of today's students*, London: Penguin.

Boeckelman, K. *et al.* (1995) 'Messenger or Message – David Duke in the Louisiana Legislature', in J. Kuzenski and C.S. Bullock, *David Duke and the Politics of Race in the South*, London: Vanderbilt, pp. 23–34.

Boulard, G. (1995) 'The Man Behind the Mask', *The Advocate*: 29–34.

Bourdieu, P. (1984) *Distinction: a social critique of the judgement of taste*, London : Routledge and Kegan Paul.

Bouvier, L. (1991) *Fifty Million Californians*, Washington, DC: Federation for Immigration Reform.

Brah, A. (1996) *Cartographies of Diaspora: contesting identities*, London: Routledge.

Braham, P. (1982) 'How the media report race', in M. Gurevitch, T. Bennett and J. Currans (eds), *Culture, Society and the Media*, London: Routledge, pp. 267–86.

Brimelow, P. (1995) *Alien Nation: common sense about America's immigration disaster*, New York: Random House.

Busia, A. (1985) 'Manipulating Africa: the buccaneer as "liberator"', in D. Dabydeen (ed.), *The Black Presence in English Literature*, Manchester: Manchester University Press, pp. 168–85.

Butler, J. (1993) 'Endangered/Endangering: Schematic Racism and White Paranoia', in R. Gooding-Williams (ed.), *Reading Rodney King: reading urban uprising*, London: Routledge, pp. 15–22.

Carlson, M. (1996) 'The Soap Opera Games', *Time* 5 August: 48.

Carter, B., Harris, C. and Joshi, S. (1993) 'The 1951–55 Conservative government and the racialization of black immigration', in W. James and C. Harris (eds), *Inside Babylon: the Caribbean diaspora in Britain*, London: Verso.

Carter, B., Green, M. and Halpern, R. (1996) 'Immigration policy and the racialization of migrant labour: the construction of national identities in the USA and Britain', *Ethnic and Racial Studies* 19 (1) January: 135–57.

Cashmore, E. (1987) *The Logic of Racism*, London: Allen and Unwin.

Cashmore, E. and Troyna, B. (1983) *Introduction to Race Relations*, London: Routledge.

Cheyette, B. (1989) 'Jewish stereotyping and English literature, 1875–1920: towards a political analysis' in T. Kushner and K. Lunn (eds) *Traditions of Intolerance: historical perspectives on fascism and race discourse in Britain*, Manchester: Manchester University Press, pp. 12–32.

Clegg, J. (1994) *Fu Manchu and the 'Yellow Peril': the making of a racist myth*, Stoke: Trentham.

Cobham, R. and Collins, M. (1990) *Watchers and Seekers: creative writing by Black women in Britain*, Cambridge: Cambridge University Press.

Cohen, J. and Solomon, N. (1993) *Adventures in Medialand: behind the news, beyond the pundits*, Monroe: Common Courage Press.

—— (1995) *Through the Media Looking Glass: decoding bias and blather in the news*, Monroe: Common Courage Press.

Cohen, P. (1988) 'The Perversions of Inheritance: studies in the making of multi-racist Britain', in P. Cohen and H. Bains (eds), *Multi-Racist Britain*, Basingstoke: Macmillan, pp. 9–118.

Collins, P.H. (1990) *Black Feminist Thought*, London: HarperCollins.

Conot, R. (1974) *American Odyssey*, New York: William Morrow.

Cose, E. (1993) *The Rage of the Privileged Class*, New York: Harper Perrenial.

Crenshaw, K. and Peller, G. (1993) 'Reel time/real justice', in R. Gooding-Williams (ed.) *Reading Rodney King: reading urban uprising*, London: Routledge, pp. 56–70.

Curtis, Lewis (1971) *Apes and Angels: the Irishman in Victorian caricature*, Newton Abbot: David and Charles.

Curtis, Liz (1984) *Nothing but the Same Old Story*, London: Information on Ireland.

Dabydeen, D. (1987) *Hogarth's Blacks*, Athens, GA: University of Georgia.

Daniels, J. (1997) *White Lies: race, class, gender, and sexuality in white supremacist discourse*, London: Routledge.

Davion, V. (1995) 'Reflections on the meaning of white', in L. Bell and D. Blumenfeld (eds), *Overcoming Racism and Sexism*, Lanham, MD: Rowman and Littlefield, pp. 135–9.

Davis, A. (1981) *Women, Race and Class*, London: Women's Press.

Dees, M. (1996) *Gathering Storm: America's militia threat*, New York: HarperCollins.

Dent, G. (ed.) (1992) *Black Popular Culture*, Seattle, WA: Bay Press.

Diamond, S. (1989) *Spiritual Warfare: the politics of the Christian right*, Boston, MA: South End Press.

Diawara, M. (ed.) (1993) *Black American Cinema*, London: Routledge.

Dijk, T. van (1991) *Racism and the Press*, London: Routledge.

—— (1993) *Elite Discourse and Racism*, London: Sage.

Dines, G. and Humez, J. (eds) (1995) *Gender, Race and Class in Media: a text reader*, London: Sage.

Dinnerstein, L. (1994) *Antisemitism in America*, Oxford: Oxford University Press.

Dirlik, A. (1996) 'The local in the global', in R. Wilson and W. Dissanayake, *Global/Local: cultural production and the transnational imaginary*, Durham, NC: Duke University Press, pp. 21–45.

D'Souza, D. (1992) *Illiberal Education: the politics of race and sex on campus*, New York: Vintage Books.

—— (1995) *The End of Racism: principles for a multiracial society*, New York: Free Press.

Dulaney, W.M. (1996) *Black Police in America*, Bloomington, IN: Indiana Press.

Dunhill, C. (1989) 'Women, racist attacks and the response from anti racist groups' in C. Dunhill (ed.) *The Boys in Blue: women's challenge to the police*, London: Virago: 68–79.

Duran, L., Gallegos, W., Mann, E. and Omutsu, G. (1994) *Immigrant Rights and Wrongs*, California: Labor Community Strategy Center.

Dyer, R. (1988) 'White', *Screen* 28 (4): 44–64.

Eatwell, R. (1992) 'Why has the extreme right failed in Britain?' in P. Hainsworth (ed.) *The Extreme Right in Europe and the USA*, London: Pinter.

Edelman, M. (1988) *Constructing the Political Spectacle*, London: University of Chicago Press.

Edgar, D. (1977) 'Racism, fascism, and the politics of the National Front', *Race and Class* XIX (2): 111–31.

Edwards, J. (1995) *When Race Counts: the morality of racial preference in Britain and America*, London: Routledge.

Eisenstein, Z. (1996) *Hatreds: racialized and sexualized conflicts in the 21st century*, London: Routledge.

Essed, P. (1991) *Understanding Everyday Racism: an interdisciplinary theory*, London: Sage.

Ezekiel, R. (1995) *The Racist Mind: portraits of neo-Nazis and Klansmen*, New York: Viking.

Faludi, S. (1992) *Backlash: the undeclared war against American Women*, New York: Anchor books.

Fanon, F. (1986) *Black Skin, White Masks*, London: Pluto.

Feagin, J. and Hahn, H. (1973) *Ghetto Revolts: the politics of violence in American cities*, London: Collier-Macmillan.

Feagin, J.R. and Vera, H. (1995) *White Racism*, London: Routledge.

Featherstone, M. (1995) *Undoing Culture: globalization, postmodernism and identity*, London: Sage.

Federation for American Immigration Reform (1992) *Immigration 2000: the century of the new American sweatshop*, Washington, DC: FAIR.

Fiske, J. (1994) *Media Matters: everyday culture and political change*, Minneapolis, MN: University of Minnesota.

Foot, P. (1969) *The Rise of Enoch Powell*, Harmondsworth: Penguin.

Foucault, M. (1971) *Madness and Civilization: a history of insanity in the age of reason*, London: Tavistock.

—— (1979) *Discipline and Punish*, Harmondsworth: Penguin.

Fox, R. and Mehlman, I. (1992) *Crowding out the Future: world population growth, US immigration and pressures on natural resources*, Washington, DC: FAIR.

Frankenberg, R. (1993) *The Social Construction of Whiteness: white women, race matters*, London: Routledge.

Fredrickson, G. (1981) *White Supremacy: a comparative study of American and South African history*, Oxford: Oxford University Press.

Friedman, M. and Narveson, J. (1995) *Political Correctness: for and against*, London: Rowman and Littlefield.

Frye, M. (1995) 'White woman feminist', in L. Bell and D. Blumenfeld (eds), *Overcoming Racism and Sexism*, Lanham, MD: Rowman and Littlefield, pp. 113–34.

Fryer, P. (1984) *Staying Power: the history of black people in Britain*, London: Pluto.

Gabriel, J. (1994) *Racism, Culture, Markets*, London: Routledge.

—— (1996) 'What do you do when minority means you', *Screen* 37 (2), Summer: 129–51.

Gellner, E. (1983) *Nations and Nationalism*, Oxford: Blackwell.

Gibson, J. (1994) *Warrior Dreams: violence and manhood in post-Vietnam America*, New York: Hill and Wang.

Giddens, A. (1991) *The Consequences of Modernity*, Cambridge: Polity Press.

Gillborn, D. (1995) *Racism and Anti-racism in Real Schools*, Buckingham: Open University.

Gilman, S. (1991) *The Jew's Body*, London: Routledge.

—— (1992) 'Black bodies, white bodies: towards an iconography of female sexuality in late nineteenth century art, medicine and literature', in J. Donald and A. Rattansi (eds), *Race, Culture and Difference*, London: Sage, pp. 171–97.

Gilmore, R.W. (1993) 'Terror austerity race gender excess theater', in R. Gooding-Williams (ed.), *Reading Rodney King: reading urban uprising*, London: Routledge, pp. 23–37.

Gilroy, P. (1987) *There Ain't No Black in the Union Jack*, London: Hutchinson.

—— (1990) 'The end of anti-racism', in W. Ball and J. Solomos (eds), *Race and Local Politics*, London: Macmillan.

—— (1993a) *The Black Atlantic: modernity and double consciousness*, London: Verso.

—— (1993b) *Small Acts: thoughts on the politics of black cultures*, London: Serpent's Tail.

Goldberg, D. (1993) *Racist Culture: philosophy and the politics of meaning*, Oxford: Blackwell.

Gooding-Williams, R. (ed.) (1993) *Reading Rodney King: reading urban uprising*, London: Routledge.

Gordon, P. (1983) *White Law*, London: Pluto.

—— (1990) 'A dirty war: the new right and local authority anti-racism', in W. Ball and J. Solomos (eds), *Race and Local Politics*, Basingstoke: Macmillan, pp. 175–90.

Green, M. (1980) *Dreams of Adventure, Deeds of Empire*, London: Routledge and Kegan Paul.

Haines, H. (1996) *Against Capital Punishment: the anti-death penalty movement in America 1972–1994*, Oxford: Oxford University Press.

Hainsworth, P. (1992) 'Introduction. The cutting edge: the extreme right in post-war western Europe and the USA', in P. Hainsworth (ed.) *The Extreme Right in Europe and the USA*, London: Pinter.

Hall, S. (1990) 'The whites of their eyes: racist ideologies and the media', in M. Alvarado and J. Thompson (eds), *The Media Reader*, London: British Film Institute, pp. 8–23.

—— (1991) 'The local and the global: globalization and ethnicity', in A.D. King (ed.), *Culture Globalization and the World System: contemporary conditions and the representation of identity*, Basingstoke: Macmillan, pp. 19–39.

—— (1992) 'New ethnicities', in J. Donald and A. Rattansi (eds), *Race, Culture and Difference*, London: Sage, pp. 252–9.

—— (1994) 'Some "Politically Incorrect" Pathways through PC', in S. Dunant (ed.), *The War of the Words*, London: Virago, pp. 164–83.

Hall, S., Critcher, C., Jefferson T., Clarke, J. and Roberts, B. (1978) *Policing the Crisis: mugging, the state, and law and order*, London: Macmillan.

Hall Jamieson, K. (1992) *Dirty Politics: deception, distraction and democracy*, Oxford: Oxford University Press.

Harris, G. (1990) *The Dark Side of Europe: the extreme right today*, Edinburgh: Edinburgh University Press.

Harris, R. (1973) *The Police Academy: an inside view*, New York: Wiley.

Harvey, D. (1989) *The Condition of Postmodernity*, Oxford: Blackwell.

Hastie, T. (1986) 'History, Race and Propaganda', in F. Palmer (ed), *Anti-Racism: an assault on education and value*, London: Sherwood, pp. 43–56

207

Hawkins, H. and Thomas, R. (1991) 'White policing of black populations: a history of race and social control in America', in E. Cashmore and E. McLaughlin (eds), *Out of Order?: policing black people*, London: Routledge, pp. 65–86.

Herman, E. and Chomsky, N. (1994) *Manufacturing Consent: the political economy of the mass media*, London: Verso.

Herrnstein, R and Murray, C. (1994) *The Bell Curve: intelligence and class structure in American life*, London: Free Press.

Hesse, B. (1997) 'White governmentality: urbanism, nationalism, racism', in S. Westwood and J. Williams (eds), *Imagining Cities: scripts, signs, memory*, London: Routledge, pp. 86–103.

Hesse, B., Rai, D., Bennett, C. and McGilchrist, P. (1992) *Beneath the Surface: racial harassment*, Aldershot: Avebury.

Hickman, M. (1995) *Religion, Class and Identity: the state, the Catholic Church and the education of the Irish in Britain*, Aldershot: Avebury.

Hickman, M. and Walter, B. (1995) 'Deconstructing whiteness: Irish women in Britain', *Feminist Review* 50, Summer: 5–19.

—— (1997) *Discrimination and the Irish Community in Britain: a report of research undertaken for the Commission for Racial Equality*, London: Commission for Racial Equality.

Hillyard, P. (1993) *Suspect Community: people's experience of the Prevention of Terrorism Acts in Britain*, London: Pluto.

Hirst, P. and Thompson, G. (1995) 'Globalization and the future of the nation state', *Economy and Society* 24 (3): 408–42.

Hoffstadter, R. (1955) *Social Darwinism in American Thought*, Boston, MA: Beacon Press.

Holdaway, S. (1996) *The Racialisation of British Policing*, Basingstoke: Macmillan.

Holmes, C. (1979) *Anti-Semitism in British Society 1876–1939*, London: Edward Arnold.

Honeyford, R. (1986) 'anti racist rhetoric', in F. Palmer (ed.), *Anti-Racism: an assault on education and value*, London: Sherwood, pp. 43–56.

hooks, b. (1981) *Ain't I a Woman? Black Women and Feminism*, Boston, MA: South End Press.

Hornblower, M. (1996) 'Underdogs day', *Time*, 5 August: 45–6.

Howard, P. (1994) *The Death of Common Sense: how law is suffocating America*, New York: Random House.

Hughes, R. (1993) *Culture of Complaint: the fraying of America*, Oxford: Oxford University Press.

Human Rights Watch/Helskinki (1997) *Racist Violence in the United Kingdom*, London: Human Rights Watch.

Ignatiev, N. (1995) *How the Irish Became White*, London: Routledge.

Innes, C. (1994) 'Virgin Territories and Motherlands: colonial and nationalist representations of Africa and Ireland', *Feminist Review* 47, Summer: 1–14.

Jefferson, T. (1991) 'Discrimination, disadvantage and police work' in E. Cashmore and E. McLaughlin (eds), *Out of Order?: policing black people*, London: Routledge, pp. 166–88

Jewell, K.S. (1993) *From Mammy to Miss America and Beyond: cultural images and the shaping of US social policy*, London: Routledge.

Jordan, G. and Weedon, C. (1995) *Cultural Politics: class, gender, race and the postmodern world*, Oxford: Blackwell.

Jordan, J. (1995) 'In the land of white supremacy', *The Progressive*, 18, June: 21.

Jordan, W. (1974) *White Man's Burden: historical origins of racism in the United States*, Oxford: Oxford University Press.

Keith, M. (1993) *Race, Riots and Policing: lore and order in a multi-racist society*, London: UCL Press.

Kellner, D. (1995) *Media Culture: cultural studies, identity and politics between the modern and the post modern*, London: Routledge.

Koon, S. (1992) *Presumed Guilty: the tragedy of the Rodney King affair*, Washington, DC: Regnery Gateway.

Kovel, J. (1988) *White Racism: a psychohistory*, London: Free Association Books.

Kushner, T. (1989) *The Persistence of Prejudice: antisemitism in British society during the Second World War*, Manchester: Manchester University Press.

Kuzenski, J. (1995) 'David Duke and the non-partisan primary', in J. Kuzenski and C.S. Bullock, *David Duke and the Politics of Race in the South*, London: Vanderbilt, pp. 3–22.

Laclau, E. (1977) *Politics and Ideology in Marxist Theory*, London: Verso.

Lazarre, J. (1996) *Beyond the Whiteness of Whiteness*, Durham, NC: Duke University Press.

Lee, G. (1996) *Troubadours, Trumpeters, Troubled Makers: lyricism, nationalism and hybridity in China and its others*, Durham, NC: Duke University Press.

Leinen, S. (1993) *Gay Cops*, New Brunswick, NJ: Rutgers University Press.

Lemm, M. (1996) *Up from Conservatism: why the right is wrong for America*, New York: Free Press.

Lewis, G. (1996) *Gendering Orientalism: race, femininity and representation*, London: Routledge.

Lewis, R. (1988) *Anti-Racism: a mania exposed*, London: Quartet.

Liebes, T. and Katz, E. (1986) 'Patterns of involvement in television fiction: a comparative analysis', *European Journal of Communication*, 1 (2): 151–71.

Limbaugh, R. (1993) *See, I Told You So*, New York: Pocket Books.

Lull, J. (1995) *Media, Communication, Culture: a global approach*, Cambridge: Polity Press.

Lynch, F. (1989) *Invisible Victims: white males and the crisis of affirmative action*, Westport, CT: Greenwood.

Mama, A. (1989) *The Hidden Struggle: statutory and voluntary sector responses to violence against black women in the home*, London: Runnymede Trust.

McClintock, A. (1995) *Imperial Leather: race, gender and sexuality in the colonial context*, London: Routledge.

McClure, J. (1985) 'Problematic presence: the colonial other in Kipling and Conrad', in D. Dabydeen (ed.), *The Black Presence in English Literature*, Manchester: Manchester University Press, pp. 154–67.

Mercer, K. (1994) *Welcome to the Jungle: New Positions in Black Cultural Studies*, London: Routledge.

Miles, R. (1993) *Racism after 'Race Relations'*, London: Routledge.

Millward, P. (1985) 'The Stockport Riots of 1852: a study of anti-Catholic and anti-Irish sentiment', in R. Swift and S. Gilley (eds), *The Irish in the Victorian City*, London: Croom Helm, pp. 207–24.

Miyoshi, M. (1996) 'A borderless world? From colonialism to transnationalism and the decline of the nation-state', in R. Wilson and W. Dissanayake, *Global/Local: cultural production and the transnational imaginary*, Durham, NC: Duke University Press, pp. 78–106.

Modood, T. (1988) ' "Black", racial identity and Asian identity' *New Community*, 14 (3), Spring: 397–404.

Morley, D. and Robins, K. (1995) *Spaces of Identity: global media, electronic landscapes and cultural boundaries*, London: Routledge.

Morrison, T. (1992) *Playing in the Dark: whiteness and the literary imagination*, Cambridge, MA: Harvard University Press.

Multimedia entertainment (1994) *Rush Limbaugh*, New Jersey: Burrelles.

Museum of the Confederacy Journal (1996) *A Century of Collecting: the history of the Museum of the Confederacy*, Richmond, VA, no. 47.

Nairn, T. (1977) *The Break-up of Britain*, London: New Left Books.

National Advisory Commission on Civil Disorders (1968) *Report of the Kerner Commission*, New York: Bantham.

Neilson, J. (1995) 'The great PC scare: tyrannies of the left, rhetoric of the right', in J. Williams (ed.), *PC Wars: politics and theory in the academy*, London: Routledge, pp. 60–89.

Newham Monitoring Project (1995) *Fifteen Years of Community Resistance: annual report, 1994–5*, London: NMP.

—— (1996) *An Attack on One is an Attack on All: annual report 1995–6*, London: NMP.

Newham Monitoring Project/Campaign against Racism and Fascism (1991) *Newham: the forging of a black community*, London: NMP/CARF.

Omi, M. and Winant, H. (1986) *Racial Formation in the United States*, London: Routledge.

O'Shea, M. (1989) 'The policing of Irish women in Britain', in C. Dunhill (ed.), *The Boys in Blue: women's challenge to the police*, London: Virago, pp. 219–31.

O'Sullivan, J. (1994) 'America's Identity Crisis', *National Review*, November: 36–45, 76.

Ownes, T. (1994) *Lying Eyes: the truth behind the corruption and brutality of the LAPD and the beating of Rodney King*, New York: Thunder's Mouth Press.

Palmer, F. (ed.) (1986) *Anti-Racism: an assault on education and value*, London: Sherwood.

Parker, I.C. (1994) 'Myth, telecommunication and the emerging global informational order: the political economy of transitions', in E.A. Comor (ed.), *The Global Political Economy of Communication: hegemony, telecommunication and the information economy*, New York: St Martin's Press, pp. 37–60.

Pfeil, F. (1995) *White Guys: studies in postmodern domination and difference*, London: Verso.

Phillips, M. (1994) 'Illiberal liberalism', in S. Dunant (ed.), *The War of Words: the political correctness debate*, London: Virago, pp. 35–54.

Phillips, T. (1995) 'UK TV: a place in the sun?', in C. Frachon and M. Vargaftig (eds), *European Television: immigrants and ethnic minorities*, London: John Libbey and Co, pp. 13–21.

Pieterse, J. (1992) *White on Black: images of Africa and blacks in western popular culture*, London: Yale University Press.

Poulantzas, N. (1974) *Fascism and Dictatorship: the Third International and the problem of fascism*, London: New Left Books.

Powell, L. (1990) 'A concrete symbol', *Southern Exposure*, Spring: 40–43.

Rattansi, A. (1994) '"Western" racisms, ethnicities, and identities in a "postmodern" frame', in A. Rattansi and S. Westwood (eds), *Racism, Modernity and Identity: on the western front*, Cambridge: Polity Press, pp. 15–86.

Reed, L. (1993) 'The Battle of Liberty Monument', *The Progressive*, June: pp. 32–4.

Reiner, R. (1985) *The Politics of the Police*, Brighton: Harvester.

Rendell, S., Naureckas, J. and Cohen, J. (1996) *The Way Things Aren't: Rush Limbaugh's reign of error*, New York: FAIR.

Rhodes, J. (1995) 'The Visibility of Race and Media History' in G. Dines and J. Humez (eds) *Gender, Race and Class in Media: a text-reader*, London: Sage, pp. 33–9.

Ridgeway, J. (1990) *Blood in the Face: the Ku Klux Klan, Aryan nations, Nazi skinheads, and the rise of a new white culture*, New York: Thunder's Mouth Press.

Riggins, S. (1992) *Ethnic Minority Media: an international perspective*, London: Sage.

Robinson, C. (1993) 'Race, capitalism, and the antidemocracy', in R. Gooding-Williams (ed.), *Reading Rodney King: reading urban uprising*, London: Routledge, pp. 73–81.

Rodney, W. (1988) *How Europe Undeveloped Africa*, London: Bogle L'Ouverture.

Roediger, D. (1991) *The Wages of Whiteness: race and the making of the American working class*, London: Verso.

—— (1994) *Towards the Abolition of Whiteness: essays on race, politics and working class history*, London: Verso.

Said, E. (1978) *Orientalism*, London: Penguin.

—— (1993) *Culture and Imperialism*, London: Chatto and Windus.

Sartre, J.P. (1962) *Anti-Semite and Jew*, New York: Grove Press.

Saxton, A. (1990) *The Rise and Fall of the White Republic: class politics and mass culture in nineteenth-century America*, London: Verso.

Schafer, J. (1994) 'The Battle of Liberty Place: a matter of historical perception', *Cultural Vistas*, Spring: 9–17.

Schiller, H. (1986) *Information and the Crisis Economy*, Oxford: Oxford University Press.

Schwarz, B. (1996) 'The cow and the unicorn', *Red Pepper* 26, July: 14–15.

Scruton, R. (1986) 'The myth of cultural relativism', in F. Palmer (ed.), *Anti-Racism: an assault on education and value*, London: Sherwood, pp. 127–35.

Searle, C. (1987) 'Your daily dose: racism and the *Sun*', *Race and Class*, **XXIX** (1): 55–71.

Semmel, B. (1960) *Imperialism and Social Reform*, London: Allen and Unwin.

Seymour-Ure, C. (1974) *The Political Impact of the Mass Media*, London: Constable.

Shohat, E. and Stam, R. (1994) *Unthinking Eurocentrism: multiculturalism and the media*, London: Routledge.

—— (1996) 'From the imperial family to the transnational imaginary: media spectatorship in the age of globalization', in R. Wilson and W. Dissanayake, *Global/Local: cultural production and the transnational imaginary*, Durham, NC: Duke University Press, pp. 145–70.

Sibley, D. (1995) *Geographies of Exclusion*, London: Routledge.

Silk, C. and Silk, J. (1990) *Racism and Anti-racism in American Popular Culture: portrayals of African-Americans in fiction and film*, Manchester: Manchester University Press.

Singular, S. (1987) *Talked to Death: the life and murder of Alan Berg*, New York: Beech Tree Books.

Sleeter, C. (1996) 'White silence, white solidarity', in N. Ignatiev and J. Garvey (eds), *Race Traitor*, London: Routledge, pp. 257–65.

Small, S. (1994) *Racialized Barriers: the black experience in the United States and England in the 1980s*, London: Routledge.

Smith, A.D. (1986) *The Ethnic Origins of Nations*, Oxford: Basil Blackwell.

Smith, A.M. (1994) *New Right Discourse on Race and Sexuality: Britain 1968–1990*, Cambridge: Cambridge University Press.

Smith, D. and Gray, J. (1985) *Police and People in London: the PSI Report*, Aldershot: Gower.

Soja, E. (1989) *Postmodern Geographies: the reassertion of space in critical social theory*, London: Verso.

Solomos, J. (1989) *Race and Racism in Contemporary Britain*, Basingstoke: Macmillan, 2nd edn, 1993.

Sommers, L. (1984) *Michegan*, Boulder, CO: Westview.

Southall Black Sisters (1989) 'Two struggles: challenging male violence and the police', in C. Dunhill (ed.), *The Boys in Blue: women's challenge to the police*, London: Virago, pp. 38–44.

Southern Poverty Law Center (1996) *SPLC Report (special 25th anniversary issue)*, Montgomery, AL: SPLC.

Spoonley, P. (1987) *The Politics of Nostalgia: racism and the extreme right in New Zealand*, Palmerston North, New Zealand: Dunmore Press.

Sprinzak, E. (1995) 'Right Wing Terrorism in a Comparative Perspective: the case of split delegitimization', in T. Bjørgo (ed.), *Terror from the Extreme Right*, London: Frank Cass.

Stacey, J. (1991) 'Promoting normality: Section 28 and the regulation of sexuality', in S. Franklin, C. Lury and J. Stacey (eds), *Off-Centre: feminism and cultural studies*, London: HarperCollins, pp. 284–304.

Sternberg, J. (1991) 'The role of the New Orleans media in the election of David Duke', thesis presented to Princeton University in partial fulfilment of the Bachelor of Arts in Woodrow Wilson School of Public and International Affairs, Princeton, NJ.

Stevenson, N. (1995) *Understanding Media Cultures: social theory and mass communication*, London: Sage.

Street, B. (1985) 'Reading the novels of empire: race and ideology in the classic "tale of adventure"', in D. Dabydeen (ed.), *The Black Presence in English Literature*, Manchester: Manchester University Press, pp. 95–111.

Sundquist, A. (1987) *Pocahontas & Co. The Fictional American Indian Woman in 19th Century Literature: a study of method*, Atlantic Highlands, NJ: Humanities Press.

Sundquist, E. (1996) *The Dubois Reader*, Oxford: Oxford University Press.

Swift, R. (1985) ' "Another Stafford Street Row": law, order and the Irish presence in mid-Victorian Wolverhampton', in R. Swift and S. Gilley (eds), *The Irish in the Victorian City*, London: Croom Helm, pp. 179–206.

Sykes, C. (1992) *A Nation of Victims: the decay of the American character*, New York: St Martins Press.

Taylor, Simon (1993) *A Land of Dreams: a study of Jewish and Caribbean migrant communities in England*, London: Routledge.

Taylor, Stan (1982) *The National Front in English Politics*, London: Macmillan.

The 1990 Trust (1996) *Without Foundation: investigating the implications of the Asylum and Immigration Bill on Britain's black community*, London: 1990 Trust.

Thompson, J. (1995) *The Media and Modernity*, Cambridge: Polity Press.

Tomlinson, J. (1991) *Cultural Imperialism: a critical introduction*, London: Pinter.

Trachtenberg, J. (1993) *The Devil and the Jews: the mediaeval conception of the Jew and its relation to modern antisemitism*, Philadelphia, PA: Jewish Publication Society.

Trent, J. and Friedenberg, R. (1995) *Political Campaign Communication: principles and practices*, London: Praeger.

UEFA (1996) *Euro '96 Report*, London: UEFA.

Valle, V. and Torres, R. (1994) 'Latinos in a "post-industrial" disorder: politics in a changing city', *Socialist Review*, 4: 1–28.

Wallace, M. (1990) *Invisibility Blues*, London: Verso.

Wallerstein, I. (1991) 'The national and the universal: can there be such a thing as a world culture?', in A. King (ed.), *Culture, Globalization and the World System*, Basingstoke: Macmillan, pp. 91–105.

Walvin, J. (1971) *The Black Presence: a documentary history of the Negro in England 1555–1860*, London: Orbach and Chambers.

Ware, V. (1992) *Beyond the Pale: white women, racism and history*, London: Verso.

Warren, D. (1995) 'White Americans as a minority', *Telos* 104, Summer: 127–34.

Webster, D. (1988) *Look Yonder! the imaginary America of populist culture*, London: Comedia.

Wellman, D. (1993) *Portraits of White Racism*, 2nd edn, Cambridge: Cambridge University Press.

West, C. (1990) 'The new politics of cultural difference', in R. Ferguson, M. Gever, T.T. Minh-ha and C. West (eds), *Out There*, Cambridge, MA: MIT Press, pp. 19–36.

Wetherell, M. and Potter, J. (1992) *Mapping the Language of Racism: discourse and the legitimation of exploitation*, Brighton: Harvester.

Wiegman, R. (1995) *American Anatomies: theorizing race and gender*, Durham, NC: Duke University Press.

Williams, P. (1997) *The Genealogy of Race: towards a theory of grace*, Reith Lectures, London: BBC.

Williamson, J. (1995) *Hillbillyland*, London: University of North Carolina.

Winant, H. (1994) 'Racial formation and hegemony: global and local developments', in A. Rattansi and S. Westwood (eds), *Racism, Modernity and Identity: on the western front*, Cambridge: Polity Press, pp. 266–89.

The Women of Broadwater Farm (1989) 'Into Our Homes', in C. Dunhill (ed.), *The Boys in Blue: women's challenge to the police*, London: Virago, pp. 123–37.

Young, L. (1994) 'Natural selection? Ideology, environmentalism, race', *Cultural Studies from Birmingham* 3: 151–69.

—— (1996) *Fear of the Dark: 'race', gender and sexuality in the cinema*, London: Routledge.

Young, R. (1990) *White Mythologies: writing history and the west*, London: Routledge.

—— (1995) *Colonial Desire: hybridity in theory culture and race*, London: Routledge.

Zatarain, M. (1990) *David Duke: evolution of a Klansman*, Gretna, LA: Pelican.

Zelnick, R. (1996) *Backfire: a journalist's look at affirmative action*, New York: Regnery.

INDEX